FOREN

Investigation

METHODS FROM EXPERTS

CRIME SCENE DO NOT CROSS   CRIME SCENE

Kendall Hunt
publishing company

Katherine Ramsland, Ph.D.
DeSales University

www.kendallhunt.com
Send all inquiries to:
4050 Westmark Drive
Dubuque, IA 52004-1840

Published in the United States of America

To the OUGs, Sally Keglovits and Dana DeVito,
For listening, encouraging, and caring

Brief Contents

Contents

Acknowledgments

This book is the result of many years of interaction with many people, as well as of opportunities to research and write about forensic science and its history. Among those who made contributions to this book, I wish to thank:

- John Silbersack, my literary agent and close friend, who encourages me and keeps the momentum going.
- Marilyn Bardsley, my former editor at Court TV's Crime Library, who got me started writing about forensic science.
- Angela Willenbring, my efficient and enthusiastic editor at Kendall Hunt, who provided great feedback.
- Investigative and behavioral experts and researchers, with whom I've had many conversations. Those who made direct contributions to this book's content are Teresa Brasse, Carole Chaski, Sam Del Rosario, Joe Dietz, Nola Foulston, Vernon Geberth, Sally Keglovitz, Andy Kehm, Don Kneese, Julia Kocis, Maria Konnikova, Henry Lee, Lee Lofland, Zachary Lysek, Gregg McCrary, Tim Palmbach, Joe Pochron, Sandy Russell, Don Shelton, Cyril Wecht, Joe Walsh, and Seth Weber.

Also, I want to thank Leslie Myers, my research assistant, and Susan Lysek for their assistance with the manuscript. Susan, especially, gave a thorough read, good feedback, and an investigative eye.

About the Author

Dr. Katherine Ramsland directs a master's program in criminal justice and teaches forensic psychology at DeSales University in Pennsylvania. She has published over 1,000 articles, blogs, and reviews, and 59 books, including *Confession of a Serial Killer: The Untold Story of Dennis Rader*, *The Mind of a Murderer: Privileged Access to the Demons That Drive Extreme Violence*, *The Forensic Science of CSI*, *Inside the Minds of Serial Killers*, *The Human Predator: A Historical Chronicle of Serial Murder and Forensic Investigation*, *The Forensic Psychology of Criminal Minds*, *Beating the Devil's Game: A History of Forensic Science and Criminal Investigation*, *The CSI Effect*, and *The Criminal Mind: A Writer's Guide to Forensic Psychology*. She presents workshops to law enforcement, psychologists, coroners, judges, and attorneys, and has consulted for *CSI* and *Bones*. She speaks internationally about forensic psychology, forensic science, death investigation, and serial murder, and has appeared on numerous documentaries, as well as on such programs as *The Today Show, 20/20, 48 Hours*, and *E! True Hollywood*. She writes a regular blog for *Psychology Today* called "Shadow-boxing."

Website: www.katherineramsland.com
Blog: http://www.psychologytoday.com/blog/shadow-boxing
https://www.facebook.com/Kath.ramsland/
https://twitter.com/KatRamsland

Introduction:
Investigative Basics

Forensics braids the process of investigation with psychology and the law. Psychology shows the human element, while law dictates the parameters for investigative practices. This text demonstrates how these threads intertwine and offers practice with cases that apply specific insights.

Each chapter opens with a case and features experts at work in some area of investigation. They include first responders, detectives, death investigators, scientists, attorneys, analysts, technicians, psychologists, profilers, and private investigators. Each chapter also offers case-related puzzles to ponder, such as the one below, which highlights how the first leads can sometimes *mis*lead. A detective on this case offered it as a cautionary tale for other investigators.

Near Miss

In November 2010, Tina Herrmann failed to show up for work at her job in Apple Valley, Ohio. Valerie Haythorn, Herrmann's boss, had asked the Knox County Sheriff's Office to perform a welfare check, but no one responded to their knocks. Herrmann had missed work for two days, which was uncharacteristic. Haythorn knew that she was estranged from her boyfriend, Greg Borders, and was about to move out. Concerned, she went to the house on November 11 and entered (Scott, 2012).

On carpets inside, Haythorn spotted greasy black stains with reddish borders. It looked as if a large object had been dragged. She phoned the sheriff's office, and several first responders arrived.

As they walked through the house, they saw more stains, which smelled like motor oil, along with a disturbing amount of blood spatter in the bathroom. They called the local school and learned that Herrmann's children, 13-year-old Sarah and 11-year-old Kody, were absent. From clumps of fur in the bathroom, a dog appeared to live in the home, but it could not be located.

Officers protected the scene and called for detectives. Crime scene agents from the Ohio Bureau of Criminal Identification and Investigation arrived to take photos and notes. Large shoe prints showed that an adult male had stepped in the oil stains, which appeared to be from an empty gallon container left in the house. Large blood saturation areas on the rugs suggested that three people had been stabbed. In the bathroom, detectives examined blood spatter and collected a pair of gloves, a bottle of bleach, and a box of bloodstained trash bags. On a floor inside the front door were bloody wipe patterns and transfer stains. A Jeep Cherokee with bloodstains inside was parked in the garage. It was registered to a friend of Herrmann's neighbor, Stephanie Sprang. She, too, was missing. Small footprints in the garage indicated that a child was still alive. The foot size matched shoes found in Sarah's closet.

Prior to this activity, investigators had looked for Greg Borders, Herrmann's ex-boyfriend. He had left home for work on the morning that these four individuals had disappeared, followed by a golf outing. When contacted, Borders seemed unconcerned. He said he had texted Herrmann on the morning of November 10 and she had been fine.

Officers were suspicious. It seemed too coincidental that he had been away for the same amount of time that his estranged girlfriend had been missing, and his lack of alarm seemed odd. Although Borders' work records established a partial alibi, Herrmann's ex-husband, who shared joint custody of their children, also suspected Borders.

Soon, Herrmann's Ford pickup truck, missing from the house, was located near a nature area. Police searched the woods, but found nothing. When Borders heard details about the state of his home, he grew concerned, especially when he realized that Herrmann's credit card and cellphone activity had ceased just after he had spoken with her. He affirmed that he had a dog and that the garage door had been broken for a while. It was stuck in a partially open position, with a gap wide enough for someone to slide under.

Crime scene processors continued their work. In the garage, near a trash container, a Walmart bag contained two tarps and a new but opened box of heavy-gauge trash bags. A processor noticed that the bags were a different brand than those in the home, suggesting a different purchaser. Detectives asked a Walmart manager to search store records, which turned up a purchase just after midnight on November 11 (Dietz & Ramsland, 2013).

Thanks to video enhancement, investigators matched product codes on the purchased items to the items in the bag at the home. The store video showed the purchaser: a thin, dark-haired man between the ages of 25 and 40. Surveillance tapes from cameras outside showed him driving a silver Toyota Yaris. From DMV license photos, detectives identified this man as Matthew J. Hoffman.

The pressure was on to find the missing girl, Sarah Maynard. Dispatch logs revealed that a deputy had stopped Hoffman near the recovery location of Herrmann's abandoned pickup, and he claimed he was waiting for his girlfriend, "Sarah." He could not recall her last name. Detectives now had several solid leads. They arranged for SWAT to enter Hoffman's home. They arrested him and discovered Sarah, bound and gagged, in the basement. She was transported to emergency care where she stated that Hoffman had molested her. She thought he had killed her mother and brother.

Hoffman, 30, was a former tree trimmer with a reputation for being strange. He had a record for domestic assault and his neighbors avoided him. He seemed paranoid and controlling, and he liked to build fires on his lawn and dress as an ape.

At this point, investigators were aware that they had nearly missed the crucial lead that solved the mystery (Dietz & Ramsland, 2013). They had focused on the boyfriend, which logic and probability analysis supported, but an observant processor's interpretation had shifted the focus toward a less likely but still possible scenario: a complete stranger had entered a home and killed people. Involved in the decisions were first responders, detectives, technicians, and a SWAT unit. The next step required interrogation, which relies on behavioral analysis.

Hoffman was brought into an interrogation room. It was not long before he removed his hooded sweatshirt and wool cap. This "venting" suggested that he felt hot, which implied possible guilt or fear. He said that he had come home on November 11 and discovered Sarah at his house. She told him that *he* had brought her there. This had confused him.

Detectives worked in teams to question him, but Hoffman went mute, even after they took him on a ride that passed Herrmann's residence and his mother's house. He sat straight up in a chair, silent, his eyes closed. He made some gestures that were difficult to interpret, but he answered no more questions.

By day four, November 18th, after a deal made by his public defender and an appeal from his mother, Hoffman admitted to killing the two women, the boy and the dog. Yet his statement also appeared to be full of lies. He said he had meant only to burglarize the home (although the amount of time he had been in the home and his failure to take items of value suggested otherwise). He had seen a garage door partially open, he said, and had watched for everyone to leave. He entered and looked around for several hours. He heard someone return. Instead of seeking a quick exit, he pulled out a blackjack and a knife. He killed the two women. He decided to dismember them and place their parts into a tall beech tree with a long hollow hole that ran down the middle. (He said this was a spur of the moment idea, but it appears to have been planned.) Eventually, the kids came home from school and he killed the boy. Hoffman had no explanation for why he had spared the girl.

Over the next few hours, Hoffman had tried bleaching the rugs to remove the blood. Failing, he poured motor oil on the stains. He then moved Sprang's Jeep Cherokee into the garage and placed the kitchen trash bags containing the body parts inside. He took the girl to his house, purchased the tarps and heavier bags at Walmart, and took the body parts to the woods to place into the tree. Intending to torch the house to burn the evidence, Hoffman drove the Jeep into the garage and left the Walmart bag there. He placed gas cans in Hermann's pickup outside and was driving it to get them filled when the truck's transmission failed, so he abandoned it. At some point, he suspected that police were at the house, so he aborted his plan.

As officers extracted the bags from the tree hollow, Hoffman pled guilty to multiple charges and received life without the possibility of parole. The coroner collected the bodies, and the pathologist's autopsy reports indicated that Hoffman had bludgeoned and extensively stabbed all of the victims.

Despite the investigators' assurance during the interrogation that they would find the bodies, Hoffman had known they never would. Even if they found evidence against him at the house, without his help the bodies would remain hidden. It required several points of pressure during the interrogation to persuade Hoffman to cooperate (Scott, 2012).

Investigators realized they could have fixated on Herrmann's estranged boyfriend (Dietz & Ramsland, 2011). Because Herrmann had expressed concern to a friend about his reaction to the break-up, and because his plans for those two days provided a convenient way to be out of the house, he was a good suspect. Home-based murders are more likely to be committed by a relative or an acquaintance than by a stranger.

This incident highlights a mental bias to which investigators are prone: threshold diagnosis and assumptions from familiarity (also called gut instinct). This derives from what psychologists call "heuristics," or mental shortcuts (Gilovich & Griffin, 2002). Due to the efficient nature of the human brain, we use shortcuts to reduce complex information into simple rules-of-thumb. However, because heuristics form quickly, they can cause errors that hinder – even damage – a criminal investigation (Rossmo, 2008). Heuristics arise from the notion that whatever makes sense must be the truth.

Because the detectives in the case above came close to making decisions based on probabilities rather than being flexible to *possibility*, they viewed the Hoffman incident as a good teaching case. It reminded them of the power of a *likely* narrative to seduce them into a premature sense of closure. They might have missed the subtle difference in the trash bags. Thus, they could still have an open case.

Overview

In such scenarios, several investigative issues arise. All will be addressed in this book. First, there were missing people and evidence of violence. Second, there was a need for a full victimology and profiling. Third, we have the investigators' mental frame. The latter receives little attention in texts devoted to investigation, but cognitive psychology offers relevant research to investigative frames (Ask & Granhag, 2005). Cognitive biases present a persistent challenge for criminal investigators (Stelfox & Pease, 2005). Since detectives have considerable discretion in making investigative decisions, being aware of these perceptual quirks can remind them to exercise caution about haste, even if – and *especially* if – those decisions feel "right."

In addition, investigators must recognize issues with spotting, processing, and analyzing evidence, which must fit within legal admissibility standards. Investigations involve numerous layers that must all coordinate, so even when experts are singled out in the following chapters to describe and demonstrate a method, they work as part of a larger team and within the legal system. No one works effectively without knowledge of, and assistance from, multiple arenas. Even private investigators working on their own will call on resources from others when needed.

A variety of investigators are involved in the forensic process. The obvious group features detectives in a police department, but there are also military investigations involving crimes, private investigators, freelance death investigators, expert consultants, researchers, medical investigators, and even attorneys who do their own investigation.

This book begins with first responders: what must be done to prepare the foundation for a proper investigation. This involves self-awareness and knowledge about basic cognitive processes in observation and analysis. In addition, the nature and role of behavioral evidence is important but often overlooked. Certain chapters highlight each of these areas.

Besides being mindfully attuned, investigators must know how to coordinate resources, especially from scientific methods and experts, with an eye to the integrity of chain of custody, the need for careful enhancement, and knowledge about admissibility in court. Thus, it is important to understand the roles of the judge and attorneys. For criminal investigations, knowing about criminal types is also a good idea.

As cases develop, the totality of the evidence is essential for accurate reconstruction. This is where knowledge about cognitive bias is helpful. There is also an ethical imperative to protect investigations against error and fraud.

The current book is about what experts from diverse disciplines can tell investigators, to enhance their knowledge or improve their practices. It covers each area in relevant detail, encouraging readers not only to learn the methods and areas of expertise relevant to forensic investigation but also to gain opportunities to apply this knowledge. There are many books about investigation, but few include a focus on psychological information that lays a foundation.

The case that opened this introduction demonstrates the importance of being aware of how easy it is to succumb to such things as ego anchoring and confirmation bias. It is also a reminder to remain open and flexible throughout the process. We start the first chapter where it all begins, with first responders.

References

Ask, K., & Granhag, P. A. (2005). Motivational sources of confirmation bias in criminal investigations. *Journal of Investigative Psychology and Offender Profiling, (2)*1, 43–63.

Dietz, J., & Ramsland, K. (2012) Solution in the details. *The Forensic Examiner, (21)*1, 19–23.

Gilovich, T., & Griffin, D. (2002). Heuristics and biases: Then and now. In T. Gilovich, D. Griffin, & D. Kahneman (Eds.), *Heuristics and biases: The psychology of intuitive imagination* (pp. 1–18). Cambridge, UK: Cambridge University Press.

Rossmo, K. D. (2008). Cognitive biases: Perception, intuition, and tunnel vision. In K. D. Rossmo (Ed.), *Criminal investigative failures* (pp. 9–21). Boca Raton, FL: CRC Press.

Scott, R. (2012). *The girl in the leaves.* New York, NY: Berkley.

Stelfox, P., & Pease, K. (2005). Cognition and detection: Reluctant bedfellows? In M. Smith & N. Tilley (Eds.),*Crime science: New approaches to preventing and detecting crime* (pp. 194–210). Cullompton, UK: Willan Publishing.

Chapter 1
Crimes, Scenes, and First Responders

Learning Objectives

❖ Understand the roles and responsibilities of first responders.
❖ Be able to explain the basics of crime scene processing.
❖ Recognize the psychological components of crime reconstruction.
❖ Define types of evidence.
❖ State the roles of crime scene personnel.

Key Words

Evidence, crime scene, crime scene mapping, logic tree, reconstruction, chain of custody

Jocelyn Earnest's friends knew that her ex-husband, Wesley, scared her. He might live five hours away from Forest, Virginia, but he could pop up unexpectedly to terrify her. Still, this seemed like a weak motive to kill herself. It did look like a suicide to the first responders who entered her locked house in response to a call. Jocelyn lay face-up, fully clothed, with a gunshot wound to her head. Yet the caller, a friend, had insisted that Jocelyn had been murdered (Fanning, 2014). This alerted officers to pay attention to anything inconsistent with suicide.

Investigators saw items of concern right away: the heat was turned to 90 degrees and the gun was on the wrong side of the body. In addition, a drag pattern in the blood showed that the body had moved or been moved. The thirty-eight-year-old woman, still wearing her coat, had a non-contact gunshot to the back of the head. Her beloved dog was crated, unfed, and Jocelyn had gone silent that night while texting a friend. She had a job she enjoyed, had good friends, could pay her bills, was seeing a therapist, and was not depressed. Yet, police found a typed suicide note that mentioned overwhelming financial difficulties. Further investigation showed that the note had not been typed on any computer associated with Jocelyn, and her preferred mode of expression was to write by hand.

The gun belonged to Wesley and he had the original box and case, although he told police he had purchased it for Jocelyn. He insisted he had not been near her that evening. An assistant high school principal, Wesley Ernest had a serious girlfriend. He admitted that he and Jocelyn had argued over their recent divorce settlement. Thanks to a legal judgment, Wesley had shouldered the majority of debt on a second home for which they owed more than it was worth.

When the suicide note was processed, it bore two partial thumbprints that belonged to Wesley. His attorney argued that he had once lived in the home and could have handled the paper. However, behavioral evidence raised other concerns. Wesley had misrepresented himself: He had told people he was not married and had lied about his debt. After the murder, he had gone to a tire shop some distance from where he lived, used a false name, and purchased four new tires for a truck he had borrowed, although the truck had nearly new tires.

Wesley was arrested and tried for ambushing and murdering his wife. Forensics experts testified that Jocelyn had been shot in a way that would have made it impossible for her to move, so someone else had moved the body. Wesley's whereabouts could not be established for the time of the murder and he was the only person who claimed that Jocelyn had been suicidal. Everyone close to her said she was not, and her best friends knew how frightened she was of Wesley.

Jurors returned a guilty verdict. Wesley Earnest received life in prison.

The Crime Scene

Evidence Documents, statements, and all items that are included in the legal proceedings for the jury's sole consideration in the question of guilt or innocence.

A crime scene is a location that contains **evidence** of an illegal act. This might be where the act occurred or evidence was stored, or be a place from which victims were abducted. It can even be a recording or an image on a digital device (Geberth, 2015).

When a call comes in to 9-1-1, a dispatcher sends patrol officers to investigate. They assess the stability of the scene, meet immediate needs for assistance, protect the scene with barriers and cautionary tape, and decide if other personnel are needed.

If there is an immobile victim, like Jocelyn Earnest, they check first for signs of life and might call for a paramedic unit. The officers note the victim's position when found and record a description of visible wounds or injuries. (This is how they saw that Jocelyn's body had been moved.) First responders record the time, set up a personnel log, and jot down pertinent observations (such as the thermostat setting). In some jurisdictions, they also take photographs or video. They note comments from a living victim and whatever they might ask victims or witnesses (e.g., friends who discovered Jocelyn's body). They also note distinct odors, lighting conditions, and other potentially relevant factors, especially those that might change or quickly disappear. In this case, the overheated room suggested an attempt to skew the time of death.

The type of incident and its degree of severity determines whether paramedics, detectives, forensic specialists, or death investigators are necessary (Adcock & Chancellor, 2013).

Figure 1. Crime scene tape

Source: Katherine Ramsland

Law enforcement will look for evidence left by the perpetrator, as well as items from the scene that might be on the perpetrator. This is Locard's exchange principle. Criminalist Edmond Locard believed in cross-transference between criminals and crime scenes because "every contact leaves a trace." Often, the contact evidence is subtle, such as a glass fragment or a thread. Officers must look carefully, avoid contamination, and restrict scene access to primary personnel. If there are multiple scenes, all must be protected. For evidence to be useful later in court, it must be provably uncontaminated. To achieve this goal, crime scene processors might wear protective gear, such as shoe coverings, gloves, a cap or hairnet, and a coverall suit. They must also be able to show who had custody of the evidence at all times. In some cases, an expert might be called for special evidence handling (Gilbet, 2010).

If any suspects are present, and probable cause can be established regarding their involvement, officers can make an arrest. Officers also obtain names of witnesses for questioning. If there is a body that must be moved, the first responders sketch its pose and location, and take photos.

At this time, the primary death investigator will take over.

Crime scene processing reports by first responders should reflect certain acts:

1. Resisted the tendency to quickly decide what happened;
2. Recognized the principle of evidence transfer;
3. Followed protocols for preserving the scene;
4. Secured the scene and attended to living victims;
5. Understood the need to control persons at the scene;
6. Identified witnesses and prevented them from mingling;

7. Moved nothing and touched nothing without gloves;
8. Added nothing to the scene; and
9. Properly documented everything, according to their agency's protocol.

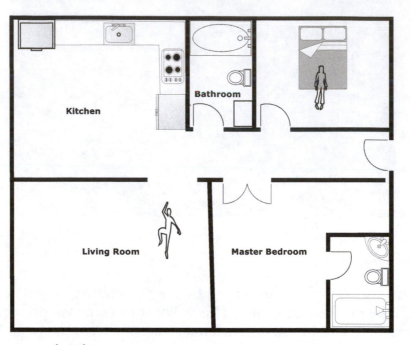

Figure 2. Crime scene sketch

Source: Katherine Ramsland

Crime Classification

Forensic investigation can be simple or complex. Criminal law (federal and state rules) divides crimes into four categories: personal, property, inchoate, and statutory. This book is concerned mostly with the first category, which involve crimes that result in mental or physical harm to another person, such as assault, battery, kidnapping, rape, and homicide. Homicide covers first- and second-degree murder and varieties of manslaughter. The next category, property crimes, lists acts that interfere with someone's right to enjoy their property; it includes robbery, burglary, arson, embezzlement, forgery, and receipt of stolen goods. Inchoate crimes are attempted crimes that would require substantial steps for completion: attempted murder, attempted rape, and conspiracy are on this list. Statutory crimes violate a state or federal statute, such as drunk driving, sexual contact with a minor, or selling alcohol to a minor.

Each state devises its own rules about how such acts are penalized. Some states might identify certain behaviors as illegal (possession of marijuana or carrying a concealed firearm) that are not included on other state lists (Lee, Palmbach & Miller, 2001). Crimes are also classified in terms of their level of seriousness. Felonies are more serious than misdemeanors and carry stiffer penalties. Some states also distinguish between violent and nonviolent crimes, and some focus on degree of criminal intent. Civil infractions include traffic violations and noise ordinance violations.

Lead detectives decide whether a search warrant is needed. If the person who controls the property offers permission to search, the search is legal. If not, the warrant must be obtained from a judge. Everything must be done according to legal procedure; if a search or seizure of evidence is made without protecting the rights of those people involved, then the evidence can be thrown out of the case, along with anything associated with it. The entire case can crumble on a technicality. Some scenes must be secured even after processors are finished, pending results. In this case, uniformed officers are usually posted at the scene until everyone connected with the case is satisfied that nothing further needs to be done.

Evidence and Documentation

Criminalistics is the analysis of physical evidence that will assist to reconstruct the incident and identify the offender. Two primary issues arise for crime scene processing. First, how were items determined to be evidence? Second, was the evidence properly collected and preserved?

After the crime scene manager has completed an initial assessment, the next step is to record the undisturbed scene. Crime scene technicians or designated photographers might take several hundred photos, because law enforcement officers who will reconstruct the scene need visual documentation of all perspectives; in other words, photos must show an overall view, a medium view, and close-ups. Photographers use digital, video, and 35-mm cameras, including those that can take black-and-white photos. Single lens reflex cameras are adaptable, and tripods offer stability. Wide-angle lenses are used for perspective and close-ups for high-resolution photos, as well as shooting in the dark. Some departments use cameras that can achieve a 360-degree image.

The skill of crime scene mapping requires experience. (This should not be confused with *crime mapping*, described in Chapter 11.) They must consider the time available to develop a map and define evidence that is most relevant or in danger of vanishing (Galvin, 2015). The more complex the scene or difficult the conditions, the more urgent the task. Investigators might rely on optical scanning and photogrammetry – the science of making measurements from photographs. Forensic CAD software and laser scanning can produce accurate 3-D scene diagrams that can be accessed later. They can also be examined from different angles. Robotic "total stations" allow operators to control the scanning remotely. This technology cuts down on the time involved to recreate scenes and some systems allow real-time viewing (and corrections) while the scan is processed. The end result of being able to "stitch together" several scans is a virtual walk-through of a crime scene that can be used for a trial display.

To begin, crime scene photographers walk through the scene to get perspective. Their task is to create an accurate representation for investigators. They discuss with the investigating officers what should be photographed in greater detail. The first photographs provide an overview of the scene from several angles, with notes made. These photos must include the position of items considered to be possible evidence.

Close-up still photos should be taken in high resolution and include a scale (sometimes two at right angles) and a frame marker, which will correspond with the item number used on the evidence custody sheet. Flash or flood lighting is adequate for general crime scenes, but some cameras are equipped with light guides that direct a narrow beam at a specific area. Some also have different filters, such as UV, which help to highlight biological evidence not easily seen. Oblique angle lighting brings out visually elusive details. Photographers shoot their way into a room or scene, focusing on those areas where the evidence has been identified. Finally, they shoot individual close-ups of each piece of evidence. Then they shoot their way out.

Other photos might include the body (if a homicide), tire treads, trace evidence, fingerprints, blood, and footprints. Impressions are photographed with flash or light sources placed at an angle. Photographers also record images of dusted fingerprints and document any evidence of a struggle.

Only after a scene has been visually and verbally documented does the search for evidence begin. Evidence can prove that a crime has been committed and reveal key aspects, including the identities of victims and suspects. It guides the type of investigation that must be performed, corroborates or undermines witness or suspect narratives, pressures suspects, and provides leads for further investigation.

The lead detective forms a plan to prioritize collection, with fragile or transient evidence collected immediately. If there appears to be a hazard, such as biohazards from decomposing bodies, special equipment and clothing are used. All evidence gets a numbered flag or marker to show where it was found, which is photographed and added to a scene diagram and a log (Lee, Palmbach & Miller, 2001).

The type of evidence to look for includes:

1. Temporary (may change or be lost)
2. Conditional (associated with specific conditions at the crime scene)
3. Associative (links a suspect or victim to a scene)
4. Pattern (blood, impressions, tire treads, or evidence of the *modus operandi*)
5. Trace/transfer (produced by physical contact with some surface)

The use of appropriate lighting is important. A bright flashlight is part of any kit, but using all available light can be helpful. For outdoor scenes in dim light or darkness, a large portable light might be required. To take shots in a pitch-black room or in the woods at night, cameras must be set up on tripods. They must also be capable of a long exposure, such as a digital single lens reflex, for "painting with light." The shutter is opened for thirty seconds while the photographer moves a bright flashlight over an area. The result is similar to an image produced in better light.

For reconstruction, investigators must know how to handle different types of evidence at the scene and how it is analyzed in a laboratory.

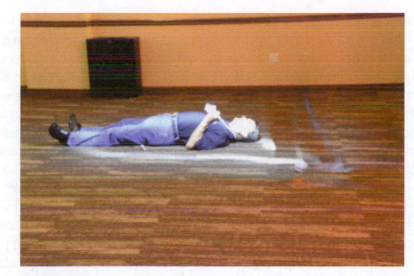

Figure 3. Painting with light in a dark room

Source: Katherine Ramsland

Logic Trees

The mission of the Henry C. Lee Institute at the University of New Haven in Connecticut is to educate and train investigators in the methods of forensic science. Dr. Henry Lee is one of the world's most renowned experts in criminalistics and incident reconstruction. Born in China, Lee studied police science in Taiwan, but went to the United States to attain a Ph.D. in biochemistry. He began to teach at the University of New Haven and established a program in forensic science. In 1979, Lee became the first chief criminalist and director of the Connecticut State Police Forensic Science Laboratory. He has innovated several methods, testified in hundreds of trials, and consulted on thousands of criminal cases around the world (Lee, Pagliaro & Ramsland, 2009).

At the Institute, a corridor separates the Forensic Science National Crime Scene Training and Technology Center from the Forensic Training Center. The virtual crime scene and virtual laboratory rooms provide a connected perspective of crime scene and lab analysis. Projections of scenes help viewers see them through the eyes of a crime scene investigator. The crime-scene training area contains furnished living, dining, bed and bath rooms, with "wounded" or "deceased" mannequins for practice with crime scene analysis and reconstruction. Across the hall are the labs for the scientific analysis of trace evidence, DNA, and fingerprints. Lee likes to say that he seeks to discover the truth, and for this, he believes that investigators need integrity, objectivity, and the ability to work under pressure. He has been associated with such famous cases as O. J. Simpson, JonBenet Ramsey, Chandra Levy, Phil Spector, and Connecticut serial killer Michael Ross.

For decision making in crime investigation, Lee uses a strategic and systematic logic tree, working from the crime scene out. The scene offers clues about the offender's *modus operandi*, as well as showing any pattern or impression evidence, so that investigators can distinguish primary from secondary scenes and determine what happened. Lee develops a flexible hypothesis that can be tested as the case evolves.

Among his most painstaking cases was the investigation into the 1986 disappearance of a Pan Am flight attendant, Helle Crafts (Herzog, 1989). Late that year, she was in the process of divorcing her husband, Richard, a commercial pilot. She suspected infidelity and had hired a private investigator (PI), confiding to friends that she was scared. Then, on the night of a significant snowstorm that produced a power outage, Helle disappeared from her home in Newton, CT. The PI contacted authorities. The responding officers learned that Richard Crafts told people that Helle had driven to a relative's house, but had never arrived. He told other stories as well, none of which resolved the mystery of her whereabouts. Helle's car was discovered at Kennedy Airport, yet she had not reported for work.

Because Richard Crafts worked as an auxiliary police officer, investigators figured that he knew how to hide evidence. They learned from the nanny that a large piece of carpet was missing from the bedroom, where she had formerly seen a large, dark spot. This sounded suspicious. She had possibly seen blood.

Yet Crafts, passing a polygraph, explained that he had spilled kerosene on the rug. The PI, in the meantime, located the missing piece of rug and had it tested at the state police laboratory, where Dr. Lee was director and chief criminalist. Elaine Pagliaro was his lab assistant. They found no blood on the rug. Then a new lead developed: Craft's credit card records showed the purchase of a large freezer and the rental of a commercial wood chipper. He had also purchased a new truck with a special trailer hitch (Lee, 2002).

A search of his home turned up more than 100 items of potential evidence. Investigators, performing presumptive blood tests, identified blood in various areas. Fortuitously, they learned about a public works employee who had seen a man parked near the river on the night Helle had vanished. Notably, this man had been using a wood chipper during the snowstorm. When detectives searched the area, they spotted wood chips, blue fibers, and scraps of paper. A shredded envelope bore Helle's name. The search team picked up strands of blond hair, human bone fragments, a finger, a tooth, and other items. In the trunk of Richard's car were similar items.

It seemed unthinkable, but to confirm that a person could be put through this type of wood chipper, resulting in pieces of this size, the investigative team put a pig's carcass through it. The fragments were similar. Crafts was arrested. After two trials in which Lee's team presented a logic-tree reconstruction from physical evidence and suspicious behavior, Crafts was convicted of murder.

Constructing a logic tree starts with evidence at the scene (or scenes). Whatever is picked up is inventoried and considered within a context that makes sense. Obvious evidence is collected first, but the type of scene determines the type and quantity of evidence collected. Lee offers logic trees for different types of crime, such as rape and sexual assault, burglary, bombing, arson, and poisoning (Lee, Pagliaro & Ramsland, 2009). In some cases, such as a suspected staged suicide, research might be necessary to supplement the logic, since logic alone can sometimes rely on common myths. Investigators learn to think according to their own experience, but a logic tree can keep things organized.

Search protocols, too, are based on type.

1. A common indoor search is the "strip search," which involves walking from one end of an identified scene to another, turning and walking back, aiming slightly to the right or left.
2. A spiral search takes a circular path, beginning in the outer perimeter and working inward.
3. Sector searches assign an investigator or a team to a specific area.
4. Grid searches involve criss-crossing specific areas.

A logic tree for the Crafts case first recognized potential evidence, such as a missing person, the report of a man acting strangely with a wood chipper at the same time she went missing, the lies the man subsequently told, and the items found where the wood chipper would have placed them. This produced a four-way linkage between the victim, the suspect, the evidence, and the scene. The items of evidence were identified and examined for significance to a reconstruction and uniqueness. Lee's team surmised that on the night Helle died, she was wearing a blue bathrobe and carrying envelopes in her pocket. Richard bludgeoned her, accounting for the blood in the house, and placed her body in a freezer to await transport. When the storm approached, he saw an opportunity to chop the body into pieces without anyone seeing him (because who would be out in such a storm?) and to use the accumulating snow to obliterate evidence. He had a truck and a wood chipper, which would accommodate a frozen corpse.

To ensure evidence integrity, each piece must be placed in an appropriate container, labeled with the case number, the victim's (or suspect's) name, and all signatures of people who have handled it. Until 1924, when the "murder bag" was introduced in England, detectives used whatever packaging they could find and handled evidence with their bare hands. The case that changed this practice was that of Patrick Mahon, who murdered his pregnant mistress. When investigators went to the rather gory scene, famed pathologist Bernard Spilsbury noticed that they touched the remains, which exposed them to potential infection. He thought they should carry gloves. His concern opened discussions about other items that would be useful to carry. Hence, they would need a bag for transport to the scenes.

To collect evidence, technicians today need tweezers, rubber gloves, tape, sterile swabs, evidence vacuums, and an assortment of envelopes and containers appropriate for different types of evidence.

Vacuums equipped with special filters can pick up fiber, dirt, glass fragments, and hair.

Different types of kits ensure that everything is properly documented and collected (Ramsland, 2001). Kits exist for different proposes, such as gunshot residue, rape, fingerprinting, detecting the presence of blood, biological specimen collection, entomology, and hazardous situations. Some kits are large and comprehensive, while others are packed with a few items that are used for a specific purpose.

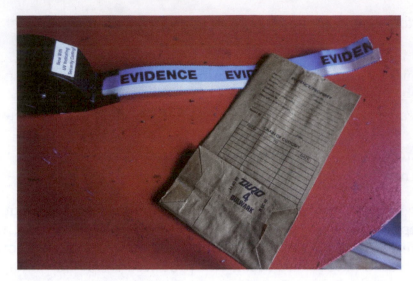

Figure 4. Evidence bag and tape

Source: Katherine Ramsland

Figure 5. Crime scene kit

Source: Katherine Ramsland

A basic kit should contain crime scene tape, a bright flashlight, sketch pads, a digital camera, clean paper sacks, disposable masks, surgical-type gloves, scales or measuring implements, fingerprinting items, casting items, markers to place next to evidence, white butcher paper, an alternative light source, and emergency phone numbers.

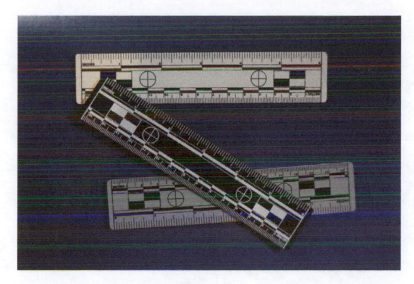

Figure 6. Scales

Source: Katherine Ramsland

A basic fingerprinting kit will have disposable gloves, fingerprint powder, clean fiberglass dusting brushes, camelhair brushes, lifting tape, latent print cards and elimination print forms, a magnifying lens, an ultraviolent light, evidence rulers, and evidence seals, tags, and bags.

Figure 7. Items from a fingerprint kit

Source: Katherine Ramsland

A casting kit for impressions would include casting compound, mixing bowls, casting frames, and fixatives for different conditions. Each kit should include a knife for scraping dried evidence, and a wide variety of containers.

Figure 8. Casting kit

Source: Katherine Ramsland

Before collecting evidence, investigators must ensure that the size and type of container corresponds to the evidence, and that there are containers for wet and dry evidence, as well as ways to air-dry wet evidence. Plastic bags or containers should be avoided for organic material, because they accelerate biological deterioration and evaporate accelerants. All evidence containers should be sealed with tape or a sealing agent.

Investigation and Reconstruction

Officer Samuel Del Rosario opened a black plastic case to show a group of students the different parts of a polygraph. Poised in a pinstriped gray suit, he explained his work as the local department's certified polygraph examiner. A former death investigator for the Lehigh County Coroner's Office, Del Rosario is currently a patrol officer with a master's degree and over thirteen years of experience. He seeks opportunities to educate himself in areas relevant to policing, such as security, crimes against children, and digital forensics.

As a member of the Bethlehem Police Department, Del Rosario hopes to bring affordable training opportunities to other officers, so he took over as program director at the Northeast Forensic Training Center (NFTC). The facility offers a regional hub for learning practical basic and advanced skills, such as fingerprint examination, crime scene photography, digital forensics, firearms, blood spatter pattern analysis, interview and interrogation, and other law enforcement investigative techniques. The NFTC provides training and assists first responders in effective methods for preserving crime scenes and laying the groundwork for advanced processing. The facility has served local, national, and international agencies with lab space, a wet room, classrooms, and a scenario apartment.

Del Rosario has over 4000 hours of advanced training in investigations, including the Department of Homeland Security's Criminal Investigator Training Program. He also gives talks to local groups to increase awareness of what police officers do. He invites instructors from a variety of disciplines to teach about fingerprint examination, crime scene photography, blood spatter pattern analysis, firearms, interview and interrogation, and anything else that might assist with better incident reconstruction.

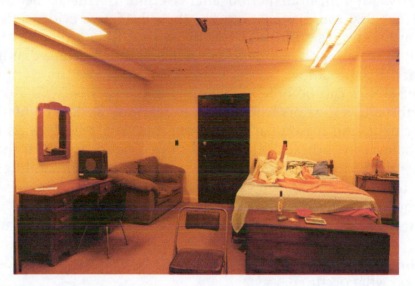

Figure 9. NFTC reconstruction room

Source: Katherine Ramsland

Because defense lawyers might scrutinize the initial collection and preservation of evidence, as well as the evidentiary chain of custody, Del Rosario knows that proper protocol must be followed. **Chain of custody** means that each person who handles evidence signs off on it, records what is done with it (with dates and times), and replaces it in its secure storage location. The evidence that is submitted to court must be provably the same evidence that was collected from the scene.

> **Chain of custody**   The method used to keep track of who is handling a piece of evidence, and for what purpose.

Each piece must be recorded on an inventory. It is assigned an item number, which should correspond to the number placed next to the item in any photographs. More will be said in the following chapters about specific types of evidence analysis.

For reconstruction, investigators pair criminalistics with behavioral evidence. This combination might provide early indications of motive and also predict the possibility of a recurrence by the same offender(s). Reconstruction depends on the incident, but in general, the procedure is (Lee, Palmbach & Miller, 2001):

1. Observe everything
2. Clarify the problem
3. Consider all potential evidence to be important until proven otherwise
4. Note the initial evidence and its location at the scene

5. Form a guiding and testable hypothesis
6. Interpret the data and add more, if available
7. Evaluate the investigation

The initial twenty-four-hour period after a crime is crucial, because aside from transient evidence that can dissipate quickly, the substantive evidence is still relatively undisturbed and witnesses still have clear memories (unless they were traumatized). The suspect's trail is fresh and reporters have not yet printed details that might alert this person to what the police know.

Some crime scenes can be processed with general expertise, while others require a team of specialists. Investigators listen to witnesses, look at documentation, develop a feel for the incident, and reason backward from it to devise likely ways to replay what happened. Whatever hypothesis is devised, it must account for all of the evidence but also be sufficiently flexible to change if new information requires a different approach. Crime scenes in which several people have moved around or gone elsewhere can be difficult to sequence. Pattern evidence is often part of reconstruction, which requires specialized knowledge. This includes blood spatter, glass fractures, behavioral patterns, burn residue, projectile trajectories, and other impressions. The goal is to identify a suspect, link the suspect to the victim or crime, and prove with proper evidence collection and preservation what occurred.

Summary

The work of the first responder is key to the quality of the work that can be done by those who come later to process the scene, analyze the evidence, and reconstruct the incident. Quality and care should be emphasized in their training, which should involve not just information but also plenty of practice.

Before we discuss methods, analysis, enhancement, and criminology, we must start at the most basic level: the psychology of investigation. Ideally, the way evidence is interpreted and used as the basis for a hypothesis should be objective and easy to replicate with the same methods and principles. However, human beings have cognitive biases, some of which can significantly affect the direction an investigation takes. "I-contact" is ground zero for observing and interpreting a scene that, as Dr. Henry Lee puts it, gets us to the truth.

Exercise #1.1

Assuming that first responders have secured the scenes and criminalists have collected the evidence, what initial steps would you take to investigate each of the following?

1. Kaye R. was raped and repeatedly stabbed in her home for three hours by an intruder that she was able to see. Miraculously, she survived and recalled that he had said he

lived in the same complex and, like her, had a son. Oddly, he had used her blood to paint a happy face on her back. Three full fingerprints were lifted from a plastic cup and a rape kit was processed. After news coverage offered a composite sketch, a man who strongly resembled Kaye's attacker came to Kaye's home, got down on his knees outside and prayed that someone would find the perpetrator. When police brought him in for questioning, he asked for a job application and signed it with a happy face. He had no alibi for the night of the rape and he was a person of interest in an earlier murder case. Kaye and her son both identified him in a line-up, and Kaye said his voice was the same. He also resembled the composite drawing for which she had provided details. Under arrest, he said, "Tell her I didn't mean to do it." Yet, his fingerprints and DNA did not match the evidence.

2. Arby Little Soldier was riding through his back pasture when he saw an object on the ground. It was the remains of his prized white buffalo calf. The animal had been gutted and skinned, he reported, and the pelt was gone. This had caused a significant financial loss, because Arby had invested a lot in an upcoming ceremony to honor the calf's first birthday. In Native American folklore, the rare white buffalo is a sacred animal. A lot of preparation had gone into the big event. However, the calf was dead and, per Native American custom, quickly buried.

    Arby wanted an investigation. He said the carcass' head was facing east and the feet were facing south, which suggested a Native ritual. He suspected rival tribal leaders of killing the calf to discredit him. They were jealous that the calf had been born on *his* land. He suggested that the perpetrator was someone who had known he was going out of town during the period when the calf was killed.

    Arby dug up the calf's skull and a rib bone to show the officers, claiming that the calf had been skinned and the hooves were missing. In fact, the whole sacred family was gone. The calf's father had died a month earlier, seemingly struck by lightning. The mother had died a month after the calf, apparently from a wound suffered during the attack on the calf.

    Arby received many condolences and gifts. He started a reward fund to help find the killer, receiving $45,000. The Powwow that Arby arranged drew many people, and he charged $5.00 for parking. He predicted that the calf's killer would die in a bad way. The crime was categorized as criminal mischief.

References

Adcock, J. M., & Chancellor, A. S. (2013). *Death investigations.* Burlington, MA: Jones & Bartlett.

Fanning, D. (2014). *Under cover of night.* New York, NY: Berkley Books.

Galvin, R. (November, 2015). Getting more detail from crime scene diagrams. *Evidence Technology Magazine.*

Geberth, V. (2015) *Practical homicide investigation: Tactics, procedures, and Forensic techniques,* 5th ed. Boca Raton, FL: CRC Press.

Gilbet, J. N. (2010). *Criminal investigation,* 8th edition. Upper Saddle River, NJ: Prentice Hall.

Hall, M. (2013, January). The mystery of Lightning Medicine Cloud. *Texas Monthly*.

Herzog, A. (1989). *The woodchipper murder*. New York: Henry Holt & Co.

Lee, H. C. (2002). *Cracking cases: The science of solving crimes*. Amherst, New York: Prometheus.

Lee, H. C., Palmbach, T., & Miller, M. T. (2001). *Henry Lee's crime scene handbook*. San Diego, CA: Academic Press.

Lee, H. C., Pagliaro, E. & Ramsland, K. (2009). *The real world of a forensic scientist: Renowned experts reveal what it takes to solve crimes*. Amherst, NY: Prometheus.

Ramsland, K. (2001). *The forensic science of C.S.I.* New York: Berkley.

Chapter 2
I-Contact: The Psychology of Investigation

Learning Objectives

❖ Recognize the role of bias and cognitive distortion in observation and decisions.
❖ Learn the importance of the spotlight of attention.
❖ Be able to describe a mental map.
❖ List the key mental shortcuts that affect an investigation.
❖ Describe one's personal style of processing information.

Key Words

Attentional drain, cognitive interference, confirmation bias, heuristics, high need for closure, inattentional blindness, mental map, mindfulness, observation, threshold diagnosis, tunnel vision

In Lansing, Michigan, eighteen-year-old Rose Larner would hang out with suspected drug dealers John Kehoe and Bill Brown. She considered Kehoe her boyfriend, but he did not agree. On December 6, 1993, the last time Rose talked to her mother, Rose Markey, she said she was going to visit a friend. Her mother believed she meant Kehoe. Then Rose vanished. Resolving this case required a highly observant investigator.

The local police questioned Kehoe and Brown. Kehoe admitted he had spoken to Rose on the night she disappeared, but he was on a date, so she had left. Brown said he knew nothing. The case went cold. When the Michigan State Police reviewed it three years later, they leaned on Brown. He resisted, but finally said Kehoe had killed Rose.

They had taken Rose to the home of Kehoe's grandparents, who were away. She had showered with them but resisted sex. Kehoe had strangled her in the shower stall, slit her throat, and dismembered her. Brown had helped to clean up. Kehoe said they could take the body parts to his family's cabin. There, Kehoe prepared a fire and burned Rose's body. He allegedly ate some of her roasted flesh. When the fire died out, they collected the ashes to toss along the road as they drove away.

Brown said Kehoe scared him, so he had kept this story to himself. Police located Kehoe in Mexico and returned him for trial. He claimed that Brown had killed Rose.

Despite the passage of time since the murder, investigators searched Kehoe's grandparents' house. Luminol revealed a bloody ring on a carpet that matched the size of a bucket's bottom, corroborating Brown's story. One of the investigators went carefully over the patterned wallpaper and noticed a small brown spot that stood out. A DNA test confirmed that it was Rose's blood. The basement sump-pump and the campfire ring yielded human bone fragments from a young person ("Out of the Ashes," 1998).

John Kehoe was convicted of first-degree murder and went to prison for life. Brown served one year as an accessory. Kehoe is currently seeking a new trial.

Without the spot on the wall, it would have been difficult to corroborate Brown's story, and such a tiny spot was easy to overlook. Patient observation is an essential investigative skill. In this chapter, we look at aspects of human perception and cognition that can enhance observational skills, as well as thwart them. The ultimate goal is greater cognitive suppleness, to be able to process data quickly but without subversive shortcuts. Although it is difficult to be self-reflective during the heat of an investigation, exercises like those below can prepare investigators to do this as part of their routine.

The Psychology of Observation

Being close to crime on a regular basis, especially violent crime, can either dull the mind or sharpen it. Those investigators who seek to excel in their jobs will appreciate the importance of patient, exacting observation. However, certain mental quirks can undermine the effort, and it is just as important to be aware of them. We start with the art.

Scottish surgeon Joseph Bell had learned that the finest nuances matter. He told his students that they could not do better than to develop a finely honed sense of observation. However, this skill requires practice. Bell urged students to "use your eyes, sir, use your ears, use your brain, your bump of perception." He expected them to be able to figure out details about patients without even talking to them. Then they had to verify, or match their ideas against the facts (Liebow, 1982).

Bell liked to bring a beaker to class that he had filled with an odd-looking fluid. He told students that it tasted bitter, but insisted that they should learn how various liquids tasted and smelled. Within this context, he told them to "follow my example." Then he dipped his finger into the fluid, tasted it, showed with a sour expression that it was indeed bitter, and passed it to a student. Each stuck in a finger, tasted it, winced, and gave it to the next one. Then Bell would deliver the punch line: he had not tasted the liquid. He had dipped a finger into it, yes, but had placed a different finger into his mouth. The students who tested the liquid had not observed him carefully. It was an impressive lesson.

Yet mere sensory acuteness is not enough. The best observation skill is based on knowledge. Bell insisted that students study subjects that would help them make distinctions among such things as weather patterns, medicinal odors, geographical terrains, styles of carriages, or different tread patterns from boots and shoes. Bell dedicated significant time to learning about items that would enhance his ability to "see more." His student and clerk, Arthur Conan Doyle, watched Bell with admiration. He went on to base a fictional character on him – Sherlock Holmes.

Figure 10. Sherlock Holmes statue in London

Psychologist Maria Konnikova (2013) describes the skills of investigative observation, critical thinking, and decision-making in *How to Think Like Sherlock Holmes*. Konnikova is a psychologist and journalist who explores topics in psychology for mainstream scientific publications.

She illustrates in detail how the iconic detective, like Bell, honed his mental processes into a precision machine: observe, hypothesize, test, and deduce. In Holmes' world, she observed, nothing is taken at face value. What characterizes Holmes' thinking is skepticism and inquisitiveness. Holmes was also attentive to errors of thinking from subconscious influences, such as the tendency to see what you want to see or drawing quick conclusions to gain closure.

Konnikova recognizes that, by neurological default, we tend to be "Watsons," with lazy thinking habits, content with "autopilot," and reacting as things catch our attention rather than being proactive. The normal human mind is not highly focused, but we all can improve our minds with training. The first step is to be motivated to make a practice of "reflective alertness." In investigative work, this means a habit of vigilance. This will clarify the mind. Holmes warns against taking too much "lumber" into the "brain attic," because it crowds out information that is genuinely useful.

"The most powerful mind," says Konnikova, "is the quiet mind. It is the mind that is present, reflective, mindful of its thoughts and its state. It doesn't often multi-task, and when it does, it does so with a purpose" (p. 73).

She offers three rules that will facilitate better observational skills:

1. Institute a daily mindfulness practice: at least 10 minutes, every morning. It will make you more observant throughout the day, not just immediately following the practice.
2. Eschew multitasking. Practice focusing attention on only one thing.
3. Be wary of the influence of emotion. Never make decisions while angry, upset, thrilled, etc. It biases your observation, and you don't end up seeing what you think you're seeing" (personal communication, 2015).

Mental vigilance also needs context. Dr. Joel Katz, a professor of medicine at Harvard Medical School, realized that observational skills among new students were declining, thanks to dependence on laboratory tests and radiological exams. He wanted to find a way to teach them how to keep their skills honed. Before he went into medicine, Katz had been a graphic designer. He knew that, as with art appreciation, the inherent ambiguity of interpreting medical conditions forces observers to make judgments from incomplete data sets. This gave him an idea (Ramsland, 2012).

Katz and his colleagues paired diagnostic instruction with Visual Thinking Strategies (VTS), an active thinking approach to art interpretation. They developed a ten-week course and invited twenty-four students in pre-clinical training to participate. Half formed the control group.

Each student took a pre-experiment visual skill examination. While the control group continued with the typical medical curriculum, students in the experimental group went to Boston's Museum of Fine Arts for weekly lessons on how to observe critically the characteristics of various sculptures and paintings. The exercises encouraged the students to develop their own ideas.

At the end of ten weeks, all participants retook the visual skill exam. Compared to the control group, students who completed the art course made more frequent observations. There was an average increase of 5.41 observations per image, as well as a higher level of sophistication in critical reasoning.

However, as Joseph Bell pointed out, proactive training in observation is not enough. Aspiring super-observers must also understand personal cognitive quirks that can undermine close observation. Bell himself described tunnel vision as the mistake of getting one's theory before one's facts, and then bending the facts to fit. Holmes calls this "arguing in front of your data." It is all too easy to cherry-pick or reshape facts.

Let us consider some potential snags in the process of becoming a good observer.

Cognitive Snags

Criminologist Kim Rossmo (2008, 2011) has studied how quirks of the human mind can negatively impact investigations. He notes that all investigators arrive at scenes with a perceptual set (a.k.a, a mental map), based on education, culture, and personal experience. This helps them to make decisions. Yet, even the most experienced can make a hasty judgment, and the investigation can become anchored in early data. This is called a threshold diagnosis. People react to a scene, compare it with what they know, decide what it means, and then look for support. They often see what – and only what – they expect to see. More important, they fail to see things that might be present because their judgment shuts it out. Add to this an emotional layer, and you can mire an investigation in some very poor judgment.

Consider this case:

Mark and Donnah Winger appeared to be the perfect couple. The recent parents of an adopted baby girl, they lived in Springfield, Illinois. Life seemed fine until August 29, 1995. At 4:40 PM, Mark called 9-1-1. He needed help, fast! A maniac had attacked his wife! When paramedics and police arrived, Mark showed them an unconscious man and woman lying five feet apart on the dining room floor. Both were still alive. One officer took three Polaroid photos as they awaited the ambulance.

Mark said he had been in the basement fitness room when he heard commotion upstairs. On his way to respond, he grabbed his .45 semi-automatic gun. In the dining room, he saw a man standing over his wife, hitting her with a hammer. Mark shot the intruder and ran over to Donnah, to check her. When the intruder raised his head, Mark shot him again. When this man moaned, Mark grabbed the hammer and beat him in the chest.

Mark called 9-1-1, mumbled, and hung up. He called again.

Police noted that Mark had blood on his arms, hands, and neck. He did not know the identity of the intruder until police found the man's wallet and told him it was Roger Harrington. He was a limo driver for BART. A coffee mug on the table bore the company's label. A car parked in the front of the house belonged to Harrington. Inside it were a knife and a crowbar. A note lay on the front seat with the Wingers' address and a time, 4:30 PM.

Both victims died at the hospital. To investigators, Mark offered a theory. Six days earlier, Harrington had shuttled Donnah from the airport, talking crazy and driving so erratically he had frightened her. Mark had urged her to write down the details. They had complained to the shuttle company. Then they received hang-ups. Wary, they asked for police protection and purchased a dog. Mark had kept his gun loaded and ready. The hammer

Figure 11. Winger scene reconstruction

Source: Katherine Ramsland

that Harrington used to strike Donnah had been on the dining room table, to remind Mark to finish a project. He thought that Harrington had arrived, intending to hurt them. He got into an argument with Donnah, saw the hammer, and used it.

When police investigated Harrington, they discovered he had a record of domestic abuse and talked about demons ordering him to kill. Harrington had requested that the shuttle company give his phone number to Mark for a possible reconciliation, but Mark said that when he had called Harrington, the man spoke strangely to him.

Police also queried Wingers' neighbors. Their accounts did not add up, but the inconsistencies seemed minor. One had seen a man in a junky car drive up and wait for a few minutes before going inside. Another heard two shots, 40 minutes apart. There was no sign of forced entry, so Donnah must have opened the door. The Wingers' guard dog had been locked in the garage.

The incident was ruled a justifiable homicide in defense of home and family. Officers viewed Mark as a hero, defending his wife and child.

However, Officer Doug Williamson had reservations. He thought the investigators had not fully considered some issues. Williamson wondered why the guard dog had been locked in the garage and why Donnah would invite a man in who scared her. Why had Harrington brought in a coffee cup with his company's logo and a pack of cigarettes? Why had he brought no weapon? He would not have known that a hammer was handy on the table. If he had intended harm, he would have parked in a more isolated spot, not in front of the Wingers' house in the wrong direction. In addition, not only had he written down the address and time on a note, he had told his roommate where he was going. These were not the behaviors of someone intent on assault or murder.

Williamson confided his doubts to his partner, Charlie Cox, but Cox and other officers assured him that all cases had holes. The overall totality of the evidence supported Mark's story. Williamson, a rookie, did not have enough experience yet to judge. "They discounted everything I had to say," Williamson would later tell a correspondent from the *48 Hours* television program (Zimmerman, 2008). Even his request to look at Winger's phone records was denied.

But Cox started listening. They discussed the case for months. Cox maintained that Williamson was over-thinking; simple answers were best. Yet Cox started to wonder. Could Mark have planned such an elaborate scheme? Why? Eventually, the "no-brainer" case with the simple answers fell apart. Williamson was right.

Winger filed a civil lawsuit against the shuttle company for hiring Harrington. The company's attorneys hired a forensic blood spatter expert, Thomas Bevel, who turned up evidence that Winger had lured Harrington to his home in an elaborate set-up. Among the items was the fact that Winger's bloodied hand showed a clean area that appeared as if he'd held something thick, like a hammer. The photographs from the scene contradicted his story, from body position to blood spatter to where the shell casings were picked up. Investigators surmised that, prior to the incident, Mark had considered killing Donnah. Her call about the shuttle ride gave him an idea. Then came the motive: an affair. The mistress came forward to tell police that Mark had planned to kill his wife.

Blood pattern analysis contradicted Winger's story, as did neighbor reports about the two shots fired forty minutes apart. Mark Winger was convicted of murder. The rookie detective who had refused to accept the simple closure was vindicated.

It is easy for experienced detectives to let their thought processes go on autopilot once they believe they know what happened (Lord, Ross, & Lepper, 1979). They feel satisfied, and they interpret this feeling as fact.

Rossmo (2008) points out that clear and rational thinking like Williamson had done is not automatic, because our brains are not wired for uncertainty. Thus, we take mental shortcuts, a.k.a., **heuristics** (Gilovich & Griffin, 2002). Several have the potential to derail any investigation. A few show up in the Winger investigation:

1. The simple answer is the best answer.
2. If it makes logical sense, it is true.
3. Form a hypothesis and look for whatever will make it work.
4. Use those items that support the early theory and ignore those that do not.

We arrange mental shortcuts within three key areas: cognitive interference, attentional drain, and personality frames.

1. Cognitive Interference
   Cognitive interfence is the result of two concurrent modes of processing. Rossmo states that when we experience an incident, some information moves through rational channels and some through emotional-intuitive channels. Intuition is aligned with automatic, subconscious judgment, often shaped by emotion. Conclusions are made with little or no analysis, and are often based merely on past experience. Yet what *feels* right is not necessarily right. Gut instinct, wrongly believed to be unerring, can become a threshold diagnosis: Winger's story makes sense, so Winger's story is true. However, gut instinct is rooted in what we already know. It feels right only because it is familiar. What is familiar is limited to our perspective. Although reflective reasoning is slower than emotional reasoning, it can make us consider a greater range of factors. The result of careful analysis, like what Williamson did, is usually more reliable.

   However, we are conscious of only rational thought; the emotional-intuitive channel eludes us but still influences us (Szegedy-Maszak, 2005). For example, an experiment at a wine store showed that playing German versus Italian music in the background influenced whether customers purchased German or Italian wine. Research also shows that people will pay more for the same product if the package is colorful and appealing, or they will say that coffee in a more expensive container tastes better even if it is the same coffee as in the low-priced container. Officer Cox preferred simplicity, so he was prepared to accept a simple solution. Too many details, for him, became "over-thinking," which felt clumsy and therefore something to avoid.

Once threshold diagnosis sets in, it becomes easier to succumb to confirmation bias. Investigators who believe they "already know" what happened in a given scenario look for support, and also look past anything that fails to support their hypothesis (Kebbell, Muller, & Martin, 2010). Once the Winger investigation seemed concluded, supervisors were unwilling even to look at phone records that might raise questions. They were satisfied with a clear picture, even if it was incomplete. If there are informational gaps, our brain quickly fills them in, because the brain strives to make sense of the world (Kruglanski & Webster, 1996). For example, because Harrington had a mental illness, his odd behavior of writing down a time and entering the home without a weapon seemed consistent with his irrational frame of mind.

Once the actual scenario of the Winger incident came clear, the facts were interpreted differently and unanswered questions were answered. However, it had taken a persistent young detective to go against group consensus – and orders – to bring a killer to justice.

2. Attentional Drain

Many people believe they can multi-task well, but they fail to realize that the brain's ability to focus is limited. It has evolved to use a spotlight of focus, a single bright bulb. When we multi-task, we transform the bright bulb into several dimmer bulbs. Research shows that we do not perform multiple tasks equally well; we perform multiple tasks with decreased efficiency for each. Unfortunately, our brains do not let us know that our focus has dimmed, so we do not feel the impact of reduced efficiency, or attentional drain (Chabris & Simons, 2010). We think we can pay the same attention to the road when we text or talk on the phone as when we are just driving.

Confidence that we are doing well does not mean we *are* doing well. Confidence is an emotional state and sometimes merely the product of a high self-estimation. A human weakness is that we possess no intuitive awareness of the limits of attention. Nearly half a century of research supports this.

During the 1970s, researchers found that people who simultaneously listened to different sounds in each ear could hear just one. Even if they tried to focus on the other one, they could not hear both. Psychologists Adrien Mack and Irvin Rock (1998) coined the term inattentional blindness for this phenomenon. In one of their experiments, subjects watched a cross (+) that appeared briefly on a computer screen and reported whether its horizontal or its vertical bar was longer. As they focused on this task, the researchers sent a shape of a different color onto the screen. It hovered briefly in view, yet 75% of the participants did not see it.

Chabris and Simons (1999, 2010) created a similar experiment. Participants watched a sixty-second video of a basketball exercise. They were told to count the number of times that players dressed in white passed the ball. Players in black were also present, trying to block them. Soon after the exercise began, someone in a gorilla suit walked onto the court, stopped to pound his chest, and left. When queried afterward, it was apparent that 50% of participants had not noticed him. This experiment was repeated in several variations with other subject populations with similar results.

As mentioned above, the human visual system evolved to focus our attention. To survive, we need to notice *important* things, so when we focus on an object or an action, the attentional field constricts. On the periphery, incidents or objects might fail to register. In addition, we are subject to base-rate bias: When we get used to a certain scenario, we anticipate how it will work, so our brain relaxes and lets us see what we expect to see, even if the thing we expect does not occur. Because we "know" what will happen, we fall into a cognitive stupor. You can see how this occurred in the Winger case.

In another example of expectations affecting investigations, when eighty-four-year-old Marine Calabro was found dead, on top of a bag of trash, at the foot of the stairs in her Massachusetts home in 2001, detectives relied on stereotypes about the elderly to declare it an accident. No one took photos. Nearly a year later, one of her killers confessed that he and his friends had staged the murder as an accident to get Calabro's money. Investigators had fallen into a lazy mindset: "I already know." They failed to treat the incident carefully.

The adaptive unconscious can size things up fast. This is an advantage that can also become a snag. We trust it, but it makes us lazy (Breitmeyer, 2010). When familiarity relaxes the brain, it falls back on superficial analysis. It trusts the default position, which eases anxiety about what is not yet known.

3. Personality Frames

We are each our own point of departure for how we view the world. This automatically launches a self-serving bias. Those who make judgments that affect others' lives must understand the impact of their own needs and biases. Such decisions are often so automatic that they fail to realize how their bias influences what they view as facts.

This is a mental map, or a cognitive positioning system (CPS). It is how we mentally navigate our world. Our personal CPS is composed of a unique network of influences, including physiology, education, experience, and temperament. Constructs that we learn, such as gender roles and stereotypes, have a significant subconscious impact on how we see the world. Repeated experience with them forms the mental maps from which we "script" situations with specific expectations.

By default, the human brain prefers clarity to ambiguity, but some people want more clarity than others. They are inclined to accept the first thing that makes sense and feels satisfying. This relates to specific traits. This is where this book gets personal.

Kruglanski and Webster (1994) offered a 42-item assessment scale (now revised) that used a 6-point rating between "strongly agree" and "strongly disagree" for assessing the level of one's personal need for closure (the Need for Closure Scale, or NFCS). Among the scale's items are such statements as "I hate to change my plans at the last minute," "I feel uncomfortable when someone's intention is unclear," and "I prefer interacting with people whose opinions are different from my own." Five subscales organize the items into specific areas: preference for structure, decisiveness, preference for predictability, discomfort with ambiguity, and being closed-minded.

Kruglanski and Webster believed that a need for closure derives from one of two tendencies: urgency and permanence. Urgency is about attaining closure as soon as possible, which inspires *seizing* on early information. Permanence is about *freezing* or maintaining closure for as long as possible.

A high need for closure (sometimes called HNC) can influence thinking by encouraging quick decisions without full consideration. Thinking tends to be superficial, producing fewer options for what might have happened, especially as situations grow more complex (Ask & Granhag, 2005). HNCs also tend to anchor in an early judgment and look for things to support that position (confirmation bias). HNCs prefer decisions made by people they consider their peers, in terms of perspective and characteristics, and they prefer leaders (and teachers) who provide clear rules. They tend to blame people for their situations and are aligned more closely with competitive than cooperative behavior. They tend to be inflexible and unwilling to compromise. In their minds, considering opposing opinions risks loss of clarity. They also rely on categories to understand and predict others, rather than looking at individuals, and they favor people whom they consider to be members of their group.

A low need for closure (LNC), in contrast, is found in people who enjoy complex thinking and are more willing to reexamine initial notions in light of new information. They might be attracted to art, theoretical disciplines, and philosophy. However, because they prefer process to product, they can take a long time to come to a decision – if they decide at all. They tend to second-guess.

We can see how personality styles can affect investigative decision-making. A strong need for closure can encourage shortcuts and subject people to errors of judgment – and justice. It leaves us vulnerable to the "decoy heuristic": in the face of anxiety that arises over choice, we are attracted to options that restore security.

Another Holmes, economist Jamie Holmes (2015), wrote *Nonsense: The Power of Not Knowing* to encourage us to gain a greater comfort level with a lack of clarity. The need to act rather than just observe activates our HNC. Feeling rushed, bored, or fatigued increases our discomfort with ambiguity. HNC can impact some of our most critical decisions: how we deal with threats, who we trust, whether we can admit being wrong, and whether we stereotype others.

There are advantages to quick decision-making and resolute commitment, just as there are disadvantages to thinking too hard about every facet of a situation. However, there is a difference between a need for closure based in fear or habit and closure based on genuine skill in efficient analysis (like Sherlock Holmes or Joseph Bell might do). The Winger case demonstrates this: Cox preferred simplicity and wanted closure, but he also wanted to give his partner due consideration. What he viewed as over-thinking quickly became good investigation skills. Officer Williamson had observed seemingly minor details that made no sense and allowed himself to float in uncertainty so he could fully consider what these items meant.

In an experiment, 50 homicide investigators and 68 undergraduates were given evidence from a murder and offered two potential hypotheses. The students showed bias that reflected their initial hypothesis, but they were open to evidence that could contradict it. Investigators – especially those who had a high score on the Need for Closure Scale – were more likely to view evidence as automatically incriminating. They accepted disconfirming evidence *only* if it aligned with their initial hypothesis. Otherwise, they did not remain open to new evidence (Stelfox & Pease, 2005).

Individuals with HNC tend to anchor: they form strong initial impressions and resist information that arises later.

To review, the cognitive quirks that can undermine a solid investigation are threshold diagnosis, confirmation bias, base-rate bias, anchoring, inattentional blindness, and personal needs. How can investigators overcome these issues?

Solutions

Some training points and mental exercises can hone focus, vigilance, and attention. Motivation is key. Practice develops skill. The more practice, the easier it is to realign the adaptive subconscious. Joseph Bell was automatically vigilant only because he made it his goal to be so until it became a habit. At first, this requires working against the path of least resistance, which can be uncomfortable, but better habits can form until the process of focused attention becomes easier, even preferable. Rapid decisions can include critical analysis. This will also diminish the impact of cognitive snags.

Rossmo (2008) writes that with training and effort, investigators can improve. His suggested strategies include:

1. Teach investigators about the impact of cognitive shortcuts.
2. Create exercises that can help investigators to form and analyze two or more competing hypotheses.
3. Devise case checklists of key assumptions and identify poor ones.
4. Identify areas of uncertainty or ambiguity, which attract mental shortcuts.
5. Examine the impact of fatigue, ego, and group pressure.
6. Study good investigations – especially those where skills made the difference.
7. Dissect mistakes in problematic investigations, such as the Winger and Calabro cases, to identify how such errors occurred.

Summary

Cognitive factors matter. Investigators are rarely trained about their influence, although more agencies and law enforcement associations are recognizing their impact, especially the effect of bias and tunnel vision. Understanding one's own response to investigative situations helps to minimize the negative effect of mental shortcuts, so mindful awareness should become as much a part of the investigative toolbox as any other aspect of crime scene processing and reconstruction.

We turn now to those who take charge of investigations. In police agencies, this would be the detective. For other types of investigations, we have experiences and advice from private investigators. In the next chapter, we look at the foundation for best practices.

Exercise #2.1

Your OQ, or observational intelligence, depends on understanding your unique way of seeing. Below is a quick self-assessment, meant to reveal your orientation. You have 3 options for each item: **0** = not true of me, **1** = sometimes or sort of true, **2** = that's me! Answer carefully.

I am:
_____**1.** alert to the environment around me.
_____**2.** aware of my preferences for furnishing a room.
_____**3.** good at following directions to specific places.
_____**4.** generally not curious about the contents of a sealed envelope.
_____**5.** only basically skilled at assessing another person's moods.
_____**6.** quite perceptive about subtle changes in a room or property.
_____**7.** only vaguely attuned to how I feel.
_____**8.** attentive to the significance of items in someone else's home.
_____**9.** aware of where the exits are in any room I enter.
_____**10.** easily distracted during a long project.
_____**11.** observant of the color of the walls when I enter an unfamiliar room.
_____**12.** confident of arriving at unfamiliar destinations.
_____**13.** able to draw quick inferences from appearances.
_____**14.** unable to quickly adopt another's perspective.
_____**15.** attuned to scene details in a novel.
_____**16.** able to estimate quickly the number of people in a room.
_____**17.** uninterested in keeping a dream journal.
_____**18.** alert to what people are wearing.
_____**19.** aware of my thoughts most often when I'm stuck.
_____**20.** alert to subtle sounds around me, even when working on a project.

Add up your score and compare it to the chart below:

30-40: You have good observational skills.

15-30: You have some good observational skills, so you can improve your OQ quickly. The higher your score, the more easily you can achieve this.

Below **15:** You're more internally than externally attuned. To improve as an investigator, you need to practice being aware of what's around you. Create reminders for yourself whenever you enter a new place or meet a new person to learn five new things.

Exercise #2.2

Consider the following case:

Around 8:00 in the evening, Joseph made an emergency call. When paramedics arrived, Joseph said he had found his twenty-one-year-old wife, Valerie, hanging from the showerhead, nude, with a nylon rope around her neck. He had ripped down the shower curtain and sent his son to get a neighbor to help him place Valerie onto it. But it was too late. She was deceased.

Responding officers saw that Valerie's hair was damp, but her body was dry, as was the bathroom and shower curtain. Ligature marks on her neck suggested that she had looped the cord twice around her neck before putting a loop over the pipe to the showerhead. Her skin was still warm to the touch.

According to Joseph, Valerie had been in a bad mood all day, and was often depressed. She had declined his invitation to go out, and when he heard her talking on the phone, she had sounded upset. Joseph did not know the identity of the caller. At times, Valerie acted aggressively, and police had a record of it. But Joseph insisted that he loved his wife of three years. He admitted that she had recently ended an affair after he gave her an ultimatum. He said she had mentioned suicide on several occasions.

On the afternoon of the incident, Joseph had heard the shower running. He thought Valerie had changed her mind and was getting ready to go out with him. When the water ran for a long time, he went to check. He found her hanging.

The next morning, the lead investigator gathered the team. He agreed that suicide was plausible. The medical examiner backed him up. Yet despite appearances, he said, "Something doesn't fit."

1. What might an observant investigator have noticed?
2. What research might be valuable for this investigation?
3. Should investigators speak with anyone besides Joseph?

References

Ask, K., & Granhag, P. A. (2005). Motivational sources of confirmation bias in criminal investigations. *Journal of Investigative Psychology and Offender Profiling, 2*(1), 43–63.

Breitmeyer, B. (2010). *Blindspots: The many ways we cannot see.* Oxford, UK: Oxford University Press.

Chabris, C. & Simons, D. (2010). *The invisible gorilla.* New York, NY: Crown.

Gilovich, T., & Griffin, D. (2002). Heuristics and biases: Then and now. In T. Gilovich, D. Griffin, & D. Kahneman (Eds.), *Heuristics and biases: The psychology of intuitive imagination* (pp. 1–18). Cambridge, UK: Cambridge University Press.

Holmes, J. (2015). *Nonsense: The power of not knowing.* New York, NY: Penguin.

Kebbell, M. R., Muller, D., & Martin, K. (2010). *Understanding and managing bias.* Canberra, Australia: ANU Press.

Konnikova, M. (2013). *Mastermind: How to think like Sherlock Holmes.* New York, NY: Viking.

Kruglanski, A. W. & Webster, D. M. (1996). Motivated closing of the mind: 'Seizing' and 'freezing.' *Psychological Review 103* (2): 263–83.

Kruglanski, A. W., Webster, D. M., & Klem, A. (1993). Motivated resistance and openness to persuasion in the presence or absence of prior information. *Journal of Personality and Social Psychology, 65*(5), 861–876.

Liebow, E. M. (1982). *Dr. Joe Bell*. Bowling Green, Ohio: Bowling Green University Press.

Lord, C. G., Ross, L., & Lepper, M. R. (1979). Biased assimilation and attitude polarization: The effects of prior theories on subsequently considered evidence. *Journal of Personality and Social Psychology, 37*, 2098–2109.

Mack. A. & Rock, I. (1998). *Inattentional blindness*. Cambridge, MA: MIT Press "Out of the ashes," *Forensic Files*, Season 3, Episode 13 (#39), aired December 24, 1998.

Ramsland, K. (2012). *Snap: Seizing your aha! moments*. Amherst, NY: Prometheus.

Rossmo, K. D. (2008). Cognitive biases: Perception, intuition, and tunnel vision. In K. D. Rossmo (Ed.), *Criminal investigative failures* (pp. 9–21). Boca Raton, FL: CRC Press.

Rossmo, K. D. (2011, June). Failures in criminal investigation. *Police Chief Magazine*.

Stelfox, P., & Pease, K. (2005). Cognition and detection: Reluctant bedfellows? In M. Smith & N. Tilley (Eds.), *Crime science: New approaches to preventing and detecting crime* (pp. 194–210). Cullompton, UK: Willan Publishing.

Szegedy-Maszak, M. (2005, February 28). Your unconscious is making your everyday decisions. *U. S. News and World Report*.

Chapter 3
Detecting

Learning Objectives

- ❖ Be able to describe the role of a police detective.
- ❖ List the steps of the investigative pyramid.
- ❖ Recount the stages of an investigation.
- ❖ Understand the importance of a thorough victimology.
- ❖ Describe the difference between a detective and a private investigator.

Key Words

investigation, surveillance, victimology

Frederick Porter Wensley had joined the Metropolitan Police in 1888, the year of Jack the Ripper. An expert on London's East End, his obsession with solving crime paid off. Over the next three decades, Wensley had closed all his murder cases. One from 1917 demonstrates his careful approach.

Sent out to Regent Square near the University of London that November, he opened a bloody sheet that was wrapped around the trunk and arms of an adult female. A brown paper parcel nearby produced the dismembered legs, while the sheet yielded a laundry mark. This directed Wensley to 50 Munster Square. Inquiries resulted in information about Emilienne Gerard, and a search of her room turned up bloodstains, as well as a photo of a man. Wensley identified him as a French butcher, Louis Voisin, Gerard's lover. At Voisin's home, detectives found him with Berthe Roche. Voisin claimed he knew Gerard only from feeding her cat.

Wensley thought he was lying, and his questions to neighbors supported his hunch. His team had found a torn piece of paper on the corpse that had "Blodie Belgiam" written on it, so Wensley asked Voisin to write this phrase five times. Voisin showed the same spelling errors. Wensley searched Voisin and found a key that opened his cellar door.

Behind it was a cask filled with sawdust, along with the dead woman's missing head and hands.

This case shows the importance of accepting nothing at face value. The job of a detective requires *active* thinking skills, vigilance, self-awareness, and constant testing.

Voisin was convicted and hanged, while Roche was sentenced to seven years as an accomplice (Ramsland, 2007).

The Basics

Detectives on a police force gather facts for incident reconstruction and the eventual prosecution of a perpetrator. They conduct interviews with witnesses and persons of interest as well as interrogate suspects. They examine documents, observe suspect activities, conduct searches and raids, and make arrests. They might also do follow-up investigation, such as for cold cases. When demand is high for experts in specific types of crimes such as homicide or sexual assault, they might specialize.

Detectives are required to participate in regular in-service trainings to keep up with changes in law and relevant developments. They receive intensive training in crime scene investigation, evidence collection, evidence preservation, bloodstain pattern analysis, crime scene photography, ballistics, and techniques of interview and interrogation. At times, they might receive specialized education, such as symbology for gangs, mass disaster incidents, or occult crimes. Some will go undercover, perhaps for long periods of time.

Figure 12. Northeast Forensic Training Center blood spatter room

Source: Katherine Ramsland

After the initial notification that detectives are needed at an incident, they arrive to take charge and make their own observations. They use a notebook for pertinent data, so that the early steps are methodical and easy to use for later reference. They must remain detached and objective. If first responders have not already done so, detectives should record the names of everyone present and make a note of license plate numbers of vehicles. They make a note of weather conditions and lighting, look for potential sources of surveillance video, and ensure that fragile evidence is recorded or collected immediately. They also document a full description of the scene.

For incident reconstruction, detectives gather the potential pieces for a coherent and accurate picture, properly recording and filing all evidentiary items. These might be as fragile as dust particles from a foreign environment or as obvious as a weapon. Sometimes the evidence is sparse, other times overwhelming. Detectives must use appropriate investigative logic to arrive at the proper conclusions, without falling into cognitive errors.

The process of investigation, according to some detectives, moves through stages of a pyramid, as it crystallizes and becomes more refined (Keppel & Birnes, 2003). The pyramid's base is *knowledge*, which involves gathering information from many sources. As items stand out, the next level is *comprehension*. Following this is *application and analysis*. At the top is the process of *synthesizing* what is known.

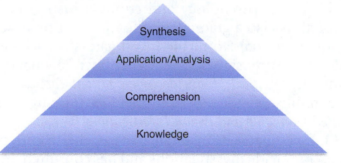

Figure 13. The investigation pyramid

Source: Katherine Ramsland

The goal is to pull everything together into a single explanatory narrative, without violating known facts or leaving out something significant. However, they must also remember that facts are interpretable: different contexts put different faces on them. A scene that appears to be a suicide will fit the facts into that narrative (the hanging victim had been anxious so she must have been depressed), but as a homicide staged to be a suicide, those same facts will look different (the hanging victim was anxious, for good reason, because someone killed her).

Ground Floor

Francois Eugene Vidocq is often credited as the founder of the world's first detective agency, undercover network, and even the first detective novel (Edwards, 1977). A keen observer and master of disguise, he also innovated many methods that improved investigations.

Born in France in 1775, Vidocq's minor infractions got him several stints in jail, and he eventually learned to escape. He got into more trouble and kept escaping, but was always caught. Eventually, he made a deal with the head of the Lyon police and acquired the position of police informant. His success won over Parisian officials, who supported his efforts in 1809 to establish the world's first police detective agency, the *Brigade de la Sûreté*. Among Vidocq's accomplishments were the use of elaborate undercover disguises and female informants, and the invention of footprint casts and indelible ink. Later, he established the world's first *private* detective agency. By the mid- to late nineteenth century, many large cities were using detectives as crime investigators.

Today, uniformed police officers might work toward becoming a detective. Sometimes, this occurs through a promotion after passing a test and application process. Other times, the investigative role is a rotated assignment, with focus on misdemeanors as well as felonies.

Vernon J. Geberth refers to himself as a "Murder Cop." He is a retired lieutenant-commander of the New York City Police Department (NYPD). As commanding officer of the Bronx Homicide Task Force, he supervised more than 400 murder investigations annually. With retirement, he became an educator and consultant. To date, Geberth has personally investigated, supervised, assessed, consulted on, or researched over eight thousand homicides. His maxim for all investigators is: "Do it right the first time. You won't get a second chance."

With master's degrees in psychology and criminal justice and a B. A. in business administration, Geberth is also a graduate of the F.B.I. National Academy. He is a charter member of the International Homicide Investigators Association and is a Fellow in the American Academy of Forensic Sciences. Geberth wrote what has been referred to as the "Bible" of homicide, *Practical Homicide Investigation: Tactics, Procedures and Forensic Techniques*. He also published the *Practical Homicide Investigation Checklist and Field Guide*, and *Sex-Related Homicide and Death Investigation: Practical and Clinical Perspectives*. As president of P.H.I. Investigative Consultants, Inc., Geberth currently provides state-of-the-art instruction on homicide investigations and has consulted on some of the nation's most notorious cases, including O. J. Simpson, JonBenet Ramsey, Jeffrey Dahmer, David Parker Ray, and the Long Island Serial Killer.

In his seminars, Geberth offers photos, documents, and exhibits related to murder, autoerotic deaths, and suicides. When he needs other experts to discuss certain types of evidence, such as DNA or 9-1-1 calls, he invites them to co-present. He stresses the importance of getting authentic experience.

"Before you get to be a homicide detective," Geberth tells attendees, "You need to spend some time in the streets rolling around with some of the folks who you are going to meet later" (personal interview, 2016).

Geberth's career in law enforcement began with an assignment to the elite Tactical Patrol Force (TPF), the "Green Beret of the NYPD." He soon earned his detective shield and went to work on the Bronx Narcotics Division, Manhattan's Fifth Division Robbery, and the City-Wide Street Crime Unit before being assigned to a precinct detective squad. He served as a TPF Squad Patrol Sergeant until he was transferred to the Special Investigations Unit of the Organized Crime Control Bureau. As a result, Geberth was promoted to Detective Sergeant and assigned to Manhattan North Narcotics. Finally moving to Homicide, he became a member of the City's busiest unit, the Seventh Homicide Zone, composed of four precincts in the South Bronx. "We had over two hundred and twenty homicides a year," he said.

Geberth decided he needed to catch up, so he selected his sharpest detectives and shadowed them. His habit of recording everything laid the basis for his books. "This was the nucleus of *Practical Homicide Investigation*. I created the checklists so I could be on top of the investigations and properly supervise my detectives in the field."

The NYPD had basic guidelines for how to use forms and make notifications, but not how to solve crimes. In 1978, Geberth became a contributing author for *Law and Order Magazine*. "On my days off," he said, "I would go to the various libraries and seek out and acquire any information on homicide investigations and forensic techniques that I could locate. I would take my own photographs of crime scenes as well as take the official crime scene pictures home to analyze them. I used to keep a Rolodex of all the experts that I had met in different locations. I would call them up for advice and involve them in the case. I was the first person to use forensic entomology in the police department on a murder case."

At his first murder scene, Geberth realized that he had little to work with and no idea how to proceed. "The best that I could come up with at the time," he recalls, "was that the person was dead. It was a drug-related shooting in an alleyway in West Harlem, and basically there were no forensics at all." At the time, the only procedure for solving these types of crimes was to pay or pressure informants to provide leads. Thus, as a supervisor, Geberth improved the approach. He was the first law enforcement professional to devise standard guidelines and protocols for proficient death inquiries.

One day, Geberth's team investigated an apparent suicide. "We had an individual who was a graduate of John Jay College of Criminal Justice, so I guess he thought he knew all about police work. He'd decided that he wanted to kill his common-law wife and get himself a new girlfriend. He put together a scenario suggesting that his wife who had been 'depressed' since the birth of their latest child had committed suicide."

This man had set up that he had to leave the house by 7:00 A.M. to get to the Unemployment Office. When he returned nearly three hours later, he claimed he had found the door to his apartment unlocked. As he rushed inside, he heard his baby crying and found his wife drowned in the tub. He attempted mouth-to-mouth resuscitation, he said, but could not save her. He called his brother to report the suicide, and the police and an ambulance crew soon arrived.

The protocol that Geberth had devised for such unattended deaths necessitated that the patrol officer call for the uniform sergeant, who would then notify a detective to conduct an investigation. "When I got there," said Geberth, "the place was in pandemonium. No one was doing their respective jobs. The patrol sergeant had already decided that the death was a suicide based on the 9-1-1 call. The husband had given the sergeant a story that his wife had been depressed and had placed an empty vial of a prescribed antidepressant next to her body to suggest an overdose."

Geberth was uneasy. "When you get a gut feeling that there's something wrong, there's probably something wrong." He ordered the patrol sergeant to clear the bathroom area so he could examine the decedent. "I pulled back the sheet that the ambulance crew had draped over her body and leaned down. I pulled her eyelids back and saw evidence of petechial hemorrhage. I realized we had a potential homicide. I immediately ordered the entire apartment cleared as a crime scene and directed the patrol sergeant to find out exactly who lived in the apartment."

An eight-year-old girl lived there. She had gone to school. "I went to the school with a female relative from the victim's side of the family and got her out of class. The little girl told us that when she had gotten up that morning, her four-year-old sister was watching cartoons on television. Her mommy had cleaned and bathed the newborn baby and she and mommy had breakfast together and then she went to school around 8:25 A.M. Daddy had still been in bed, but he was yelling at Mommy." Geberth also interviewed the younger child. "She told us that she saw Daddy grab Mommy's neck and squeeze her neck and that Daddy took Mommy's clothes off and put Mommy in the tub. She'd seen the whole thing. By making that observation of petechial hemorrhage, I was able to get a 24-hour jump on the bad guy."

The man knew that an autopsy would have undermined his story, but by then he would have gotten an attorney and placed the children off limits. Geberth's quick thinking gave him the advantage.

He believes that the best homicide detectives look at their work as a spiritual calling, a duty to seek justice. The lead detective (or the detective supervisor) is responsible, Geberth states, for maintaining professional standards throughout an investigation. This begins with the right attitude, including awareness of ethical standards. The attitude should encourage teamwork.

Important steps include conferring with the first responders, prioritizing the proper handling of witnesses and suspects, preparing assignment sheets, establishing a command center (if needed), disseminating all the necessary information to appropriate units (including alarms and BOLO [be on the lookout] alerts for missing suspects), and controlling the personnel involved. In a case that attracts the media, there may be a need for deciding which information to make public (keeping secret the information known only to the offender and investigators). In addition, a canvass, or door-to-door inquiry, should be implemented. A canvassing questionnaire form can help to organize the information.

Detectives should learn how to keep witnesses from mingling and to interview them effectively with a standard witness form. Good interviewing technique involves a knowledge of basic psychology, including deceptive and deflective behaviors. One of the most significant factors to consider is the victim. When **victimology** is short-changed, Geberth has found, mistakes are made.

> **Victimology** A study of victim information to find clues about the offender's opportunity and selection process.

Geberth lists the five primary components of an investigation:

1. Teamwork
2. Documentation
3. Preservation of evidence
4. Being flexible
5. Using common sense

"During the early stages of an investigation, detectives should not consider themselves certain of anything," he says, "and must therefore be flexible and open to new information. To establish the size of the scene, they should clear the largest area possible, and narrow down later if necessary. Make an objective evaluation of the scene as a whole, based on visible physical evidence, natural boundaries, and eyewitness statements. There are no definite rules for establishing boundaries of all possible crime scenes, especially as new information is still coming in." During the process of observing and recording evidence, investigators should develop a mental image of the crime, which becomes the foundation for later work.

In one scenario, the relatives of a decedent whose death the police had reported as a suicide hired Geberth to reinvestigate. The family was suing the life insurance company, which they believed had used a deficient police report to support its decision not to pay.

"The victim had not shown up for work for two days," says Geberth, "which was highly unusual. His family and people who knew him noticed things were amiss. The young man lived in a mobile home in a rural area on the same property as his parents. A down-the-road farmer noticed the deceased's car parked in an unusual manner, but he didn't think much about it until the following morning when he noticed that the car had not moved. He drove over on his tractor and heard loud music blasting from the trailer, which was uncharacteristic. Also, the heat had been turned up as high as possible. The car was unlocked, which was also uncharacteristic. The farmer knocked on the front door, but no one answered, so he got the mother to accompany him back to the trailer.

"She looked into the trailer and down the hallway, where she saw blood on the floor. She saw a pair of feet and assumed it was her son. She backed out and called the Sheriff's Department."

The officers arrived and observed the young man on his back on a bed, with a Remington .308 model rifle lying between his legs. There were two spent shell casings in the room and two bullet holes in the ceiling. Various amounts of blood, skull and brain matter were found in the room and a portion of the victim's head was blown away. On the floor near the rear door lay a large chunk of brain matter. Geberth noted that it would require a series of impossible maneuvers to arrive at this location. However, because the weapon and ammunition belonged to the decedent, the deputies had decided that the incident was a suicide.

"Their ridiculous conclusion," says Geberth, "was that the victim had shot himself in the head, twice. They did no victimology."

Geberth undertook a full investigation of the decedent's circumstances. He reviewed over 300 interviews of friends and relatives, and personally interviewed the victim's mother, sister, and brother-in-law. He learned that the victim had a fiancée. The victim had made both long-term and short-term plans. He had paid his union dues in advance and was repairing and remodeling his mobile home in anticipation of his fiancée's visit. He had purchased paint and wallpaper, had applied for a loan, and was preparing for a trip to clear property for a house they hoped to build. Two days before his death, he had purchased groceries. He was not in debt and had no history of depression. The decedent fit no suicidal profile.

In addition, he had kept at least $1000.00 in cash in his trailer, had recently withdrawn $200 from his bank account, and had received $50 from his sister, but just $2.50 was recovered. A prized gold calculator was missing, as was a card from his sister with $50 in it. Numerous behaviors were also out of character: keys in the ignition of his unlocked car, cigarettes in an ashtray, empty wallet on the floor of the car, and tools and a radar detector missing from the car. The calculator turned up in a pawnshop.

However, the deputies did not know this because they had not performed an investigation. They did not even search for the bullets. An open box of Remington .308 ammunition was found in an adjoining room, with six cartridges missing. Inside the closet was evidence of velocity blood spatter, but the officers had not noticed. There was also no follow-up for family reports about missing money and items. There was no test for gunshot residue or ballistics reconstruction to determine how the shells had been ejected to where they were found. No scene sketch was made and no evidence documented. The autopsy was equally deficient, undertaken by an ordinary hospital pathologist.

From the sheriff's office, Geberth received lame responses. They produced an alleged suicide note that consisted of 2 lines: "Depressed over a girl. Nothing to live for." The sergeant stated he showed this note to the mother and verified that it was her son's writing, but he added, "I realize she will probably deny this." As predicted, she stated that she was never shown any such note, had verified nothing, and had been repeatedly told there was no note. The investigators had not documented a note in a report.

A cleaning service had taken photographs, which assisted with a proper reconstruction. Geberth saw blood and brain matter on the walls, ceiling, and closet wall. The cleaners had found a piece of scalp and skull bone imbedded in the closet's back paneling. He believed that the shots fired into the ceiling were intended to make the incident appear to be a suicide.

"In my professional opinion as an expert in homicide and death investigations," he wrote, "the inquiry into the death of the deceased was perfunctory and inadequate according to the recognized standards of professional death investigation. It was readily apparent that this particular crime scene had been staged and it was a reasonable assumption based on the facts that the deceased had not committed suicide."

The investigative strategies that Geberth offers to prevent such perfunctory efforts are to take each factor to its ultimate conclusion:

1. Assess the victimology of the deceased.
2. Evaluate the types of injuries and wounds of the victim in connection with the type of weapon employed.
3. Conduct the necessary forensic examinations to establish and ascertain the facts of the case.
4. Conduct an examination of the weapon(s) for latent evidence, as well as ballistics and testing of firearms.

5. Evaluate the behavior of the victim and suspects.
6. Establish a profile of the victim through interviews of friends and relatives.
7. Reconstruct and evaluate the event.
8. Compare investigative findings with the medicolegal autopsy and confer with the medical examiner.
9. Corroborate statements with evidential facts.
10. Conduct and process all death investigations as if they were homicide cases.

"It all begins at the crime scene," Geberth says, "and this is where most of the errors occur. The investigator's mission is to create the perfect record of the scene so that we can apply the very best advances of forensic science."

Police Academy Conference

Lee Lofland is a former police detective who now conducts immersion workshops in law enforcement procedures for writers. Having published *Police Procedure and Investigation* as a guide for learning the finest details, Lofland also sets up authentic experiences at various police training centers. His annual conference is known as the Writers' Police Academy (WPA). He knows that the "CSI effect" is real. Television shows, movies, and novels influence millions of viewers and readers into believing that they know exactly how investigations work. Many serve on juries and might make decisions based on erroneous notions. Writers who learn from professionals how it should be done will presumably have a trickle down effect, including on young minds who aim to become detectives. Lofland hopes for such a result from his conference.

"The Writers' Police Academy," Lofland said, "was established in 2009 as a hands-on, interactive training event designed to enhance understanding of police procedure, forensics, firefighting, and EMS. Participants quickly discovered this extremely popular and novel approach to research – participating in never-before available access to inside and behind the scenes police, fire, forensics, and EMS training – added a new depth and level of realism to their narratives.

"In 2010, the WPA moved to an actual police academy near Greensboro, N.C., where writers participated in an expanded curriculum featuring hands-on workshops and sessions that included fingerprinting and the how-to of homicide investigation. Ride-alongs with on-duty officers and deputies, firearms and driver simulation training were also added, as well as top instructors. The hands-on workshops incorporate firearms training, evidence collection, bloodstain pattern investigations, ballistics, toxicology, and emergency vehicle driving, including high-speed pursuits and PIT maneuvers" (personal interview, 2015).

The three-day event allows participants to visit jails, see an interrogation room, learn self-defense, fire a variety of handguns and rifles, and watch equipment demonstrations.

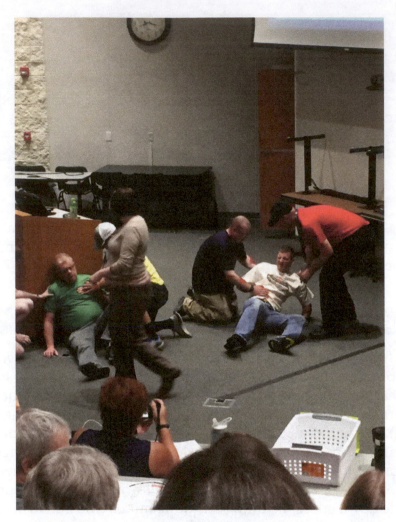

Figure 14. Mass assault scenario training, WPA 2016

Source: Katherine Ramsland

They might see a K-9 team at work, go to a prison, clear a building, operate alternative light sources, explore a mobile command post, participate in an arson investigation, watch a medical response to an accident scene, and even see a dive team demonstrate underwater crime scene investigations. A rare opportunity is the firearms simulation training. As animations of people on a screen jump from behind walls and around corners (maybe just to point out the direction of the primary scene), the armed practitioner must make snap judgments as to whether or not they're an imminent threat.

Law enforcement officers who aspire to be writers meet writers who want to learn law enforcement techniques, or law enforcement personnel who have already become writers. Even bestselling writers attend, not only to offer tips from their experience but also to add to their knowledge base for future work. So do the professionals who instruct.

"Cops, especially detectives, must be the best used car salesman, ditch digger, auto mechanic, florist, circus dung shoveler, and warehouse box stacker in the world," says Lofland. "Investigators absolutely must be able to fit in by walking the walk and talking the talk no matter where they are and to whom they're speaking. Dialogue is a huge key to solving crimes. Cops have to be able to 'BS the BS'ers.' So having the ability to carry on a meaningful conversation with anyone and everyone is an extremely important part of the job."

This is one way that police and the public can mingle and learn. Among those who participate as teachers are private investigators. They have a different approach to investigation, often having to be a bit more creative in their approach.

Private Investigators

Not all investigators are part of a police force. Private investigators (PI) also assist with, and benefit from, basic crime scene procedure. Most states have regulations governing their licensing, certifications, training, and practices. They also have active professional associations for continuing education and censure of misconduct. Many PIs are former police officers. They are allowed to travel to other states on behalf of clients, but they must know and follow those state requirements. A few states have reciprocity agreements. Some PIs carry guns; others think weapons are unnecessary. Should they decide to carry, they must follow state laws.

One PI job description stated simply, "You find people, you interview them, you write it up." PIs might work for attorneys, tracking down information. They can also be hired to document the behavior of private individuals, such as those engaged in adultery or skipping bond (skip-tracing). They might help to locate a missing person, prescreen a job applicant, check investment legitimacy, research a cold case, pursue evidence of fraud, reinvestigate an incident on behalf of a family that questions official procedures, perform psychological autopsies, locate stolen property, perform surveillance, and access records. Cases range from divorce to money laundering to murder. At times, PIs can even assist the police.

They learn the best databases and records for locating someone, but they also develop innovative methods for finding those who prefer not to be found. Public records, social media, credit reports, along with associates and angry spouses are among the best sources. Some websites are set up specifically to help find someone, usually for a fee.

Sandy Russell is a private investigator in North Carolina and has long been a leader in that state's PI association. A former police officer, she was inspired to become an investigator from her interest in puzzles. "If a piece didn't fit, I had to follow the path, piece by piece till I found the slot" (personal interview, 2015).

As a law enforcement officer, she was in field operations and rose through the ranks to lieutenant. "I was a first responder. I answered the calls, I supervised the work, and most of the time we had all the work done before a detective ever arrived on the scene. All that was left for CID was to bring the charges, and in some cases, we had already done that, too. For me, law enforcement was a great primer. It also helps to be curious or just plain nosey. Prior to being in law enforcement/security I was just a simple housewife, but I believe it helped prepare me for what I'm doing now, because my former spouse was one of those cheaters that I so often catch."

When Russell considers her top three most valuable skills, she identified patience as number one. Since there is a lot of surveillance work, this makes sense, but she also needs knowledge of the law. "You need to know it and follow it." Her third-ranked skill is empathy. "This may just be an assignment to a PI, but it could be life changing for the client." Russell finds a case resolution satisfying, but it can also be sad. "If it is 'a domestic,' somebody is going to be hurt emotionally. If it is a case involving a child, either domestic or criminal, it is difficult for me to wrap my head around the logic or lack thereof."

Many of her cases involve cheating spouses, child custody issues, and problems with alimony payments. "I have also conducted background investigations, insurance fraud, missing persons, criminal defense, nursing home abuse. I have worked undercover for attorneys that contract with HBO, Showtime, Cinemax, etc. to discover establishments that are illegally obtaining programming for such things as boxing matches. This involves going into a restaurant or a bar that has not purchased a license to show these events but is doing so anyway. I find this both exhilarating and dangerous. Most of the locations are little hole-in-the-wall places where patrons are heavily armed. I'm usually successful in covertly videoing the fights or games."

When asked about a particularly challenging case, Russell recalled, "One of my very first clients was an independent female professional. She was divorced from her spouse, but they had a small child together. She was fairly well-to-do and her ex, although from a wealthy family, was not. There had been allegations of child abuse when the minor was visiting the father. Allegations against the father and the new wife mostly sprang from social media where the new wife constantly posted about her dislike for the former Mrs., as well as the child. She talked about giving the child small amounts of alcohol as well as Xanax to keep him quiet while visiting. She would show pictures of the child lying on the floor asleep, or perhaps passed out and say things like, 'Glad the little bastard finally shut up.' Consequently, the courts issued a restraining order stating that although the child could continue visiting the father, the stepmother could not be present when the child was in the house. So began the quest to prove that this restraining order was being violated.

"It was a difficult case for several reasons. My client had retained a couple of investigators prior to me that had not been discreet. Therefore, both individuals had a suspicion they were being watched. The house was like a fortress. It sat on a lot, surrounded by established trees, which provided a nearly impenetrable fence. The blinds were always drawn and the garage doors were always closed, which made it impossible to see if any other vehicles were inside. This was one of those puzzle pieces for me.

"I began by thoroughly investigating the neighborhood. I was looking for places to park, and breaks in the trees so that I could see the house from the back. I drove. I walked, including taking my dog a few times so as not to look out of place. I wore wigs, used different cars and always had a story, in case a neighbor approached me.

"This case went on for months. Then one rainy night while parked nearly a block away on a road behind the residence, I saw her. I knew the child was there, I knew the father was there, and now I took video of the stepmother being there. She was smoking and drinking, which was forbidden to be happening while the child was there. I got video from between two trees and through the woods. It showed what was needed.

"I immediately called the client, who called her attorney. We were seeking an immediate return of custody based on the violation of the court order. What we got was as far away from that as could be. The attorney, it seems, wasn't as excited as we were and decided things could wait until Monday. This was Friday night and for the child to be exposed to this situation all weekend was unbelievable. My client called the Sheriff's Department and was told that, without authorization, they couldn't touch it. The client had the paperwork, but the officers wouldn't act. Monday came and nothing happened. By now, I was totally invested, which is not a good thing. I had let myself become personally involved. I was angry and frustrated.

"But I got another chance a few weeks later. The father was taking the child on vacation, but was not divulging where. I devised a plan to place a GPS unit in the bottom of the child's suitcase. I followed them to the Outer Banks of North Carolina. For the first few days, it was just the two of them. On about the fifth day, they traveled to South Carolina where there was a big family get-together in progress. I took a hotel room on the top floor and lucked out. The balcony overlooked the house they were renting. The stepmother was there. She was drinking and smoking. I advised the client and once again the authorities (especially since we were across state lines) would not intervene. I thought to myself, what else can I do?

"Oddly enough, not more than a week after they returned to North Carolina, the father and the stepmother separated and the whole investigation became a non-issue. Nothing was ever done to the father for violating the court order. I was so frustrated with the 'system' that I thought about just quitting. An attorney, a court system, and law enforcement that should have had this child's safety as its utmost concern had failed him. This situation gave me a different perspective."

Female detectives face some challenges. "A universal disadvantage," says Russell, "is that a lot of male PIs don't take me seriously. I grew up with this type of male attitude as prevalent in my generation." Yet there are also advantages. "I am a woman, and in my case, a mature woman. Most people do not even suspect that I could be a PI. Most would view me as retired and would never consider that I could have a more sneaky side."

To conduct business efficiently and safely, investigators must learn about surveillance and recording devices that will serve their needs. Don Kneece, the owner and senior investigator for Kneece Investigations in Saluda, South Carolina, tests, demonstrates, and sells investigative equipment. A personable, enthusiastic individual with a confident presence and booming voice, he has learned what works in various conditions. "Until I show you," he said in a PI seminar, "it won't sink in." He offers instruction in the classroom and in the field. "Hands-on training," he stated, "allows investigators to utilize the equipment with confidence and to conduct a cost-effective and productive investigation."

Kneece served twenty years in the military, including in the role of police investigator, and was a member of the Department of Defense Counterdrug Mobile Training Team. He has received extensive training in interview and interrogation techniques, as well as in the use of technical surveillance equipment. In addition, he has worked for the Institute of Investigative Technologies as a certified senior instructor for local, state, and federal law enforcement.

In his workshops, participants are assigned investigative goals. They must select the appropriate pieces of equipment from those that he has demonstrated to meet those goals. In other words, they have a scenario that requires critical thinking and they must decide how best to approach it. They gather information about an alleged activity or a specific location, for example, and decide how to acquire close, medium, and long-range imagery of mobile and fixed subjects from a remote location. When selecting equipment, they must consider such things as size, shape, weight, lens types, noise potential from signals, and infrared sensitivity.

The equipment Kneece demonstrates includes an array of covert video cameras, recording systems worn on the body, handheld recording systems, and GPS tracking systems. He offers low-light cameras, pocket DVRs, GPS loggers and live GPS trackers, a cellphone data recovery device, counter-surveillance detectors, several cleverly hidden cameras (including clocks and glasses), and weatherproof cameras for recording outside. Then there's the "iStranger" voice changer, compatible with cell phones, to disguise voice pitches. He even offers a semen detection kit.

Figure 15. Cameras can be placed in items such as outlets and glasses frames

Source: Katherine Ramsland

Kneece has many stories about how such items have helped with his cases. For example, he followed a woman engaged in an affair who had some savvy about how to deflect anyone from following her. She kept her car in a closed garage, so it was difficult to attach a GPS. She drove on gravel roads and stopped often to listen for cars following her. Still, she made a mistake and got caught.

Urging investigators to be creative in unusual situations, Kneece demonstrates his own ingenuity. To camouflage his recording equipment, he has used utility boxes, outlets, and canisters, among other things. "The use of covert surveillance equipment is an ever-changing science," Kneece states. "It should be the objective of each of us to use the available technical equipment in order to obtain the best results possible" (personal interview, 2015).

He tells another story to demonstrate: "I was working a domestic case where the wife (we'll call her 'Sue') had moved out of the home where she and her husband (we'll call him 'Tom') lived together. Tom had no idea where Sue was staying and needed to know if she was having an affair with someone else. The only place we knew we could find Sue was at her work location. We located her car there and installed a GPS tracker.

"Through information obtained, we learned that she was staying in a home that was in a neighboring town. It was in a housing development where no vehicles were allowed to park on the roadside and the homes were only twenty feet apart. Property records and other database searches were conducted and we found that Sue was living in a home with a single man (we'll call him 'Larry'). Several attempts to gather video evidence that Sue and Larry were living together failed, because there was no place to establish a manned surveillance location.

"By using available technology and a little brain power we installed a camera, DVR, and batteries in a metal toolbox. We painted the box red, and with yellow paint we stenciled the words 'Acu-Count Traffic Monitoring.' This box was placed across the road from where Larry and Sue were living. A rubber hose was stretched across the road and secured to the pavement on each end. The toolbox was placed next to a pole and was chained and locked to the pole. We placed yellow traffic cones at the box and across the street where the rubber hose ended.

"The installation was accomplished during the middle of the day. We drove a white truck with several traffic cones in the back of the truck. We wore yellow safety vests and hard hats. During the installation, Sue walked out into the front yard and started talking to us. Our cover story was that the roads in the area were being evaluated for re-surfacing and an accurate count of the traffic on this road was needed. As we were telling her this, Sue stated that she had recently moved in with her boyfriend and had noticed the potholes. She hoped our study would help get the road re-surfaced.

"The camera was left in place for three days and, when recovered, we had video of Sue and Larry arriving at the home and staying overnight together, and we even had them sitting on the front porch together. On one occasion when they were sitting on the porch, Larry was seen kissing Sue. This case could not have been made without the use of surveillance equipment and the knowledge of how to install it to gather evidence over an extended period of time.

"Another case that also required the use of unmanned surveillance equipment to document activity was where a man was believed to be bringing his girlfriend to the marital home at lunchtime while the wife was at work. By first doing some surveillance of the husband as he entered the housing area where he and his wife lived, only one person could be seen in the vehicle. When the husband arrived at home, he parked in the garage and closed the garage door as soon as he entered. By placing a camera in a small box used to package wood screws and then placing the camera on a shelf in the garage, we were able to get a view of the husband's car as he entered and parked. The view was such that we would be able to see directly into the windshield of the car when it parked.

"When the car arrived we witnessed the girlfriend as she sat up in the front seat. She had been lying down in the seat with her head resting on the husband's leg. Once she sat up, they kissed, got out of the car, and went into the home. About forty-five minutes later, they were seen re-entering the car. The girlfriend used the car mirror to fix her hair before again lying down in the front seat so no one would see her in the car as the husband drove from the garage."

Now it is time to apply some of this wisdom, before we turn in the next two chapters to what investigators must know about science and the courts.

Summary

No matter which sort of detective one might become, there are basic protocols for careful investigation. Stay attuned to the tendency to solve a mystery before conducting a full investigation and learn the trade as deeply as possible. Practice and test observation skills, and work on mental puzzles that require critical and creative thinking.

Exercise #3.1

In 2005, Greg M. called 9-1-1 to report that his brother Peter had shot himself in the head in Greg's home. When officers arrived, Greg was calmly smoking a cigarette and had removed his bloodstained T-shirt. Detectives thought something was amiss. Although Peter was dead and there was blood and brain matter splashed all over a wall and ceiling, he had been shot in the back of the head with a powerful .50-caliber semi-automatic handgun, which lay on a desk six feet from the body. The gun's safety latch was turned downward, indicating that it had reengaged.

1. How should the lead detective handle this scene?
2. How can the team avoid the error of a threshold diagnosis?
3. What questions might they form for those who knew Peter?
4. How might they preserve evidence for the forensic analysts?
5. What practices during reconstruction might help avoid errors of interpretation?

References

Brown, M. (2001). *Criminal investigation: Law and practice.* Boston, MA: Butterworth-Heinemann.

Edwards, S. (1977). *The Vidocq dossier: The story of the world's first detective.* Boston, MA: Houghton Mifflin.

Geberth, V. (1996, February). The staged crime scene. *Law and Order, 44*(2).

Geberth, V. (2005). *Sex-related homicides and death investigation.* Boca Raton, FL: CRC Press.

Geberth, Vernon J. (2015). *Practical homicide investigation,* 5th ed. Boca Raton, FL: CRC Press.

Keppel, R. D. & Birnes, W. J. *The psychology of serial killers: The Grisly Business Unit.* San Diego, CA: Academic Press, 2003.

Lofland, L.(2007). *Police procedure and investigation.* Cincinnati, OH: Writers Digest Books.

Maurek found not guilty. (2008, January 22). ABC News. http://www.kswo.com/story/7758647/maurek-found-not-guilty-in-murder-trial

Ramsland, K. (2007). *Beating the devil's game: A history of forensic science and criminal investigation.* New York, NY: Berkley.

Chapter 4
Science, Technology, Standards, and Fraud

Learning Objectives

❖ Describe the purpose of the NAS report.
❖ Explain the scientific method.
❖ List the key court decisions about scientific admissibility.
❖ Discuss why labs should be independent from police departments.
❖ Understand the oversight organizations.
❖ Explain how scientific fraud harms the entire justice system.

Key Words

AAFS, admissibility, AFIS, CODIS, Daubert decision, dry labbing, fraud, Frye standard, NAS, NCAVC, NCVS, NIBIN, NIBRS, NIST, OSAC, quality assurance, scientific method, SWG, UCR, ViCAP

Teresa Halbach was missing. She had been assigned to meet Steven Avery to take photos of a car he wanted to sell. Investigators located her car in his salvage yard. A thorough search of Avery's northern Wisconsin property turned up bone fragments, teeth, a burnt camera and pieces of a cellphone in a burn pit behind his home. Officers from the Manitowoc Sheriff's Department said they found Halbach's car key, with blood on it, inside. More blood was in her car, and Avery's DNA was on a latch. Police matched a bullet collected from the garage to a rifle in Avery's house. It seemed like a solid case against him.

However, Avery told reporters that the officers had planted evidence to frame him for the murder because he was suing them for millions for a wrongful conviction from two decades earlier, for which he had spent eighteen years in prison. The police charged Avery with Halbach's murder and with mutilating a corpse. More evidence seemed to implicate him, although there were problems with the manner in which the search and evidence handling was conducted. During Avery's 2007 trial, defense attorney Dean Strang offered an elaborate theory: Law enforcement had engineered the whole thing.

The jury deliberated for three days before convicting Avery of first-degree intentional murder. They acquitted him of the charge of mutilating a corpse. Since then, this case has been the subject of intense scrutiny, due to a documentary that focused on investigative error.

One item brought out in the trial was a directive to the Wisconsin State Crime Lab DNA analyst, Sherry Culhane, on February 26. It demonstrates the reason there is potential for bias even within scientific analysis. Culhane knew the suspect's name and admitted receiving phone and email messages from Special Agent Tom Fassbender, from the Wisconsin Division of Criminal Investigation. The defense attorney showed Culhane a case communication record from November 11, 2005. She acknowledged the exchange between Fassbender and herself. The attorney continued, "And the very first thing that is indicated on [line] 12 here is, he is telling you that there's some evidence that is going to be coming or is already here, right?"

She affirmed this and acknowledged that some items from the Avery house and garage would come to the lab.

"And then he says – or you wrote down, I assume that's him telling you – try to put her in his house or garage, correct?"

"Correct."

"So you are being told, before you do any of these tests, that Mr. Fassbender wants you to come up with results that puts Teresa Halbach in Mr. Avery's house or garage, isn't that right?"

"I had that information, but that had no bearing on my analysis at all."

"That's what Mr. Fassbender told you he hoped you would be able to do with your tests, isn't that right?"

"Yeah, I assume so." (*Wisconsin v. Avery*, 2007)

There should have been no such communication between an investigator and a lab analyst (Guerra Thompson, 2016). Lab analysts should operate in an arena free of knowledge about what the investigators hope will occur. It was not until 2009 that a report from the National Academy of Sciences on the overall state of the forensic sciences strongly recommended that crime labs be independent of police departments. What follows is the legal and interdisciplinary context for investigators to minimize opportunities for such potential compromises. However, independence is just part of the story. Proficiency testing, accountability, and protocols add further credibility.

We now look at admissibility standards from the time that the role of science first became an issue for legal proceedings, as well as the protocols for quality assurance and control, the need for watchdog groups, and the importance of databases. All of this ensures that whatever evidence is found, it will be admissible in court, without being subject to later scrutiny that could result in reasonable doubt. We include some of the cases of high-profile fraud.

An Investigator's Guide to Basic Science and Admissibility

The aim of science is to approach facts with an attitude and method that can be objectively replicated by peers under controlled conditions, so as to identify genuinely influential or causal factors. Science is not necessarily about certainty. The goal is to devise a testable hypothesis that best fits the full array of facts, without distorting them. Scientific knowledge relies on systematic observation to make reliable deductions and create formulas from established physical laws. The intent of admitting scientific expert testimony into the courts is to assist fact-finders in dealing reliably with complex information for which they have no background (Shelton, 2011). So, we look at the first case to provide a standard for science in U. S. courts.

A commonsense assumption is that physiological changes will reveal lies. To place this in a scientific context, psychologist William M. Marston invented a device in 1917 that would measure specific changes. He claimed that systolic blood pressure changes provided a standard and reliable way to detect deception. A case in 1923 put his notion to the test.

James T. Frye, convicted of murder, had appealed the conviction because the court had not allowed evidence from a systolic blood pressure deception test. The District of Columbia Court of Appeals upheld the conviction. In the process, the *Frye* standard was articulated: "The thing from which the deduction is made must be sufficiently established to have gained general acceptance in the particular field in which it belongs." The lie detection device had not gained this status (*Frye*, 1923). Marston's belief about the reliability and validity of this device was not substantiated by general acceptance in criminal justice.

Eventually, critics claimed that the *Frye* standard excluded theories that were unusual but well supported. Several attempts were made to rephrase the standard, including the Federal Rules of Evidence 702, which replaced the phrase, "general acceptance," with knowledge, skill, training, or experience, and allowed judges to determine relevance. However, the *Frye* standard held sway in one form or another throughout the United States until 1993, when another case yielded a new standard for many jurisdictions.

The parents of Jason Daubert and Eric Schuller sued Merrell Dow Pharmaceuticals, alleging that its nausea drug, Bendectin, had caused birth defects. The company's epidemiologist reviewed more than thirty published studies involving over 130,000 patients and found no evidence of this. The petitioners' legal team offered eight experts to contradict this finding, but the judge decided that their methods fell short of the *Frye* standard. The Ninth Circuit Court of Appeals affirmed this ruling.

The petitioners brought their complaint to the U. S. Supreme Court, asking for a clearer standard for scientific reliability. In what has come to be known as the *Daubert* decision, the Court spelled out conditions under which scientific evidence would be admitted in federal jurisdictions: "scientific" means having a grounding in scientific methods and procedures that are sufficiently established by general acceptance in a relevant field, and "knowledge" must be stronger than subjective belief. Trial court judges would determine this by focusing on methodology, not conclusions, and on whether the method applied to the facts of the case. In other words, judges now had to determine whether 1) the theory can be tested within scientific criteria; 2) the potential error rate is known; 3) peers have reviewed the method, attracting widespread acceptance within a relevant scientific community; and 4) the testimony was relevant to the issue in dispute. Some *Daubert* analysts add another condition: standards controlling the discipline's operation are maintained (*Daubert*, 1993).

The Dauberts lost the case, because their experts had prepared evidence specifically for their litigation, not as independent research. Attorneys took note.

Two subsequent cases, *General Electric Co. v. Joiner* (1997) and *Kumho Tire Co. v. Carmichael* (1999), clarified the judge's role and applied the same criteria to other types of specialized knowledge and technical expertise. These cases are known collectively as the *Daubert* trilogy. *Daubert* became the federal standard and replaced the *Frye* standard in many states.

However, this ruling laid a significant burden on judges. A survey in 2001 involving 400 state trial judges found that only four percent grasped the demands of their role as the gatekeeper. Few knew what it meant to test a hypothesis, establish an error rate, and perform a statistical analysis. They also tended to misapply the concept of reliability. Another problem is that many reputable journals publish studies based on unrepresentative samples or inappropriate methods. Judges do not have the training to spot these problems (Shelton, 2009; Vidmar, 2011).

In truth, guidelines are slippery. As long as the practitioner has credentials, is experienced, and seems unbiased (not acting as a "hired gun" on behalf of some attorney), the results are deemed trustworthy and acceptable to the relevant scientific community (Shelton, 2009).

Behavioral science presents even more problems, due to interpretive ambiguity and the malleable error rates of probability analysis. Because clinical opinion derives from observation and subjective analysis, important questions are raised over whether it could meet the *Daubert* definition of reliable science (Brodin, 2004; Dahir, 2005; Faust et al., 2010; Goodman, 2010).

One area of psychology that *is* grounded in measured research involves experiments with eyewitness memory. More than a century of research has shown that juries often erroneously trust eyewitness testimony, especially confident testimony. However, only when witnesses express a high degree of confidence when initially questioned following an incident are they accurate up to 80% of the time. More often, their confidence builds after a few words of encouragement by investigators. A high percentage of people exonerated by DNA evidence over the past two decades were convicted with considerable support from eyewitness misidentification (about 75%), so memory issues should be taken seriously. Research psychologists can educate juries about factors that influence the quality of recollection (Murname, 2015).

During the mid-2000s, concerned parties gathered into committees to examine the state of the forensic sciences, particularly regarding the cases of false convictions. Expertise had been presented as science under the umbrella term, "forensic science," which gave fact-finders a weightier impression of certain disciplines than was warranted.

Even fingerprint identification, accepted in the courts for a century, has been challenged. All investigators should take note!

The National Academy of Sciences (NAS) Report

In 2009, the National Academy of Science's National Research Council published the results of a two-year study that found that the country's forensic science system needed a substantial overhaul. In a sweeping 254-page report, "Strengthening Forensic Science in the United States: A Path Forward," the National Academy of Science (NAS) stated that there was too much variability in terms of expert qualifications, reliability of findings, and proof of claims. Among the worst offenders were those methods that relied on eyeballing a pattern match. The Council recommended that the collective forensic sciences develop a better foundation, mandate accreditation, and improve accountability for claims made, as well as form a national oversight agency. For many disciplines that touted themselves as "science," the report was a wake-up call. Other, more recent reports, have affirmed these needs.

Technically, forensic science is the application of scientific perspectives and methods to the investigative and legal process. However, the phrase has evolved into an umbrella term that encompasses disciplines that use no controlled conditions, reliable data collection, peer-reviewed studies, or testable hypotheses. More alarming has been the serious backlog of work in some areas and the lack of resources to address immediate needs. The community is fragmented, the NAS Research Council found, its practices inconsistent and its quality controls lacking.

Although the "gold standard" DNA methods have been rigorously validated, few other forensic disciplines have received this treatment. This included analyses for bite marks, tool marks, some areas of ballistics, handwriting, hair, blood patterns, arson, and behavior. Labeling many of these procedures as "science" misrepresented them and made them falsely appear in court to be highly reliable.

The NAS recommended the formation of a National Institute of Forensic Science, empowered to uphold "best practice" standards and to set up mandatory certification and accreditation programs. In addition, crime labs should be independent of police departments and more rigorously peer-reviewed research should be undertaken. Overall, there should be more integrity. People's lives were at stake, evidenced by the hundreds of exonerations of the wrongly convicted.

The Board of Directors of the American Society of Crime Laboratory Directors (ASCLD) issued a response. Pleased that forensic science has been prioritized, ASCLD advised lab directors to prepare staff. Changing the perception that science is lacking could be accomplished only with collaboration. Some forensic science leaders called for an international think tank and a strategic plan. The primary issue was integrity: unbiased procedures, qualified experts, and scientifically verified facts.

Scientific working groups (SWG) formed. SWGs consist of subject-matter experts who collectively decide on the discipline's best practices and standards. Among them were SWGs for anthropology, firearms, toxicology, and facial identification. There was even a SWG for wildlife forensics.

In 2013, in consultation with the Department of Justice, the National Institute of Standards and Technology (NIST) sought input from the forensic science community for a registry of standards for practitioners. The ultimate goal was to offer a transparent account that minimized the impact of "junk science" and to improve oversight for the "forensic science ecosystem." NIST publishes regular newsletters to update progress and provides video recordings of past meetings. It names its consulting subject matter experts and fully describes how the National Commission on Forensic Science (NCFS) operates. The ecosystem includes law enforcement, the legal system, medical examiner and coroner offices, research facilities and institutions, and forensic laboratories.

The Organization of Scientific Area Committees (OSAC) has a governing board, a standards board, and resource committees, along with five scientific area committees. These include Biology/DNA, Crime Scene/Death Investigation, Digital/Multimedia, Chemistry/Instrumental Analysis, and Physics/Pattern Interpretation. The OSAC has two-dozen subcommittees, replacing scientific working groups. Those involved seek to improve the underlying science, the operational systems, and the applications. "The aim of the Organization of Scientific Area Committees for Forensic Science (OSAC)," its website states, "is to identify and promote technically sound, consensus-based, fit-for-purpose documentary standards that are based on sound scientific principles... A standard or guideline that is posted on either Registry demonstrates that the methods it contains have been assessed to be valid by forensic practitioners, academic researchers, measurement scientists, and statisticians through a consensus development process that allows participation and comment from all relevant stakeholders."

Figure 16. Northeast Forensic Training Center lab

Source: Katherine Ramsland

As part of this effort, the Academy Standards Board (ASB) of the American Academy of Forensic Sciences (AAFS) is forming "Consensus Bodies" for several categories: Bloodstain pattern analysis, disaster victim identification, DNA, firearms and tool marks, footwear and tire impressions, friction ridge identification, odontology, wildlife forensics, document examination, and pattern injuries.

The Forensic Science Commission (FSC) in Texas was created in the wake of a scandal, yet it now leads the way in quality assurance (Hall, 2016). The standards had been lax at the Houston Police Department crime lab, so errors made by poorly trained technicians assisted with wrongful convictions. Among the cases was Cameron Todd Willingham, convicted with unscientific arson analysis and executed in 2004. It was possible that Texas had executed an innocent man based on junk science. Politicians quickly buried the report, and there was an attempt to exonerate the investigators by finding that they had relied on the "science of the time." However, the investigators had used a technique that had never been scientifically validated.

Texas developed a plan to certify or license all state forensic examiners by independent bodies and to host forensic seminars for training in new developments. In addition, when the state of a discipline evolved and that discipline had influenced a conviction, inmates were given the right to have cases reopened. After Michael Morton was exonerated after wrongly serving twenty-five years in prison for murdering his wife, prosecutors were required to be more transparent with their files. All crime labs were mandated to become accredited. Even DNA analysis was reexamined, finding that some of the statistical claims relevant to whether a suspect's profile fit a crime scene sample were not as straightforward as often presented in court.

The interpretation and handling of methods and evidence are the key issues, which brings us back to the problem of bias in subjective analysis. In 2015, the AAFS highlighted this concern in its keynote seminars at its annual meeting. This body of scientists wants to take seriously their responsibility for individuals' lives.

Quality Assurance

With a graduate degree in investigative forensics, Teresa Brasse has more than 23 years of experience with medicolegal investigation, forensic quality management, auditing, and process improvement. Brasse worked as the quality assurance manager for Bode Technology Group, a private DNA laboratory that assisted in identifying human remains following several mass disasters, including the 9-11 World Trade Center attacks. As a quality consultant and project manager, Brasse worked at several federal law enforcement forensic laboratories, including the ATF and the U. S. Postal Inspection Services. In addition, she was appointed to the Guatemalan Forensic Anthropology Foundation DNA Scientific Advisory Board to assist with the set-up of the country's anthropology laboratory.

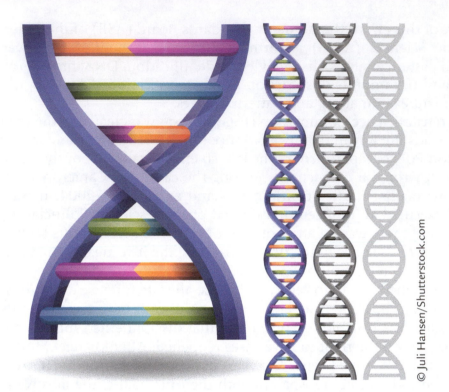

©Juli Hansen/Shutterstock.com

Figure 17. DNA

As part of several exhumation teams, she managed evidence collection and handling. No one was more careful and exacting, even on hot, dusty days next to maggot-infested or waterlogged remains, than Brasse. She logged potential evidence, used proper tape, and ensured the chain of custody. Despite her low-key manner, she was the acknowledged scientist.

"My work in forensics," Brasse said, "started with specialized investigative work as part of a volunteer exhumation team that researched high-profile cases where cause and manner of death were in question. Through investigative efforts, exhumation, autopsy and evidence collection, cause and or manner of death was determined. My interest in evidentiary issues led me to forensic quality assurance" (personal interview, 2015).

Her current focus is to assist law enforcement agencies with cold cases. She also consults on process improvement, untested forensic evidence, and quality assurance efforts with evidence handling. "Currently, I volunteer for a local law enforcement agency's Investigative Unit with open and cold cases and as chair of the Forensic Science Consulting Committee for the American Investigative Society of Cold Cases."

Brasse took a special interest in the Casey Anthony murder trial in Florida, because, as a state resident, she could stay attuned to detailed news coverage. The trial combined several forensic disciplines and highlighted good versus junk science. Even today, it remains a good study about why oversight and accountability are important.

In June 2008, a toddler, Caylee Marie Anthony, disappeared in Orlando, Florida. Her mother, Casey Anthony, did not initially report it. She became the primary person of interest, notably because she lied about a fictional nanny taking the child and had also gone about her life as if the child was not gone. She had even gone to parties. In December, the toddler's body was discovered in a wooded-area near Anthony's home. Prosecutors worked hard to compile forensic evidence to support a murder charge. Although the case was built primarily on circumstantial evidence, Prosecutor Jeff Ashton had successfully prosecuted numerous homicides similarly composed (Ashton & Pulitzer, 2011). Jose Baez, Anthony's lead defense attorney, exploited the lack of solid physical evidence and attacked new technologies (Baez & Golenbock, 2012). His alternative scenario was also circumstantial. (In Chapter 11, we will revisit this case to look at the digital analysis.)

The evidence included items collected and recovered from the trunk of Anthony's car, which had been abandoned at the time the child went missing. The items and procedures became a source of debate among experts, with the defense claiming that the prosecution's case rested on "fantasy forensics," or junk science. In some instances, expert testimony was unique and had to prove itself as science (Ashton & Pulitzer, 2011; Baez & Golenbock, 2012).

To highlight these courtroom battles, Brasse focused on the entomological evidence recovered from the trunk and the body dump site. She spoke with experts from both sides.

The prosecution team had consulted with Dr. Neal Haskell, a leading entomology expert, shortly after the discovery of the defendant's abandoned car. The defense had consulted Dr. Timothy Huntington, a professor. Although both experts met the education requirements and were two of only fifteen certified forensic entomologists in the country, Haskell had more experience.

Haskell received entomological or insect evidence removed from a fluid-stained paper towel inside a white plastic trash bag that had been in the trunk of the defendant's car. He determined that the insects were coffin flies. Haskell consulted a weather report and concluded from an analysis of the insect developmental stage that approximately four days of decomposition had occurred. After the body was discovered, he also collected samples from the disposal site (Haskell, 2008).

"He told me," said Brasse, "that the insect evidence recovered from the disposal site crime scene and the items [he took to] the medical examiner's office were consistent with the insect evidence collected from the plastic trash bag in the trunk of the car."

At a later date, Huntington examined four containers of insects from the trash bag and looked at Haskell's report (Huntington, 2010).

"In court," said Brasse, "Dr. Haskell testified that coffin flies found in the trunk of the car were consistent with the coffin flies found at the disposal crime scene. Based on Dr. Haskell's observations at the crime scene in the swamp area and the evidence he'd examined from the car trunk, he believed that the body had been dumped in the swamp area during mid-summer but had been in the car trunk prior to this."

Haskell's opinion was based on the lack of first early insect colonizers at the disposal site, which suggested that the early decomposition, attracting insects, had occurred in another location. Yet, there was a lack of proliferation of early insect evidence in the car's trunk, and he explained that this had been the result of the body being wrapped in a plastic bag in a sealed trunk, which would limit insect activity (Haskell, 2008).

"The insects recovered from the plastic bag in the trunk," said Brasse, "and specifically from the paper towel previously determined to contain decomposition fluid was reported as evidence of decomposition in the trunk."

Huntington contradicted Haskell's interpretation. He said that coffin flies are common and the flies recovered from the trunk were not forensically significant. They had merely been attracted to a bag of rotting garbage. A corpse, he insisted, would have attracted a lot more flies.

"Dr. Huntington had performed an experiment with a pig carcass," said Brasse. "He placed it in the trunk of a car to decompose to replicate the evidence found in the defendant's trunk. He said it produced large amounts of insects. But cross-examination [in court] exposed the weaknesses of his method. The experiment was not performed under the same environmental conditions or in concordance with the state the body was found, wrapped in a blanket, plastic bag and laundry bag."

In addition, the trial focused on odor evidence. Huntington attributed the smell that came from the trunk of the car to garbage, yet he had not examined the contents of the trash. He deduced from a photo that the odor came from a package of salami. "Then," said Brasse, "the actual empty package of salami was brought into evidence. His smell theory was not supported."

Brasse pointed out that, while forensic entomology is a generally accepted science, more challenges to its reliability (and admissibility) might occur in the future. "Although the 2009 NAS Report does not specifically mention recommendations for the field of forensic entomology," she said, "it does address all qualitative forensic disciplines that are open to subjectivity and human error. Therefore, entomology has the potential to be scrutinized in the courtroom and its expert testimony subject to challenging admissibility hearings."

The real issue, she said, is "how is a jury that hears two opposite opinions and interpretations of important evidence expected to come to an educated determination of which expert is credible and reliable? The fact that an opinion from a less qualified entomology expert that insect presence historically attributed and generally accepted as proof of decomposition could be attributed instead to an empty package of a salami meat suggests [the need for] further research and published studies to refute coffin flies as a reliable and valid test of decomposition."

Current admissibility standards fail to touch on some of the key issues. "We are left with the question of why the investigators were not able to piece together the evidence in the trunk with supporting entomological evidence in this case. The prosecution's insect-derived evidence appeared to corroborate the other expert testimony. But when you compare the knowledge and experience of the two entomologists in this case, it's difficult to challenge who is more qualified to render an opinion." One expert had more experience and was not caught in problematic testimony like the other one was, but jurors place experts into the whole package. Whichever package they prefer, that expert will be preferred, even if not superior.

"As procedures for governing expert testimony are progressively becoming more stringent," said Brasse, "a general acceptance of forensic evidence may require higher legal tests of admissibility."

For investigators, the take-away lesson is to ensure that all methods for evidence collection maintain integrity, and to ask important questions about lab independence and procedures. Investigators tend to appreciate having a connection with the labs, but this can end up with a wrongful conviction, a case that is easily dismantled with the charge of junk science, or a case that wins an appeal. Best practices dictate getting it right in the early stages, with no appearance of compromise.

Databases and Crime Reports

For complex cases, judgments based on expertise have traditionally been considered the best practice, but information from databases can contradict such judgments. An expert's experience, no matter how extensive, is limited. Their mental habits can also move a case in the wrong direction, as we saw in earlier chapters. If a database or extensive classification system exists for a specific type of analysis, investigators should consult it.

The earliest classification system is the *Uniform Crime Reports* (UCR), which the Federal Bureau of Investigation (FBI) prepares with the Department of Justice. Formed during the 1920s as the *Uniform Crime Records*, this annual roundup of statistics in the United States gives law enforcement, attorneys, researchers, and journalists perspective on the rates, volume, and locations of homicides. In 1989, the FBI created the National Incident-Based Reporting System (NIBRS) to expand on the UCR. It is more reliable, as it gathers details on incidents and adds more details than what usually go into the UCR. The NIBRS consists of incident and arrest information collected from law enforcement agencies and has twenty-two categories of offenses in Group A and ten additional offenses in Group B. The National Crime Victimization Survey (NCVS), which began in 1972, surveys victims. This adds yet another dimension. The latest version improved estimates of domestic violence and sexual assaults.

The Bureau of Justice Statistics (BJS) also offers U.S. homicide trends since 1976. Homicide rates are considered a reliable barometer of other violent crimes. The National Center for Health Statistics (NCHS) collects mortality data, which includes those who have died by homicide. This information is available via a publication, *Vital Statistics*. It comes from coroner and medical examiner offices across the country. The accuracy is dependent on the thoroughness of the death investigations.

Databases have been developed in many areas of forensic science, especially where comparisons are crucial. We will describe some in other chapters. The oldest and best-known set of records is for fingerprints. Once stored on cards that could be time-consuming to sort through, fingerprints are now digitally stored on the Automated Fingerprint Identification System (AFIS) in each state.

For spent bullet casings from a crime, examiners compare unique drag marks left by a specific gun. Investigators at police departments can upload images of the marks into the National Integrated Ballistics Information Network (NIBIN), operated by the Bureau of Alcohol, Tobacco, Firearms and Explosives. NIBIN might make a match from another incident. Then a firearms examiner inspects the shell casing under microscopic enhancement to look for individualizing characteristics and matching striations or grooves. Although such marks will not necessarily reproduce with 100 percent accuracy, the database still provides law enforcement with an important crime-solving tool.

DNA, tire impressions, footwear, carpet fibers, drugs, and paint chips have databases as well, as do specific types of behavior, such as linguistic analysis. The American Association of Suicidology, for example, provides extensive data on suicides in many different cultures and populations. Consulting these studies can minimize harm done from investigations that accept superficial stereotypes or cultural myths.

In 1967, the FBI started the National Crime Information Center (NCIC), a computerized index that permitted state and local jurisdictions access to FBI archives on such items as license plate numbers and recovered guns, as well as the ability to post notices about wanted or missing persons. It also provided a way to coordinate certain types of national investigations. During the late 1970s, the FBI established the criminal profiling unit at Quantico for a better approach to the investigation of serial crimes. (See Chapter 8.)

By the mid-1980s, the Bureau had set up the National Center for the Analysis of Violent Crime (NCAVC) and developed the Violent Criminal Apprehension Program (ViCAP). It was slated to become the most comprehensive computerized database for homicides nationwide. Its purpose is to assist with linking cases across jurisdictions to a single offender or group of offenders, and to provide officers with a way to communicate on cases. Police departments from around the country, having free access, contribute solved, unsolved, and attempted homicides; unidentified bodies in which the manner of death was suspect; and missing-persons cases involving suspected foul play.

Many information-based items, such as DNA in the Combined DNA Index System (CODIS), have been digitized and are searchable. Numerous databases exist for literature searches as well, such as for unidentified decedents or biomedical data.

Computers also allow for evidence enhancement, image restoration, three-dimensional reconstruction, surveillance analysis, and numerous types of informatics. At the heart of any digital investigation is access to some type of gathered, categorized, and analyzed information. (See Chapter 10 for more about enhancements.)

Forensic Fraud and Self-Policing

In North Carolina in 1993, Greg Taylor was convicted of murder and given a life sentence. A crime analyst testified that the victim's blood was in the bed of Taylor's truck. However, not only was the analyzed substance *not* the victim's blood, it was not even blood. The eyewitness testimony had been faulty, as had testimony from a jailhouse snitch. Taylor served seventeen years before an Innocence Project attorney worked to free him in 2010 (Zucchino, 2010).

Taylor's is one of many stories about innocent people convicted on faulty or false methodology. In 2015, even the FBI lab took a hit. DNA testing was halted in its crime lab and soon thousands of cases involving the FBI's hair analysts from the past two decades showed a 95% rate of "exaggerated testimony." Thirty-two of the defendants had been sentenced to death. Some had been executed (Kohn, 1999).

In one case, a victim even insisted that seventeen-year-old George Perrot was not her rapist. However, an FBI hair analyst testified that he was. The analyst based his claim on a single hair found in the victim's bed. The supposed power of the expert trumped the victim – until Perrot was exonerated two decades later in the sweeping examination of hair analysis cases (Segura & Smith, 2016). The FBI admitted that the method it once had used and described as cutting-edge science was significantly flawed and that agents had given the impression that hair matches had greater weight than they actually did. Juries had believed them. Unfortunately, other methodologies are in the same boat.

Innocence Projects all over the United States have found erroneous forensic techniques to be at fault in wrongful convictions, with some people spending as long as three decades in prison for something they did not do. This is what led to the FBI hair analysis scandal. An analyst in 1978 had stated that a hair found in a stocking mask from a killer matched suspect Santae Tribble "in all microscopic characteristics" (Enserink, 2016, p. 1129). The analyst gave the odds against it matching someone else: 1 in 10 million. Yet, there was no basis for such a claim, and in 2009, a DNA analysis proved the analyst wrong. Tribble was awarded $13.2 million.

The age of junk science and false expert testimony started with West Virginia's State Trooper Fred Zain, a supervisor in the State Police laboratory (Hodel, 2001). He had attended many workshops and claimed to have compiled impressive collections of materials for comparisons in his casework. He testified in numerous cases, state to state. Eventually, scientists at the West Virginia lab discovered that Zain was "dry labbing" – not actually testing the items. Hundreds of his cases were reviewed and Zain was charged with fraud.

Then there was Joyce Gilchrist. When Jeff Pierce, once convicted, was found to be innocent, an investigation revealed that her work had put hundreds of people behind bars. In Pierce's case, Gilchrist had falsely testified about matching hairs. In fact, she had often gotten the results that law enforcement needed. It appeared that bias had affected her work.

Police laboratories have been under fire over the past decade and some have been shut down, pending external audits. In 2013, a lab tech in Massachusetts admitted to falsifying tests in literally thousands of cases over a nine-year period that had assisted with convictions (Segura & Smith, 2016).

Such fraud often arises from a conflict between the objectives of science to be neutral and the needs of the prosecution to support a case. The notion of an error rate and a probability analysis conflict with courtroom expectations of certainty. In addition, the system resists being second-guessed, even for correcting injustices.

So, how did this shocking state of affairs happen? Although forensic science has roots in toxicology and biology, eventually more technical disciplines such as fingerprint matching and the subjective judgments involved in other matching or reconstruction methodologies became prominent. Techniques that were useful and required some degree of training and expertise became subsumed under the label of science. There was little accountability for actually proving scientific methodology, in part because attorneys and judges had a poor understanding of scientific methodologies. Once precedents were set in the courtroom, it became easier for technicians to be viewed as "scientists" when they were not. Many forensic tests were never subjected to stringent scientific scrutiny, the NAS report concluded. "With the exception of nuclear DNA analysis … no forensic method has been rigorously shown to have the capacity to consistently, and with a high degree of certainty, demonstrate a connection between evidence and a specific individual or source" (p. 7).

In response to criticisms from several studies about bite-mark matching, the American Board of Forensic Odontologists (ABFO) developed a decision tree to demonstrate its standardized methodology. They posed 100 case studies to thirty-nine participants, all of whom were ABFO-certified. However, on only four cases was there solid agreement that the impression they had analyzed was a bite mark. At least two-dozen false convictions have been linked to an error in bite-mark testimony (Segura & Smith, 2016). It remains unknown how many more there might be. When judges accept junk science, appeals courts rarely deal with it.

Even DNA has come under criticism. When done right, it has a high degree of integrity. DNA methodology has been tested and retested more than any other method grouped among the forensic sciences. Because interpretations can be proven incorrect, the method has a verifiable error rate. However, DNA labs can fail to maintain protocols and analysts can still give faulty testimony (Garrett, 2016). Some examiners were found to have failed their proficiency tests. Unfortunately, some had already falsely testified (Hsu, 2016). In San Francisco in 2016, thousands of convictions were thrown out for this reason.

In March 2016, after the hair analysis debacle, the Justice Department expanded its review of the FBI Laboratory to pattern-matching techniques such as fingerprint examinations, handwriting analysis, and bullet-tracing. If it finds systematic problems in one of the techniques, it might review expert testimony from other labs. "What has crept into the forensic field are forensic sciences that are not sciences, and that is one of the basic problems," said Texas Forensic Science Commission member Vincent Di Maio (Hsu, 2016).

Fingerprint examiners have taken the call for standards seriously. Studies are underway to examine match-error rates and to quantify degrees of matching correspondence. In addition, examiners are cautioned about their testimony. They no longer individualize a print to a specific person, as they did in the past, and no one can state that the method is error-free (Segura & Smith, 2016).

Statisticians also acknowledge the NAS report criticism, because so many claims made in a courtroom invoke statistical measurement and analysis. During the early days of DNA, prosecutors quoted stunningly high odds about the findings, and many had no idea what they are actually stating.

NIST awarded a grant to a team of legal professionals and statisticians, the Center for Statistics and Applications in Forensic Evidence, to develop tools that will reliably analyze the strength of a supposed match between, say, a shoe and a footprint impression.

In other words, they want to replace eyeballing and subjective judgment with math. This will be difficult, since many disciplines are affected and the variability of patterns in most is unknown. Some areas of evidence do not have large databases, and there might be no established standard for when a match definitely suggests a common source (Servick, 2016). However, an effort must be made to develop a model based on those areas for which it can be done, because studies now being conducted show more false positives and negatives than expected. The aim is to develop "likelihood ratios."

Among claims that experts can no longer make are:

1. "It's a match."
2. "It's a reasonable degree of scientific certainty."
3. "The error rate is 0%."
4. "I'm never wrong."

It will be important to educate juries about statements that *are* allowable and what they actually mean. The aura of science influences fact-finders, so genuinely using scientific methods matters.

Some disciplines dismiss the NAS report and continue to insist that their methods are sound, even if not scientifically verified. In addition, new disciplines have jumped in to make statistical claims similar to those that have come under fire. In part, this is because if a method proves useful in court, attorneys will use it. An absence of oversight in the forensic system provides this opening. When judges, as gatekeepers, are also uneducated in science, this exacerbates the situation. When attorneys and judges depend on jurors to make sense of the testimony, they rely on people who, on average, are as uneducated in science as they are.

Benforado (2015), a legal scholar, proposes that all experts be independent, due to what we know about unconscious bias that influences judgment. Money spent on the criminal justice system should support the improvement of impartiality, not the proof of guilt. We should focus on quality and integrity in the methods (Frost, 2016).

The National Registry of Exonerations, which collects data differently than DNA-based Innocence Projects, is based at the University of Michigan Law School. The Registry was founded in 2012 in coordination with the Center on Wrongful Convictions in Illinois. Since 2011, the annual number of exonerations has doubled, with approximately three per week. A statement on the website offers their mission: "We study false convictions – their frequency, distribution, causes, costs and consequences – in order to educate policy makers and the general public about convictions of innocent defendants … Our primary goal is to reform the criminal justice system and reduce if not eliminate these tragic errors in the future. We also aim to make police officers, prosecutors, defense attorneys and judges more sensitive to the problem of wrongful convictions and more willing to reconsider the guilt of defendants who have already been convicted when new evidence of innocence comes to light." At this writing, there were 1,909 exonerations since 1989.

Summary

Forensic science today is about standards. To protect individuals as well as the general public, the NAS report recommends a National Institute of Forensic Science, empowered to uphold best practices and set up mandatory certification and accreditation programs. If more states follow the example of Texas, and if more investigators become educated in admissibility standards and scientific practices, investigations will gain greater integrity. With greater integrity, there will be fewer false claims, false convictions, and people falsely imprisoned. There will also be increased trust in the forensic system. More peer-reviewed research should be undertaken to support the scientific foundation of all methodologies that claim scientific status. In addition, there should be better – even mandatory – science education for attorneys, judges, and investigators. No investigator operates outside these parameters. The need for integrity begins with the crime scene.

Next, we look at the courtroom itself and how it impacts investigations.

Exercise #4.1

John Sweek was stabbed to death in his home in Dallas in 1987. A mark on his arm appeared to be a bruise made by human teeth. Two forensic odontologists examined the mark against the primary suspect, Steven Chaney, and declared that his teeth impressions matched the bruise. One expert claimed that the odds were a million to one that the bite mark would match anyone but Chaney. Nine alibi witnesses tried to help Chaney prove his innocence, but he was convicted. He spent twenty-eight years in prison before the Texas Forensic Science Commission (FSC), along with the Innocence Project, examined his case.

1. How would the FSC examine the evidence?
2. Bite mark analysis has been allowed in court since 1975. Why isn't this sufficient to validate it?
3. If evaluations of bite mark cases have discovered error rates as high as 64%, how can odontologists show the FSC that this discipline is a science?
4. How does reliance on precedent, which is often how courts proceed, hinder the improvements of science for forensic purposes?
5. What is the judge's role in this circumstance?

Exercise #4.2

One of the key questions in forensics is measuring the accuracy of facial forensic examiners. A research study proposes to use standard laboratory methods and tools to evaluate their performance. They recruit practitioners to compare faces in twenty image-pairs and answer a background survey. In addition, they ask non-examiner face experts and fingerprint examiners to take the same study. They believe that the two latter groups will serve as adequate controls. "By participating in this research study," they say, "you will assist in developing a scientific measure of performance of facial forensic comparison. These results may help meet the *Daubert* standard for the admissibility of expert witness testimony."

Questions

1. Does this study meet standards of scientific rigor?
2. How could it be improved?

References

Ashton, J. & Pulitzer, L. (2011). *Imperfect justice: Prosecuting Casey Anthony.* New York, NY: HarperCollins Publishers.

Baez, J. & Golenbock, P. (2012). *Presumed guilty: Casey Anthony: The inside story.* Dallas, TX: BenBella Books.

Benforado, A. (2015). *Unfair: The new science of criminal injustice.* New York, NY: Broadway Books.

Brodin, M. S. (2004–05). Behavioral science evidence in the age of *Daubert*: Reflections of a skeptic. *University of Cincinnati Law Review, 73,* 867–943.

Dahir, V. B. (2005). Judicial application of *Daubert* to psychological syndrome and profile evidence. *Psychology, Public Policy, and Law II*(1), 62–82.

Daubert v. Merrell Dow Pharmaceutical. 509 U.S. 579 (1993).

Enserink, M. (2016, March 11). Evidence on trial. *Science, 351*(6278), 1128–1129.

Frost, D. J. (2016, Spring). Raising your standards. *Evidence Technology Magazine.* 20–25.

Frye v. U. S. DC Circuit, 1923, vol. 54, 1013 pp.

Garrett, B. L. (2016, March 17). Even with DNA in hand, crime lab results are deeply flawed. Bostonreview.net

Goodman, M. (2010). A hedgehog on the witness stand – What's the big idea? The challenges of using *Daubert* to assess social science and nonscientific testimony. *American University Law Review 59,* 6:35–685.

Guerra Thompson, S. (2015). *Cops in lab coats: Curbing wrongful convictions through independent forensic laboratories.* Durham, NC: Carolina Academic Press.

Hall, M. (2016, January). False impressions. *Texas Monthly,* 102–108.

Haskell, N. (2008, August 28). *Caylee Anthony – missing person.* In *Forensic entomology investigations report of diagnostic laboratory examination.* Case 08-069208, FEI#1187(A). Retrieved http://www.examiner.com/crime-in-national/casey-anthony-read-the-forensic-entomology-report. Rensselaer, IN.

Hodel, M.B. (2001, September 4). Crime lab chemist goes on trial in West Virginia for alleged fraud. *Athens (GA) Banner-Herald.*

Hsu, H. S. (2016, March 21). Justice Department frames expanded review of FBI forensic testimony. *The Washington Post.*

Huntington, T. (2010). Homicide, Caylee Anthony. In *Preliminary entomological evidence report. Orange County Sheriff's Office.* Case 08-069208.http://www.scribd.com/doc/50549784/Anthony-Case-Discovery-Trunk-Report

Kohn, D. [Producer] (1999, January 28). Expert witness. CBS *48 Hours.* http://www.cbsnews.com/news/expert-witness/

Murname, K. (2015, Dec. 21). "I think this is the guy" – the complicated confidence of eyewitness memory. Artstechnica.com.

National Research Council (NRC). (2009). *Strengthening forensic science in the United States: A path forward.* Document No.: 228091. Washington, DC: National Academy of Sciences, National Academic Press.

Segura, L & Smith, J. (2016, March 55). In Las Vegas, embattled forensic experts respond to scandals and flawed convictions. *The Intercept.* https://theintercept.com/2016/03/25/in-las-vegas-embattled-forensics-experts-respond-to-scandals-and-flawed-convictions/

Servick, K. (2016, March). Sizing up the evidence: Statisticians are on a mission to reverse the legacy of junk science in the courtroom. *Science, 351*(6288), 1130–1132.

Shelton, D. E. (2009). Twenty-first century forensic science challenges for trial judges in criminal cases: Where the "Polybutadiene" meets the "Bitumen." *Widener Law Journal 18*(2): 309–396.

Shelton, D. E. (2011). *Forensic science in court: Challenges in the 21st century.* New York, NY: Rowman & Littlefield.

State of Wisconsin v. Steven Avery. (2007). http://www.stevenaverycase.org/wp-content/uploads/2016/02/Full-Jury-Trial-Transcript-combined.pdf

Vidmar, N. (2011). The psychology of trial judging. *Current Directions in Psychological Science, 20*(1), 58–62.

Zucchino, D. (2010, February 17). North Carolina man exonerated after 17 years. *Los Angeles Times.* http://articles.latimes.com/2010/feb/17/nation/la-na-innocence18-2010feb18

Chapter 5

The Courtroom

Learning Objectives

❖ Understand the prosecutor's function and needs.
❖ Explain the judge's role for investigators.
❖ Understand the difference between interview and interrogation.
❖ List types of interview strategies.
❖ Describe the signals of potential deception.

Key Words

Cognitive interview, competency, deception, interrogation, interview, kinesics, malingering, micro-expressions, PEACE, polygraph, prosecution, Reid Technique

On July 30, 1990, nine-year-old Nancy Shoemaker went on an errand near her home in Wichita, Kansas. Her younger brother, an infant, was sick and she wanted to buy him a 7-Up at the Phillips 66 gas station nearby. Her mother had to stay with the boy, so Nancy ventured out alone. She did not return. A massive search commenced, but there was no sign of her.

The investigation continued, involving the District Attorney's Office and DA Nola Tedesco Foulston. In this section, we look at how the prosecutor works with investigators for preparing a case. This process involves educating the team in the proper procedures and maintaining organized coordination, especially as new complications occur.

"We were alerted to this investigation," says Foulston, "and we kept in close touch with the officers. In any critical incident like this, investigators need to be collaborative with the prosecution, who will weigh and measure the type of evidence brought in. The officers reported directly to us. They couldn't get a search warrant without asking us. Our interest was making sure that nothing was compromised and everything was done well. Law enforcement complemented how we worked. We needed everyone on the same page" (personal interview, 2016).

Seven months later, on February 18, 1991, some of Nancy's skeletal remains were found near Belle Plaine, Kansas, twenty-five miles south of Wichita. Her clothing was missing. "At this point, we brought in an anthropologist, Pier Moore-Jansen, to analyze the skull. They found an appliance that an orthodontist identified as one he had made for Nancy. Pier could see there was a pink tinge in the teeth, so there was suspicion of strangulation."

A tipster pointed police to a dishwasher named Doil Lane. He was mentally challenged, but could drive and hold down a job.

"We brought in the FBI to assist," said Foulston. "We worked with the Behavioral Science Unit [BSU]. We were looking for a child killer and wanted to make sure we were doing it right. We wanted to prepare before bringing anyone in. The police put together a room, as the BSU special agents suggested, with flyers of the missing girl. We would bring suspects in there."

In April 1991, officers invited Lane in for questioning. He waived his rights to silence and an attorney, and agreed to talk. He also gave consent to search his home and car. He offered an alibi for his whereabouts on the day Nancy had disappeared and said that, at the time, he had no means of transportation. Lane now asked for an attorney.

Since he had signed a consent, officers searched Lane's home and found "missing child" posters that featured Nancy's photo. Lane had helped to distribute them, but had kept some. He also had boxes of children's clothing, including about two hundred pairs of girls' panties. He insisted that he was not involved in Nancy's murder.

Lane's mother, Murlene Broughton, was upset over what she viewed as harassment. She went to the DA's Office to express her anger and was directed to see Foulston's chief attorney, Greg Waller. During that meeting, with Doil also present, she complained that the police were harassing her son "just like they did in San Marcos, Texas, when that other little girl went missing."

This statement sent up red flags. "Having this information," says Foulston, "we immediately contacted the San Marcos Texas Police Department to confirm that there had been another little girl abducted and killed over eleven years before Nancy Shoemaker."

In 1980, eight-year-old Bertha Martinez was last seen riding her bike outside her home in San Marcos, the town where Lane had lived at the time. Reportedly, Bertha had followed a man and woman who were asking local kids about a missing dog. Six days later, Bertha's body was found inside a shed. She had been beaten, strangled, sexually assaulted and stabbed to death. Missing were her glasses and underwear.

Lane's alibi for the time of Nancy's disappearance proved false. To try to prove his innocence, he kept calling the investigators to give them names of people to contact, including girls who had accused him of molesting them. Lane hinted that Nancy's killer was sick and would probably do it again. Eventually, he admitted that he "had a problem" and needed to dress in the underwear of little girls. He said that his mother had dressed him as a girl when he was young. Finally, Lane said he was involved with Nancy's murder, but added that a friend named Donald Wacker had killed her.

Wacker was brought in. He melted quickly under questioning, admitting his part as an accomplice but turning on Lane as the killer. He was driving when Lane pointed out the girl on the street and ordered him to stop. Lane forced the girl into the car.

Wacker drove to a secluded spot and watched Lane assault the girl. He said he tried to stop it, but failed. Given the circumstances, he was more credible. "We charged him with aiding and abetting," said Foulston. "We knew it wasn't him who had killed her."

Lane was arrested and held in the Sedgwick County jail. That July, Foulston's office invited Texas investigators to interview him. He confessed to Bertha's murder, implicating his mother and stepfather (never prosecuted) as the instigators. He said they had forced him. He showed police where he had left Nancy's body, giving them a pair of panties that he had taken from her. He admitted to the murder.

"We determined that it would be to the State's advantage to have the Bertha Martinez murder tried first," said Foulston, "so that any conviction in that case could be used in the Shoemaker case as evidence of same or similar acts." The DA sent Lane to Texas in February 1993. He was tried, convicted, and sentenced to death before returning to face trial in Kansas.

"By this time, Wacker was already convicted for his part," said Foulston. "I wanted to make sure he would work with us, so I would visit him. He connected with me, so he was willing to speak against Lane at the trial."

Lane was tried and convicted for the aggravated kidnapping, rape, and murder of Nancy Shoemaker. He went into custody in Texas, but his death sentence was later commuted to life, due to diminished mental capacity (Radostitz, 2003; *State v. Lane*, 1997).

Procedural Justice

When a crime has been committed and a suspect identified, there's an arrest. This involves booking, fingerprints, records checks, mug shots, and, in some contexts, collecting biological samples for analysis. Arrestees are advised of their right to remain silent and to engage an attorney (which they might waive), perhaps placed in a holding cell, and allowed to call someone, such as an attorney. If they waive the right to an attorney, there might follow an interrogation and/or a search.

Prosecution teams examine evidence to decide about a formal charge. In criminal cases, they know they will have to prove this person to be guilty beyond a reasonable doubt. Thus, they need good evidence and solid logic.

A grand jury might be convened in federal felonies and other complex cases, and a preliminary hearing is arranged to consider probable cause. At arraignments, defendants learn the charge(s) and might be asked for a plea of guilty, not guilty, or whatever the jurisdiction legally allows. The court might also decide whether to set bail or release defendants.

After pretrial motions are resolved, there may be an attempt at a plea bargain before the case moves into court. Both sides collect evidence, form a narrative, and line up their supporting witnesses. Defense attorneys might make plans for pre-trial hearings on evidence or a change of venue (trial location).

Defendants have the right to see the results of the investigation, including their own oral or recorded statements, a copy of their records, all material items used for the case in chief (in which the party with the burden of proof presents its evidence), the results of scientific testing, and all reports of mental and physical examinations. In turn, defense attorneys must show the prosecutor any items or experts they intend to use. An obligation exists to comply with the expectation of transparency, although some attorneys have their own interpretation of what this means.

A set of rules and procedures govern all courts. Many rules can be complex, and some evolve with new decisions. The United States Constitution specifies due process and acceptable rules of procedure.

Presenting evidence begins with the prosecution. Opening statements inform the jury of what to expect. Then the prosecutor presents the direct evidence, with cross-examination by the defense. Nola Foulston, mentioned above, was the elected District Attorney in Kansas for twenty-six years. She served as the Kansas State Director for the National District Attorneys Association Board of Directors and is a member of the American Academy of Forensic Sciences. Among her other notable cases were "BTK" serial killer Dennis Rader and the Carr brothers, who went on a crime spree in 2000 that resulted in rape, robbery, kidnapping, sexual assault, and the murder of five people.

In 1994, Foulston was the lead trial counsel in the prosecution of the landmark case of *State of Kansas v. Leroy Hendricks,* which focused on the state's right to institutionalize a convicted sexual predator under Kansas' recently enacted Sexually Violent Predator law. When it went up on appeal in Kansas, the Supreme Court declared the sexual predator act, as applied, to be unconstitutional. The case was successfully argued before the U. S. Supreme Court. Foulston was co-counsel in the case of *Michael Marsh v. the State of Kansas,* which challenged the constitutionality of the Kansas capital punishment statute. The U.S. Supreme Court affirmed it.

A natural teacher and storyteller, Foulston is active in law enforcement and prosecution advisory capacities. She has served with the American Prosecutors Research Institute (APRI) DNA Legal Assistance Unit and was appointed as the Committee Chair and Editor for the APRI publication, *The Prosecutor's Deskbook.*

"Those who choose prosecution as a career in law," Foulston says, "often live their lives in a fishbowl. Each step or misstep is an event in any community, and each fall from grace is a tragedy. Charged with the responsibility of gatekeeper for the criminal justice process, on a daily basis the prosecution office plays a major collaborative role in sorting out crime and consequence, and in fair dealing and responsible legal action. If there is a singular charge directing the work of the prosecutor it may be found in the concept that there must be *justice for all.*"

Foulston helped to standardize investigative practices by citing rules adopted by the Kansas Supreme Court for her office's responsibilities. Notably, they must "refrain from prosecuting a charge that the prosecutor knows is not supported by probable cause." While they do not control the investigation, "we recommended things for making it better for the case we needed to make. It's important to keep the priority in mind: making a solid case. When the officers work with us, we're responsible for them." Her office provided regular trainings for officers and for their own staff on how to operate effectively as a team.

A second important issue is the publicity that surrounds high profile cases. "We stuck close to professional rules of conduct. There was no discussion of evidence, pre-trial.

We had to be careful about the information we offered to the press, and this applied to everyone on the team. We were particular about making police understand that professional conduct was a dual obligation."

Laws exist to protect people, but perpetrators have rights as well. In the United States, suspects are guilty only after being so proven. This right, among others, dictates legal protocol in arrest procedures and evidence handling, so investigators must know the right thing to do. Even if their work assists in a conviction, any missteps can be scrutinized later, with a potential for having a conviction overturned and their reputations tarnished. Investigators should learn to work with prosecutors, who are part of the process from the start.

Figure 18. Courtroom

Source: Katherine Ramsland

Among other special responsibilities for the prosecutor that would affect investigators are to 1) advise the accused of their rights, and 2) respect these rights. Any misstep could derail the process. In addition, no one on the team is to make extrajudicial comments that could negatively affect the case or influence the public, who might become jurors. The defendant is to be accorded procedural justice, so that guilt is decided on sufficient evidence.

Seth Weber, a practicing attorney in the Commonwealth of Pennsylvania, received his Juris Doctor (J.D.) degree from Temple Law School. He began his legal career in the Bucks County Public Defender Office, and became an Assistant District Attorney in the Bucks County District Attorney's Office. For twenty-six years, Weber acted as Assistant United States Attorney in Philadelphia. He has personally tried over 150 jury trials as lead attorney, all of which involved state or federal criminal offenses, including drug conspiracies, drug gangs, environmental crimes, white collar crimes, and violent crimes. He has some advice.

"Criminal investigators need to realize that once they have made an arrest, that is not the end of their work," said Weber. "Quite the opposite. Indeed, it's actually the beginning of the case, because now they are part of the prosecutor's team as they prepare for court.

"First, the investigator needs to realize that although they are both on the same team, their roles are different. The prosecution team starts by questioning the criminal investigator, and there are a lot of questions. We want to know, what is the evidence? Are there search warrants, DNA, fingerprints, confessions, witness statements, cell phone analyses, computer evidence, forensic evidence, and on and on? Why do prosecutors ask so many questions? Because they must be fully prepared for court. They must follow the rules of criminal procedure and rules of evidence, which qualify how the case is presented. It's not just storytelling. This is all done in the legal arena and we follow rules.

"Second, the prosecutor will need to review *all* of the police reports. This doesn't mean just a piece of paper that lays out the facts. Investigators must understand that their report is a defense lawyer's best friend. The report can easily create reasonable doubt, unforeseen to the investigator. Although we all know that a report is just a 'summary' of the information, it is *their* summary. The investigators pick and choose what facts and information to put in the report, what 'spin' or phrasing they want to use. And just as important, what they choose to leave out of the report. I always says, 'Be sure you review your report before making it final, and ask yourself what will a defense lawyer ask me about what's in and what isn't? A few days before trial, they should read over their reports so they know what they said. They can't say they don't remember something in their own report!"

Weber insists that everything must be checked for completeness and consistency, right down to times and dates. Long delays between the incident and writing the report, which can happen, could end up causing serious credibility issues during the trial.

"We also look at the information in the report. Is there too much, or too little? Are there errors (even just typos) that can undermine the case? Are there facts missing from the report, and should they be included? This raises the question of whether a supplemental report is needed to clarify potentially confusing material, or to correct an earlier error or fill in something that was omitted.

"Third, criminal investigators must be mindful not to rely only on the evidence that they have. They also need to think about evidence they can additionally obtain. For prosecutors, the more evidence there is of guilt, the stronger the case.

"Finally, remember that despite all of the annoying questions, additional tasks assigned to you and the reality that you as an investigator might think all or some of the prosecutor's requests are unnecessary, you need to be on board. You need to think like a team member. You're not a lone player. Meet with the prosecutor. Get to know what they need. Bring coffee. (Donuts wouldn't hurt either.) Try to anticipate. Be prepared for questions and more questions, and additional work that you may never have thought about. Prosecutors have a method to their seeming madness, so for the team to be strong, and the end result to be the best that it can be toward the goal of a guilty verdict, the members must all work together."

He recalled working on a white-collar case with an Environmental Protection Agency (EPA) agent who had formerly worked for the Drug Enforcement Agency (DEA). "All I really thought about were the witness statements and documents creating a paper trail so I could prove the crime in court. I met with the agent during the investigation stage. Before any indictment, charges, or arrest, he asked, 'Why don't we wire up a witness to record the suspect?' He meant make a face-to-face recording. I had never heard of this at the time. 'Really?' I asked. 'Use a typical drug investigation tool in a white collar case?' We did and we obtained tape-recorded statements of the target not only talking about the crime we were investigating but also discussing how to get rid of evidence. That agent's great suggestion made the case. He was a team player. He wanted to make our case strong."

Interview and Interrogation

As a case develops, investigators must question people while also observing their behavior. They provide this information to the prosecutor, and it might get into court as evidence. Interviews can involve an eyewitness, a crime survivor, a suspect's associate or relative, or a person of interest. Someone who develops into a serious suspect would be interrogated. There is a difference. Interviewing centers on acquiring information, whereas extracting a confession relies on a different procedure, described below.

No matter who is questioned, issues of memory can interfere with accuracy. Investigators should be educated about psychological research on memory, because handling someone's memory is like handling trace evidence. Memory is fragile and can easily be corrupted. Once it is corrupted, there is no returning to the original form. Experts have established that memory is the result of a process of construction, organized around a cluster of facts and experiences (Loftus, 1979). A witness's memory of an incident can be distorted from a variety of sources. For example, exposure to new information between the time an incident occurred and the time when the memory is retrieved can influence recall, even if the new information contains errors. It can even result in gaining false memories of things that never happened (Loftus & Hoffman, 1989).

If an incident involves several witnesses, they must be separated, so as not to influence any individual's recall. Each witness should be asked to describe fully his or her account without interruption. In addition, investigators should be trained about how the phrasing of questions can significantly affect the narrative (Loftus, 1979).

The best advice for an interview is to be prepared and to stay open to the possibility of unanticipated responses. Listening, especially to people with whom one feels no sympathy, is a skill. One needs to be aware that confidence does not indicate accuracy and that logic is not the same as fact. Our minds automatically seek meaning in narratives, which form around typical story arcs, so it can be difficult to listen fully. Problems arise from a firm presumption of guilt, because it can induce tunnel vision about other options or suspects.

German investigator Hanns Scharff believed that the best way to encourage someone to talk, no matter what the ultimate purpose, is to make that person think that you are his greatest advocate. Scharff's method, developed interrogating captured American fighter pilots during World War II, involves secrecy and engagement with the suspect's perspective. The suspect is kept in the dark about the core objective and about what the interrogator actually knows. The suspect is also led to believe that whatever he says does not contribute much to the puzzle. This involves thinking like a suspect might in response to certain questions: Imagine their defense mechanism, excuses, and attempts to mislead or deflect. Imagine the face-saving they might adopt. The approach requires the investigator to figure out what the suspect might say or might want to say, but to avoid offering the opportunity to them. Remain confident and friendly, not intimidating or overly verbal (Toliver, 1997).

Another technique is the cognitive interview, which has become more popular. Instead of the sterile interrogation room, the setting is comfortable, perhaps a hotel room. The interviewer is friendly and uses open-ended questions, such as, "Tell me what happened." They might invite interviewees to change perspective and describe the incident from a different angle. The interviewers will try to revisit specific aspects of the account to draw out more detail. Finally, they summarize the account to ensure that nothing was left out. Compared to more forceful and aggressive styles, this approach has elicited good results, without as much challenge by attorneys (Fisher & Geiselman, 1992).

Figure 19. Interview room

Source: Katherine Ramsland

Most officers have been trained in the Reid Technique, which is a series of calculated manipulations (Buckley, 2004) to extract a confession. Relying on what the investigation has turned up from a scene, investigators begin with an interview to elicit more information and observe behavior. There are nine distinct stages for the interrogation, which is aggressive but not necessarily effective for getting the truth. Interrogators confront suspects with an assertion of guilt and keep up a monologue as they develop a theme that offers the suspect a face-saving, forgivable excuse. They are trained to thwart any denials of guilt and to prevent the person from withdrawing into silence. They can lie and even intimidate, but they cannot threaten injury, promise leniency, or be physically brutal.

The Reid Technique should be used with caution. David A. Harris is Distinguished Faculty Scholar and Professor of Law at the University of Pittsburgh. He researches and teaches about police behavior, law enforcement, and national security. In *Failed Evidence: Why Law Enforcement Resists Science*, Harris (2014) examines issues involving numerous areas of law enforcement, hoping to encourage more education in science. He states that the Reid Technique was not based in science, yet trainees are given a sense of certainty that they can tell truth from lies, and that once they determine the truth, they can get a confession. Problems arise from the presumption of guilt, as described in Chapter 2. Bias and certainty about a suspect can elicit false confessions (Kassin & Fong, 1999). They occur most often when a suspect is exhausted, naïve, frightened, or mentally impaired. The characteristics of those most likely to give a false confession include youth, low IQ, mental instability, a high degree of suggestibility, a trusting nature, low self-esteem, or high anxiety.

To try to avoid the influence of bias and manipulation, some investigators use a more respectful approach, such as the PEACE model (Planning and Preparation, Engage and Explain, Account, Closure, Evaluation). Officers focus on gathering information. The first stage defines the objectives, which requires knowing the evidence. Then a relationship is developed as the subject is invited to describe events of interest. The goal is to encourage the subject to review the event mentally, as with a cognitive interview. Closure helps both parties get on the same page, and finally the interviewer evaluates the material. As mentioned above, a comfortable, non-threatening setting works best.

At any stage of questioning, if suspects invoke their right to silence or request an attorney, the interrogation must stop. Any information gained thereafter might be deemed inadmissible.

Another item to keep in mind is this: Getting an admission is not sufficient, because it can be recanted, or the suspect can say it was forced or false. It is important to also acquire corroborating details about location, methods, and motives, and then appropriately collect and preserve this evidence. Never rely on just a confession.

With interviewing or interrogating, a key issue is to watch for deception, which can take many forms. It can be difficult to spot. Even professionals with repeated exposure to deception often perform no better than chance, although often they believe they are quite good at it. Thus, their sense of confidence can undermine the interview.

Lie Detection

According to extensive research, lying requires more effort than truth-telling, so it produces such physiological signals as twitches, scratching, venting, a heightened pulse rate, dilated pupils, and certain facial expressions. However, truthful but anxious people might also display such symptoms, and some liars might not. There is no Pinocchio's nose in lie detection work. No single behavior gives someone's lies away.

Polygraph   A machine used to determine through changes in physiological functions whether a person is lying.

For physiological measurements, the **polygraph** is a compact portable device that measures key involuntary physiological responses to questioning – skin conductivity, abdominal and chest respiration, blood pressure, and heart rate – while interviewing a subject. Some of the questions are designed to establish baseline responses, some are neutral, and others attempt to register "guilty knowledge." Although practitioners vouch for its accuracy, and investigators rely on it to intimidate suspects into providing information, research indicates that the polygraph does not offer the degree of certainty required for the courtroom (Krapohl & Shaw, 2015).

The American Polygraph Association states that studies prove that the polygraph's degree of validity is high, but accuracy depends on having a properly trained examiner using a good instrument, an accepted testing procedure and a standard scoring system. The scientific community registered sufficient doubt that the National Research Council conducted an independent evaluation. These scientists still found the device lacking in validity (Adelson, 2004). In most U.S. jurisdictions, polygraph evidence is *per se inadmissible*, but can be admitted in a few if the prosecution and defense stipulate this before a defendant takes the test. In *State v. Solis* (2012) in New Mexico, the court affirmed that the defense remains free to refuse a polygraph, and the prosecution is not allowed to comment on the meaning of such a refusal.

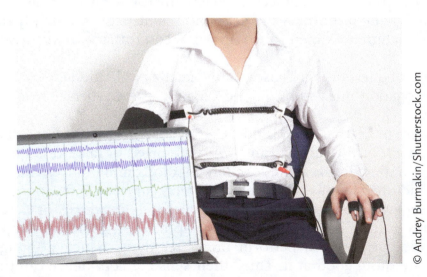

© Andrey Burmakin/Shutterstock.com

Figure 20. Polygraph

The process works like this: when a question is asked, this is marked on the paper, just before the response gets recorded. It goes on like this until all questions are asked. The resulting data are interpreted through a numerical scoring system, according to deviations from a baseline that occur when the subject shows a physiological response to a question. The examiner interprets the data according to the magnitude of the deviation and can include his or her observations of the subject during the process. Examiners decide if the subject was truthful or deceptive, or that the results are inconclusive and require another test.

The first stage of this process involves gathering data on the subject's medical background, physical condition, and psychological history. Before the test can proceed, subjects must be deemed competent to take it. Then comes a pretest, to get the subject used to the device. It is designed to make the subject nervous about being deceptive. The Control Question Test (CQT) is the most widely used format. "Relevant" questions are related to the crime, while "control" questions are based on common misdeeds such as lying, which is expected to elicit an emotional reaction. The assumption is that subjects, embarrassed about their secrets, will deny small misdeeds; it is likely that they are lying. Control responses provide a baseline "deception response." Control questions generally arouse innocent subjects, while the crime-relevant questions affect guilty subjects. That is, greater physiological arousal to questions relevant to the incident than to control questions suggests deception. Non-deception is the opposite equation. If there is no general pattern of comparative responses, the diagnosis is inconclusive.

The best research on deception detection centers on the importance of knowing the subjects' default behavior – how they answer neutral and uncomfortable questions. Then, when they deviate, especially with clusters of behaviors, investigators can hone in on the items that provoke discomfort (Vrij, 2008). With this approach, investigators can use any of a number of interrogation models. To learn default behaviors requires patience: the key is to question subjects long enough to observe baseline behaviors, so as to recognize heightened stress to specific themes and see what people do to calm it. Anxious people often freeze, seek exits, or prepare to defend themselves, and the resulting behaviors can signal potential deception. They include:

- More negative than positive statements
- Increased vocal pitch
- Overly deliberative responses
- Increased shrugs, foot movements, and nervous habits
- Venting (pulling a collar away) or protecting the throat
- Pointing feet toward an exit
- Using obstacles, hands, arms, and legs as shields
- Blanching, flushing, breath-holding

As mentioned, none is definitive, but these "red flag" behaviors occur more often in those with reason to deceive.

Statement analysis is a common investigative tool, which uses open-ended questions such as, "Tell me what happened that night." This allows the subject to pick the place to start and end the narrative. Investigators watch for the way details are offered, changes in tone or in speaking pace, types of language used, and points of reaction. They note whether subjects provide more information than necessary, avoid details in certain places, or lie for no apparent reason – especially about insignificant items, such as their birthdate.

An intriguing method is to impose a cognitive load, such as asking the suspect to tell the story backwards. This can disrupt the process of lying, because it requires more concentration, especially for rehearsed narratives. Research shows that these methods can increase the detection of lies from 42% to 60% (Vrij, 2008).

The Strategic Use of Evidence (SUE) approach assumes that guilty suspects will avoid and deflect. Interrogators present open-ended questions that elicit information, followed by questions that suggest there is evidence that looks bad for the subject. Typically, truthful people will spontaneously offer more information, while guilty subjects will try to avoid it. In research, interviewers untrained in SUE were correct in their assessment of a liar slightly more than 50%, while SUE-trained interviewers obtained accuracy rates of up to 85% (Vrij, Granhag, Mann & Leal, 2011).

No matter which method is used, all require the ability to make nuanced observations. We discussed this in Chapter 2, and now we apply it.

Observing Bodies

Kinesics is the scientific interpretation of body language (Birdwell, 1970). Spoken words convey information verbally and bodies convey it through facial expression, voice tone, gestures, posture, inflections, and vocal noises. To be successful at kinesics, observers must learn about human-centered information. This requires practice and acquiring a range of contexts and experiences.

Psychologist Paul Ekman (1992) focuses on facial kinesics. A professor of psychology in the University of California at San Francisco's Department of Psychiatry for thirty-two years, Ekman is considered the world's foremost expert on facial expressions, particularly the subcategory of micro-expressions. He offers online training to improve the ability to read subtle expressions and enhance emotional attunement.

During the 1960s, Ekman surmised that if the face was part of a physiological system, it could be studied like any other system. He aspired to catalogue every possible facial expression, so that he could become an expert face reader. The expansion and contractions of the muscle movements involved in expressions that he observed became the basis for his Facial Action Coding System (FACS).

Ekman says there are seven universal emotions: disgust, anger, sadness, joy, fear, contempt, and surprise. These can show overtly or covertly. Most difficult to spot are fleeting expressions, referred to as micro-expressions. They appear and disappear in a fraction of a second. Micro-expressions are thought to "leak" information about a person's true emotional state, and practiced experts can identify them. For recognizing emotional signals, Ekman developed the Facial Recognizing Suite, including the METT, or Micro Expression Training Tool. Ekman claims an accuracy rate for detecting deceptive expressions of 90% when combining his brand of kinesics with measurements for voice stress and speech factors.

Critical kinesic principles for investigators, then, include establishing a subject's behavioral "constants," or defaults. Then, they can watch for behavioral deviations. Those that appear in clusters, especially during key stress points, are more likely to signal deception. Behaviors of discomfort can include speech hesitations and pauses, a lack of spontaneity, taking longer to respond, and irrelevant responses. Alternatively, if they've planned well, they might actually jump in more quickly than a truth-teller (Dimitrius & Mazarella, 1998; Navarro, 2008).

To become an expert, a person must be highly motivated. The following is a "to do" list of skill-building for people who wish to develop greater "reading readiness."

1. Spend time with people, especially in a variety of contexts.
2. Listen patiently and be vigilant.
3. Reveal something of yourself as bait.
4. Know your goal.
5. Train yourself to be objective.

A few psychological tests identify specific types of deception. For example, the Minnesota Multiphasic Personality Inventory (MMPI-2) and the Structured Interview of Reported Symptoms (SIRS) detect **malingering**, or faking a mental illness.

Which brings us to a key issue for investigators working their way toward court: the issue of a suspect's mental **competency**.

Malingering
Deliberate simulation of a mental illness to obtain personal gain.

Competency
Sufficient ability to participate in proceedings, such as to stand trial, to waive rights, to testify, and to be executed. One must understand the legal proceedings involved and have the ability to consult with an attorney.

Competency Issues

There are many areas in which competency to perform a task is relevant to completing a case. In the criminal arena, one must be able to waive one's rights, agree to a search, confess, stand trial, testify on one's own behalf, plead guilty, defend oneself, refuse a specific defense, be criminally responsible, and even serve a sentence. The civil arena has several more. Those situations that require formal evaluation most often involve standing trial, testifying, and waiving rights. At any time that defendants seem unable to view the situation realistically or to ably participate, they might be tested for competence. Those judged incompetent are treated until competency is restored.

Defendants who wish to defend themselves, for example, will be asked questions to determine their level of education, ability to understand and speak English, and grasp of how trials work. They might be psychotic and still be judged competent, as the standards are quite low. One psychiatrist deemed serial killer Ted Bundy incompetent because he was so narcissistic it seemed he could not act in his own best interest. (The court ignored this finding, since by the lowest standards, Bundy intelligently and voluntarily waived his right to representation.)

Investigators can be faced with competency issues from the moment they arrest someone, so they should be conversant with the standards of their jurisdiction. This is truly where it pays to have a good relationship with the prosecutor.

Finally, investigators must know the role of the judge.

The Judge

Former Michigan Circuit Court Judge Donald E. Shelton, Ph.D. (2011) has studied the impact of the NAS report on the investigative and trial process, and has written about the role of witnesses and experts on the deliberation process. After twenty-five years on the bench, he is now Director of the Criminal Justice Program at the University of Michigan–Dearborn. He is also a member of AAFS. Shelton views jury expectations as culturally based phenomena and calls for the justice system to adapt. Jurors want experts and investigators to present facts and procedures consistent with what they know from real-world experience, which includes what they watch on television and technology they have heard about.

It is regrettable, Shelton thinks, that courts have become routine in their acceptance of the experts that attorneys proffer, because this has led to lax standards, poorly supported

© Andrey_Popov/Shutterstock.com

Figure 21. Judge

cases, and false convictions. "As more courts admitted testimony from any particular forensic science field," he writes, "other courts used those admissibility decisions to bolster the idea that the field became more 'generally accepted'" (2011, p. 9). Since jurors acknowledge the court's authority, they will often listen to testimony with the patina of science that has never been proven. The DNA exonerations that began in the 1990s have now revealed the errors of this process, at the high cost of ruining lives and tarnishing justice.

The legal community, Shelton states, has been "muted" in its response (p. 133). Some judges accept the authority of the NAS report, while others ignore it. Nevertheless, doubt has emerged about the claims of certain disciplines, as described in Chapter 4.

On the other hand, some jurors have developed impossible expectations. They want all methods and results to live up to what they hear about DNA analysis. Shelton notes that pressure on prosecutors to produce convincing results or to exclude jurors who unreasonably demand it influences how investigators will handle a case. It might make them more accountable, which is a positive development, but it can also lead to unnecessary procedures and tests, which makes for an overburdened justice system.

"With the emphasis on forensic science demands by jurors," says Judge Shelton, "prosecutors now place much more pressure on forensic science experts to bolster the government's case. Often the lawyers will try to get the expert to go beyond what the facts, the science, or the expertise of the witness will allow. First, experts must recognize their own implicit biases based on who pays their salary. Their role in our judicial system is to testify about their scientific observations and opinions and not to attempt, consciously or unconsciously, to bolster the government's efforts to convict the defendant. They must restrict the information they get, or at least the information they consider, to their scientifically observable evidence and not upon factual assertions or opinions by the police" (personal interview, 2016).

He offers some basic principles:

"Act with honesty, integrity, objectivity and *impartiality*, and declare at the earliest opportunity any personal, business and/or financial interest that could be perceived as a conflict of interest. Provide expert advice and evidence only within the limits of your professional competence, and be extremely careful about answering hypothetical questions, which can be vehicles to get witnesses to testify beyond their knowledge or competence."

As more media scrutinize the state of forensic science in light of exonerations, potential jurors will become more educated. The more educated they are, the more pressure will trickle down to investigators. No one likes to be second-guessed, but given how many cases have been bungled, scrutiny of the investigative process is likely to continue.

Summary

For any case that will potentially develop into a legal proceeding, investigators must know how to work within legal parameters. They should become informed so that they can work effectively with a prosecution team. Justice involves teamwork, with all members observing professional standards and best practices.

The exercises below make clear why standards are important. In the next chapter, we move on to a different type of investigator, those who deal with bodies, blood, and human remains.

Exercise #5.1

Professional opinions differed on the deaths of John P. and Joyce Sheridan, who were found stabbed to death on September 28, 2014, in their home, which had been set on fire. The Somerset County prosecutor, Geoffrey Soriano, looked at the medical examiner's report, which noted the hesitation marks near the fatal stab wound to John's throat, and decided that John had murdered Joyce and killed himself. An armoire had fallen, which accounted for John's broken ribs and chipped tooth, and John's DNA was on the handle of a gas can found in the bedroom. John had been CEO of Cooper Health System, a stressful job. It seemed to add up.

The couple's sons refused to accept this finding, for which no analysis for suicide had been done, so they hired forensic pathologist Michael Baden, former chief medical examiner in New York City. He determined that the evidence supported a double homicide. He believes that an individual wearing gloves entered the home, possibly to commit a burglary. Among the items of evidence he cited were a DNA sample on the bloody knife that did not match anyone in the Sheridan family, the wounds on John matched no knife in the house, the deep wound on John's neck was more consistent with an attacker than self-infliction, John's five broken ribs and chipped tooth were consistent with an attack, a fire poker was in the room although the room has no fireplace, none of Joyce's blood was on John's clothing, and a psychological investigation showed no suicidal red flags for John. There was also no bruising consistent with being hit by a falling armoire. John owned and had used the gas can in other circumstances, so his DNA would be on the can for innocent reasons. Baden did not rule out a murder/suicide, but said that the evidence does not definitively support it. This would signal the need for further investigation, due to the possibility that the killer is still at large.

1. Although the prosecutor based his decision on the evidence, where might he have failed to perform to professional standards?
2. Baden offers an alternative interpretation, but how might bias be part of his evaluation?

Exercise #5.2

On February 11, 1987, in Fort Collins, Colorado, Detective Jim Broderick led the investigation of the death of Peggy Hettrick, whose body was dumped in a field. She was last seen leaving a bar the evening before. She had been stabbed once in the back and vaginally mutilated. Two different knives seemed to have been used.

Clyde Masters and his 15-year-old son, Tim, lived in a nearby trailer. When Broderick interviewed Tim, he admitted he saw the body, but he thought it was a store mannequin, posed as a prank. Several knives were found in his bedroom, but none could be linked to the murder. Still, Broderick believed Tim was the killer. He looked at notebooks full of Tim's writing and artwork, and saw that some sketches depicted acts of violence. Tim also failed a polygraph. However, no physical evidence tied him to the murder. Broderick did not follow through on other potential suspects. He focused on Tim.

Nine years later, he reviewed the file with a psychiatrist who said that he could determine if the drawings were rehearsal fantasies for violence. Broderick selected some and the psychiatrist affirmed that they supported Tim's guilt. Tim was arrested and tried. The psychiatric evidence was a central factor. No one seemed to consider that a 15-year-old boy would be incapable of the surgical precision found in the mutilation or of carrying a grown woman's body by himself. Yet, Masters was found guilty of first-degree murder. In 2008, DNA exonerated him.

1. What is troubling about this case?
2. What questions about the investigation should have occurred to the fact finders, the defense attorney and the jury?
3. What questions about the expert witness should have occurred to the prosecutor and judge?

References

Adelson, R. (2004). The polygraph in doubt. *APA Monitor, 35*(7), 71.

Birdwhistle, R. (1970). *Kinesics and context.* Philadelphia, PA: University of Pennsylvania Press.

Buckley, J., Inbau, F. E., Jayne, B. C., & Reid, J. E. (2004). *Essentials of the Reid Technique.* Burlington, MA: Jones & Bartlett.

Dimitrius, J. & Mazzarella, M. (1998). *Reading people.* New York, NY: Ballantine.

Ekman, P. (1992) *Telling lies: Clues to deceit in the marketplace, politics, and marriage.* (2nd ed.) New York: W.W. Norton.

Ekman, P. (2007). *Emotions revealed: Recognizing faces and feelings to improve emotional life and communication,* 2nd ed. New York, NY: Holt.

Fisher, R. P., & Geiselman, R. E. (1992). *Memory-enhancing techniques for investigative interviewing: The cognitive interview.* Springfield, IL: Charles C. Thomas.

Harris. D. A. (2012). *Failed evidence: Why law enforcement resists science.* New York, NY: NYU Press.

Kassin, S. & Fong, C. (1999). 'I'm innocent!': Effects of training on judgments of truth and deception in the interrogation room. *Law and Human Behavior, 23* (5), 499–516.

Krapohl, D. J., & Shaw, P. K. (2015). *Fundamentals of polygraph practice.* Oxford, UK: Elsevier.

Loftus, E. F. (1979). The malleability of human memory. *American Scientist, 67,* 312–320.

Loftus, E. F., & Hoffman, H. G. (1989). Misinformation and memory: The creation of new memories. *Journal of Experimental Psychology: General, 118,* 100–104.

Masters, T. & Lehto, S. (2012). *Drawn to injustice: The wrongful conviction of Timothy Masters*. New York, NY: Berkley Books.

Meissner, C. A., et al. (2013) *Interview and interrogation methods and their effects on true and false confessions*. Campbell Systematic Reviews. www.campbellcollaboration.org/lib/download/2249/.

Navarro, J. (2008). *What every BODY is saying*. New York, NY: Collins Living.

Radostitz, R. (2003, October 17). Why is Doil Lane still on death row? *Austin Chronicle*. http://www.austinchronicle.com/news/2003-10-17/182180/

Shelton, D. E. (2011) *Forensic science in court: Challenges in the twenty-first century*. Landham, MD: Rowman & Littlefield.

State v. Lane, 262 Kan. 373 (1997).

State v. Solis, 2012 WL 4434153 (N.M. App. 2012)

Toliver, R. F. (1997). *The interrogator: The story of Hanns Scharff, Luftwaffe's master interrogator*. Atglen, PA: Schiffer Publishing.

Vrij, A. (2008). *Detecting lies and deceit: pitfalls and opportunities*, 2nd ed. Chichester, England: John Wiley & Sons.

Vrij, A., Granhag, A. P., Mann, S., & Leal, S. (2011). Outsmarting the liars: Toward a cognitive lie detection approach. *Current Directions in Psychological Science, 20*(1): 28–32.

Walters, S. B. (2003). *Principles of kinesic interview and interrogation*, 2nd Ed. Boca Raton, FL: CRC Press.

Chapter 6
The Body

Learning Objectives

- Understand the role of coroners and medical examiners in death investigations.
- Recognize when to use experts for specific tasks.
- Learn the stages of an autopsy and wound analysis.
- Describe the stages of death.
- List the types of research in key areas of death investigation.

Key Words

Algor mortis, anthropology, asphyxiation, autopsy, coroner, entomology, exhumation, medical examiner, PMI, rigor mortis, ScanStation, serology, time of death, time since death, taphonomy, toxicology

A homicide in 2010 in Kansas City, Kansas, presented an opportunity to try out a new piece of equipment, the touchscreen Leica ScanStation C10 3D Laser Scanner, which combines a digital camera with a 3D laser scanner and digital storage. The Johnson County Criminalistics Lab had one on loan for its crime scene investigation unit. They wanted to test the system against their usual protocols for evidence collection and analysis. The American Society of Crime Laboratory Directors (ASCLD) had accredited their lab and they were aware of the NAS report stipulations, so they went through the process of obtaining permission from their quality assurance manager. The results of the system have been accepted in many U.S. courts for criminal and civil proceedings. The device has been tested, validated, and peer-reviewed.

The incident involved a man in the front seat of a car who had been fatally shot. The team mounted the scanner on its tripod and conducted three exterior scans. They also took digital photographs. After the body was removed, the team placed the scanner on an accessory mount on the car's center console, which provided a 360-degree scan of the interior. Another scan was performed from the rear seat, for a total of five scans. It had taken just ninety minutes versus ten hours with their typical procedures.

They sent the scanner to the company for processing. The five scans were stitched together into a "point cloud." The team received back a 3D fly-through animation of the scene, along with viewing software that enabled them to navigate it and take measurements. Since this was all digitally stored, they could return repeatedly to the virtual scene, if necessary, for additional measurements or viewpoints. They could also share the data with others who have the same software plug-in. Should the case go to trial, the scan results would give a jury a vivid sense of the crime scene. This is the high-tech world of today's death investigator.

Death Investigators

Coroner/medical examiner Official in charge of death investigation, with title dependent on the jurisdiction.

In the United States, **coroners** or **medical examiners** (and occasionally freelance investigators) perform all death investigations (Zugibe & Carroll, 2005). No matter which system is used, the medicolegal officer is responsible for determining the circumstances under which someone died: the cause and manner of death, and if possible, the time of death. "The main objective is to give the police a first estimation of the time since death already at the place where the body was found" (Madea, 2016, p. 1). Examining both ante-mortem and postmortem changes, these findings should be as precise as possible, and as reliable. Medical examiners can also perform autopsies to determine the mechanism of death, whereas coroners will rely on the findings of forensic pathologists. They all develop investigative skills, similar to detectives, including observation, awareness of the stages of death in diverse circumstances, and awareness of standards and research in their field (Madea, 2016; Randall, 1997).

The earliest anatomists who dissected corpses noticed rigor mortis, or muscle rigidity; algor mortis, the body's cooling temperature; and how the blood has settled, lividity (Madea, 2016; Sachs, 2001). Today's officers might add metabolic and membrane permeability factors, as well as more advanced techniques from bacteriological studies (Greenwood, 2016; Madea, 2016; Rosier et al., 2015). Generally speaking, decomposition affects the face and neck before moving downward through the body.

Death investigation involves reconstructing an incident, with the manner of death categorized according to the NASH system: natural, accident, suicide or homicide, or undetermined. Any deaths not clearly the result of natural causes are generally investigated – and sometimes even natural deaths are investigated. The laws and the financial means of the jurisdiction in which the death occurred govern the procedures, as does the investigation's duration.

Figure 22. Double homicide training

Source: Katherine Ramsland

At the scene, medicolegal officers make preliminary notes and direct photographers to take specific photographs (Baden & Roach, 2001). They might also take the body temperature, noting obvious trauma and the presence and patterns of blood at the scene. If insects are present or the remains are skeletal, officers might consult a forensic entomologist or anthropologist (see descriptions below). Blood spatter patterns might also enter into the calculations, as well as biological evidence for DNA analysis. Death investigators determine how the remains will be handled.

Zachary Lysek has been the Northampton County Coroner in Pennsylvania since 1992. He has also been a police officer, pathology assistant, and medical investigator. In his busy office, one might catch him on a cellphone talking to an attorney while also directing a deputy coroner to look up a list of recent suicides.

"The coroner or medical examiner," said Lysek, "is charged with determining the cause and manner of death of individuals who die within their designated jurisdiction. Not all cases require full on-scene investigations, such as those who succumb under hospital or hospice care, but any unattended or suspicious death necessitates a representative from the Coroner's Office to respond to the scene. Although the coroner's main responsibility is the body of the deceased, it cannot be the only focus. The scene surrounding the actual body is also highly relevant to the process of accurately determining the cause and manner of death. Therefore, the investigation begins upon the initial notification of the death call and progresses through to the arrival on the scene, to surveying the scene, interviewing first responders and witnesses present, examining the body in place, removal of the body, ordering an autopsy if deemed appropriate, following-up with police and medical personnel as needed, and concluding with a determination of cause and manner of death. It's a multiple level process. You don't walk in and form a conclusion based on first impressions" (personal interview, 2016).

Lysek has been trained on the Leica ScanStation C10, described above, which he finds useful for accident scenes as well as homicides. "It gives us a way to visually reconstruct the scene that we didn't have before," he says. He also has a list of experts to use when necessary. An odontologist assisted with the following case.

On June 15, 2000, two female friends of Devon Guzman discovered her body in a car parked at Delaware State Canal Park, near Easton, Pennsylvania (Ramsland & Lysek, 2008). Her throat was slashed and her clothing bore strands of animal fur. The friends told police she had committed suicide. Because there was little blood in the car, Lysek determined that Devon had been killed elsewhere and placed there. In addition, the cut on her throat was too deep to have been self-inflicted. This launched a homicide investigation.

Detectives linked nineteen-year-old Devon to a married couple, Michelle Hetzel, 20, and Brandon Bloss, 26. Hetzel was one of the friends who had found her. Devon's roommate was the other. The three women had been high school friends. An investigative hypothesis formed around a love triangle gone sour. On the day before the body was found, Devon had told her roommate she was going to see Bloss and Hetzel. Hetzel called the roommate to report that Devon had not arrived.

Although Hetzel had married Bloss, she had gone to St. Croix with Devon to get married as a lesbian couple. A simple analysis suggested that Bloss discovered the affair and killed Devon, but the scenario proved to be more complicated.

It started with the physical evidence. The couple had a cat and dog with fur consistent with strands lifted from Devon, suggesting that Devon had been at their home. A bite mark on Bloss' arm was consistent with Devon's teeth. In addition, Bloss' clothing had spots of Devon's blood. This clothing was bundled with two pair of gloves in Hetzel's car trunk, so Bloss and Hetzel were arrested. They went to trial together.

It seems that Devon had sought to break up with Hetzel, which upset her. Witnesses had heard them arguing the day before Devon's body was found. Hetzel testified that Bloss had confessed to her that he had killed Devon. Bloss' attorney accused Hetzel, acknowledging only that Bloss took Devon's body to the park to stage a suicide. An acquaintance of the couple's said that Hetzel had asked *him* to kill Devon. However, Hetzel's mother reported hearing Bloss threaten to kill Devon. With two competing sides to the story, the physical evidence helped the jury to find both guilty of first-degree murder. Hetzel and Bloss received life sentences.

Lysek's advice to investigators begins with the importance of observing everything before forming a theory. "To remind myself," he said. "I put my hands in my pockets and look around. I touch nothing, move nothing, until I've examined a scene from several angles. I try to think carefully about cases, so we don't jump to quick conclusions or just accept what might seem obvious. Thinking about them during the early stages cuts down on backtracking and reworking them."

Detectives might make important decisions about cases, but in a death investigation, they must respect the coroner's authority. It benefits no one to undermine team coordination.

"To accomplish this and avoid tunnel vision, the members of the Coroner's Office must maintain objectivity from the time of the initial call-out. Often when the call comes in to our office, first responders have prematurely hypothesized a cause and manner of death. For example, if drugs are found in the vicinity of a body, the initial call will often describe a drug overdose. The responding Coroner's Office representative must resist the urge to accept this theory and must approach the scene with an open mind and form their judgment only after a thorough investigation.

"This begins with a response to the scene in a timely manner. Upon arrival, the scene should be carefully observed and noted, both for safety and investigative information. Being cognizant of such things as who is present – both officially and witnesses, and whether the type of area is residential or commercial, inside or outside, or affluent or depressed. We look at weather conditions to paint a clearer picture of the scene. The investigation starts away from the body and moves inward, avoiding damage to any evidence and at the same time looking for anything of evidentiary value. The body itself will hold evidence, both externally and internally, that must be preserved in an appropriate manner.

© Zachary Lysek

Figure 23. Human remains

"The Coroner's Office works with police investigators to secure evidence and document the scene. The more documented a scene is during the initial investigation, the easier it is to reexamine later if questions arise. The Northampton County Coroner's Office has in place a policy to document every scene that we respond to with full body photographs. Digital photography is inexpensive, so the more the better. We can't redo it later.

"Not all death investigations warrant all these steps, but if any question exists surrounding the death, it is better to err on [the side of] doing too much than [of doing] too little. Based on all evidence garnered from the scene, the body, police, medical personnel, autopsy results, interviews, and any other sources deemed necessary, a determination of cause and manner of death is made. Ensuring quality control means investigators must stay current with the ever-evolving technology, such as the Leica ScanStation C10. In addition, Pennsylvania Statute requires continuing education hours for all Coroner's Office investigators.

"Finally, one of the most important aspects in death investigations is to remember the core issue: a life has been lost, and all members of the Coroner's Office, as well as all other responders to the scene, must maintain a sense of professionalism and show respect to the deceased."

The Autopsy

An autopsy is a postmortem medical examination. The body first gets photographed and x-rayed, measured, weighed, externally examined, and fingerprinted. Identifying marks, such as piercings, scars, and tattoos, are noted. Trace evidence – strands of hair, glass fragments, foreign fibers – is collected from the clothing and body. Assistants, called dieners, place the body (if sufficiently intact) on a steel table, face-up, with a block to stabilize the head. To expose the internal organs, the pathologist makes a "Y" incision, cutting from shoulder to shoulder down toward the sternum, then straight down the abdomen to the pelvis. They might have to avoid wounds. Organs are removed, weighed, and described, and blood, urine, and stomach contents are sampled for toxicology screening. The skull is examined for external wounds or bruising before being opened to look at the brain. It is removed, weighed, and described (Zugibe & Carroll, 2005).

Figure 24. Autopsy

Source: Katherine Ramsland

"The forensic pathologist determines the legal cause of death based on a combination of factors," says Dr. Cyril Wecht. These factors include the autopsy findings, the circumstances of the death, and the victim's clinical history. "The forensic pathologist, frequently exposed to the pathology of trauma, recognizes the importance of a careful external examination" (personal interview, 2015).

Dr. Wecht, from Pittsburgh, Pennsylvania, offers the experienced eye of a longtime forensic pathologist. He performs more than 450 autopsies a year, to add to more than 40,000 autopsies from his long career. He received his medical degree from the University of Pittsburgh and his law degree from the University of Maryland. He has been certified by the American Board of Pathology in anatomic, clinical, and forensic pathology and is a Fellow of the College of American Pathologists and the American Society of Clinical Pathologists. He is also certified by the Board of Disaster Medicine and the American Board of Legal Medicine. Having served as president for both the American College of Legal Medicine and the American Academy of Forensic Science, Wecht compares the field of forensic science to a "rainbow of color and light, with new hues constantly being discovered on a regular basis." He is aware that "even fingerprint analysis is not an absolute science. A lot of things have shifted away from past claims of certainty, and mistakes have been identified. Absolute certainty is about ego." If juries better understood how forensic science and medicine work, he believes, they might be more vigilant about the interpretive nuances. To get it right takes patience, experience, and hard work. "One of the beauties of my field," Wecht says, "is that I can take my time. The body isn't going anywhere. There's no rush, and there shouldn't be one."

Wecht has published several books about his cases, some of which address popular mysteries, such as those associated with Elvis Presley, O. J. Simpson, Robert F. Kennedy, and JonBenet Ramsey. Wecht is probably most renowned for his work on the subcommittee that evaluated the assassination of President John F. Kennedy. "The assassination of President John F. Kennedy," he states, "is the best example of the kinds of problems that can develop in a homicide case where inadequate expertise is utilized." He has pointed out that the U. S. Navy pathologists who performed the post-assassination autopsy had no forensic experience. Their postmortem protocol was improper and inadequate. Thus, poor information was recorded, which contributes to questions still raised today.

"The forensic scientist, and especially the forensic pathologist," says Wecht, "is often the most important expert witness." All other members of the investigative and prosecuting team must understand the pathologist's function. In turn, pathologists must understand how to preserve and protect evidence for possible trial and must be able to speak clearly to juries.

Due to his extensive experience, Wecht is often invited into cases with unique elements, such as the death of motivational speaker Jeffrey B. Locker. The fifty-two-year-old father of three had fallen into debt and was running from creditors. He had applied for several life insurance policies, with collective payouts for his dependents of $18 million. A few weeks later in July 2009, Locker was stabbed to death in his SUV, in East Harlem. Kenneth Minor was arrested and charged with second-degree murder. Minor admitted to the act, but claimed that Locker had hired him for an assisted suicide. Locker, he said, had wanted to die. He had formed a convoluted plan to ensure that his family would get the insurance payouts. Since suicide nullified the payout, Locker had gone to East Harlem to hire someone to carry it out. Kenneth Minor came along. At first, he resisted the seemingly absurd idea, but the money was tempting and he finally agreed. Wecht testified in Minor's defense, stating that Locker's wounds were consistent with Minor's narrative. Although Minor was convicted, his twenty-year sentence was reduced in 2014 to twelve (Wecht & Kaufman, 2014).

Many homicides involve wound analysis. During an autopsy, wounds are recorded for number and type. A blunt force injury, for example, results from impact with a blunt object. The autopsy might show the direction of impact, the type of object that caused it, and how often the contact was made. If a suspect weapon is available, wound patterns can be compared to it. In one case, a cinder block from the suspect's garage matched wounds on the victim's head; in another, it was the rounded thin handle of a fireplace poker.

Lacerations have ragged or abraded edges, often with bruising. Abrasions are friction injuries, shown by the removal of top layers of skin. Contusions are ruptures of small blood vessels. Each type is noted and described for the autopsy report.

Gunshot wounds might show burns from gas or powder residue. The size of the exit and entry wounds are important, and must be carefully measured and described, as well as any internal bullet trajectory and the absence of an exit wound. If bullets or parts of bullets remain in the wound, they help to determine the type of weapon used. Entrance wounds are generally round and surrounded by some type of abrasion. Exit wounds are irregular, free of stippling, and typically larger than the entrance wound. Yet, there are cases where these wounds look similar, requiring greater care with observation. Some cases have been harmed by a pathologist's hasty examination and erroneous description.

© Corepics VOF/Shutterstock.com

Figure 25. Wound

For knife or "incised" wounds, the pathologist or ME makes a distinction between cut and stab or puncture wounds. Then they try to identify the type of piercing implement. A cut is longer than it is deep, while a stab is the opposite. Some wounds are defensive, such as cuts made on a victim's palms or fingers. Cuts associated with suicidal gestures are called "hesitation wounds," but superficial cuts, such as are seen with a cutting disorder, might be mislabeled.

Asphyxiation results the lack of oxygen to the brain, which is also seen in accidentally fatal autoerotic hypoxia. Hanging, obstruction of airways, smothering, or strangulation can cause asphyxia. Carbon monoxide poisoning can do similar damage (Zugibe & Carroll, 2005).

Although this information is for specialists, not investigators, some autopsies are now done virtually (i.e., via a 3-D image that does away with cutting open the body). A combination of CT scans and magnetic resonance imagining (MRI) can detect many ailments in the tissues, although interpretation requires a radiologist trained in forensic procedure (Greenwood, 2016).

The Science of Decay

At the scene, the homicide detective and medical examiner/coroner make an informed guess at the approximate time when the individual expired. This is known as a "time since death" evaluation, or the postmortem interval (PMI). Time since death is a measure of how much time has passed between when decedents died and when they were found (Bass & Jefferson, 2003; Benedict, 2003). This should not be confused with time *of* death. If someone has been in a room for three days before being discovered, the time *of* death might be 9 AM on the first day, but the time *since* death, or PMI, would be three days (or some number of hours). Both determinations are important for incident reconstruction, and both can be difficult to state with certainty, especially the longer the individual has been deceased or undiscovered. The rate at which stages of death occur that can provide markers depends on several different environmental factors, such as air and ground temperatures, where the body was left (on the ground, under dirt, under leaves, in water), insect activity, and geographical location.

The environment's impact involves the science of taphonomy. This discipline examines factors involved in the postmortem account of physical remains and the ways in which death-related processes have affected them. Buried corpses undergo a series of changes, which affect the types of creatures attracted to them, how the environment impacts them, and what alterations might occur under and around them (Dirkmaat & Adovasio, 1997; Ubelaker, 1997).

Different climates have different effects on decomposition rates. Obtaining useful taphonomic

Figure 26. Exhumation

Source: Katherine Ramsland

measures requires a team of professionals from different disciplines: anthropology, archaeology, botany, geology, climatology, and biology. If there is to be an exhumation, many items must be in place, such as the right type of equipment, the right experts, a secured scene, and the notification of relevant family members.

Individual features of decedents also contribute to taphonomic calculation (e.g., their height, age, weight, ancestry, clothing (or not), an illness, drug use, physical condition, and the properties of their bones). In addition, how and where a body is placed outside will result in diverse calculations. In a warm, moist place, a body can decompose to a skeleton within a few weeks, while in other conditions it might mummify.

As time passes, the PMI becomes more difficult to determine, but analyses have become more sophisticated. Total Body Score is a method that tries to quantify a variety of body decomposition measures, although accuracy decreases with advanced decomposition and for bodies in "mosaic decomposition" – having two different stages (Nawrocka, Fratczak, & Matuszewski, 2016).

If bodies have decomposed to skeletal condition, anthropologists are consulted. In April 1972, 16-year-old Steven Soden, an orphan, went on a camping trip with seventeen other kids to Bass River Park, in New Jersey. He went missing, along with Donald Caldwell, a friend. In 2000, a state trooper walking through the park found a piece of a boy's sneaker and four bones. They were turned over to the State Police Forensic Anthropology Lab. Through shared DNA databases, they were able to identify the bones as being from Steven Soden. His sister had heard that a cold case detective in Illinois was attempting to identify eight of the still-unclaimed victims from the 1978 John Wayne Gacy case. Soden's sister thought he might be among them, so she had submitted her DNA to the investigators in 2012. Her DNA failed to assist, but because it was in a database, it helped the New Jersey investigators close the Soden missing persons case.

Forensic anthropology is the identification and examination of human skeletal remains within the legal system. It can reveal a person's sex, approximate age, ancestry, and types of skeletal injury (Steadman, 2003). It can also help with facial reconstruction. The adult human body has 206 bones, which weigh 12 pounds for the average male and 10 for females. To calculate factors about skeletal remains, the bones are laid out on an osteometric board and measured with calipers (Ubelaker, 1997).

Sex is determined according to the size of the pelvis, if available. The male's is narrower than the female's. In addition, certain skull features are more prominent and larger for males. Another characteristic established by bones is age. The stages at which teeth develop and bones unify show advancing age; for older people, measuring calcium and other mineral deposits help establish age as well, along with successive changes in the pelvis or evidence of bone diseases such as osteoporosis and arthritis; other clues come from the developmental stages in the teeth for young people or from worn enamel. Ferllini (2012) states that the most reliable landmark is the pubic symphysis in the pelvic girdle. An intact corpse can be measured for stature, but a disarticulated or incomplete skeleton must be pieced together. Fordisc provides formulae for calculation, but the long bone of the leg or arm can also be a general guide. So can the spine or metacarpals. For body type, calculated tables from numerous human subjects provide an estimate based on bone characteristics for determining whether the person was slender, average, or heavy.

During the late 1970s, Dr. William M. Bass III created the Forensic Anthropology Center (FAC) at the University of Tennessee at Knoxville, a two-acre field dedicated to the study of decomposing human remains (Bass & Jefferson, 2003). An acclaimed expert on skeletal identification, Bass pioneered this research after he made a significant error for the PMI of a specific case. He miscalculated by more than 100 years! Bass realized that there was no scientific research for establishing important time lines. He wanted to change this.

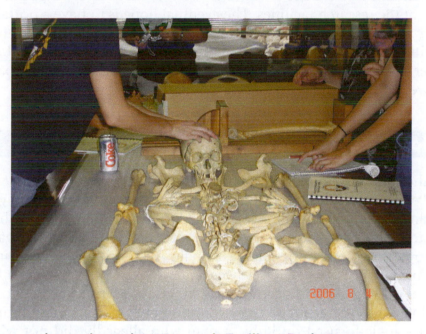

Figure 27. Class at the Anthropology Research Facility – Body Farm

Source: Katherine Ramsland

Bass acquired a plot of land from the University of Tennessee at Knoxville and laid out the unclaimed cadavers of homeless men, to expose them to weather, birds, and insects.

The ARC has become a teaching center for entomologists, investigators, cadaver odor specialists, cadaver dog handlers, anthropologists, and archaeologists. The number of corpses has substantially increased since those early days. Some are placed in the sun, some in water, some in cars, some in houses, and some underground. They might be clothed or unclothed. Researchers watch for insect and small animal activity. They also analyze soil contents throughout the stages of decomposition. (Bass & Jefferson, 2003).

Currently, six other "body farms" operate in the United States. The smallest holds about ten corpses and the largest is five acres. Some research focuses on odor, as mentioned in Chapter 4. Researchers are closing in on what it is that cadaver dogs sniff. That "smell of death" for humans derives from a combination of compounds, called esters. Elien Rosier, from the University of Leuven in Belgium, formed a team to examine these compounds. Six humans and twenty-six different animals were studied over the course of six months, including the typical pig. Organs from the human and pig remains were also removed and analyzed separately. To control for environmental impact, the team placed the remains into glass jars in a lab environment at room temperature. The metal screw caps on the jars weren't airtight, so that oxygen could enter.

During this study, Rosier's team identified 452 compounds. A combination of eight of them distinguished human and pig remains from other animal remains. Five esters helped to differentiate pigs from humans. The next step is to corroborate their findings with human remains in different conditions (buried, submerged, exposed, etc.), such as those laid out at the research facilities. The eventual hope is to have a portable electronic nose that can accurately duplicate a cadaver dog's sensitivity for odors. In addition, it could help with ways of finding lost bodies in mass disasters (Rosier, et al., 2015).

In Chapter 4, we described a case in which entomology was a key part of the evidence. Now we look more closely at a bug expert.

Entomology

In 1984, a fisherman discovered a dismembered torso in a box just after Memorial Day weekend in Perry County, Pennsylvania. The identification was made a year later. The victim was Edna Posey, a single mother who had lived an erratic life. She had come into Middletown to claim her twelve-year-old son after giving temporary legal custody for him to the boy's Boy Scout troop leader, Donald Ruby, while she went into treatment for alcoholism. Posey disappeared that weekend. Ruby said he had seen her last when he dropped her off to go shopping. An entomologist used insect activity on the body to place approximate time of death on the Friday evening when she had disappeared.

Investigative logic focused on Ruby, a man who allegedly did not wish to give up Posey's son. He was pegged as a potential pedophile, which an FBI profiler affirmed. The evidence interpretation swung toward him, especially when the boy said he had heard a loud thud on Friday night in the room where his mother was sleeping. Ruby was arrested, tried, and convicted of Posey's murder. In 1987, he was sentenced to life in prison. He claimed he was innocent.

After five years, a new trial was ordered, due to the use of unscientific profiling. DNA analysis exonerated Ruby. Semen from three different men was found in the victim's remains, none of which matched Ruby. More telling was the error found by forensic entomologist Neal Haskell, the witness described in Chapter 4 on the Casey Anthony trial. Haskell saw that while eggs from blowflies were present, no larvae had been present on the remains. This discovery shifted the timeline for the murder to Saturday evening or Sunday morning, times for which Ruby had an alibi. In addition, the fisherman had said there was no dew on the path where he found the box, which meant that the box had been pushed down the hillside after dew had formed that morning. Ruby received a new trial, at which Haskell testified (National Registry, 2014).

If insects are present (typical of bodies left outside but sometimes also on bodies inside), investigators work with an entomologist. Forensic entomology studies the developmental stages of insects and their relation to a criminal investigation

(Haskell, et al., 2001). The insects provide indicators about the time that has passed since the person's death. They also indicate something about the climate and locale in which the death may have occurred. The job of the forensic entomologist is to interpret these relationships and offer information to law enforcement officers to assist with leads.

Figure 28. Maggots on a body

Source: Katherine Ramsland

Dr. Neal Haskell was a farmer before he went to graduate school at Purdue University to study insects and decomposition. He has given hundreds of scientific lectures, seminars, and training classes internationally to provide coroners, medical examiners, death scene investigators, and others with valuable information regarding entomological evidence from death scenes. Currently, Haskell is a Professor of Forensic Science and Biology at Saint Joseph's College in Rensselaer, Indiana, and is a Diplomate of the American Board of Forensic Entomology.

Among the agencies for which he has worked include the Indiana State Police, the FBI, the Office of the Chief Coroner in Ontario Canada, the Florida Department of Law Enforcement, the New York State Police, and the Medical Examiner's Office in Seattle, Washington. He has assisted in nearly 700 cases and has offered expert testimony in approximately 100 trials and hearings. Haskell conducted research at the FAC mentioned above and he co-authored the first textbook on forensic entomology.

When a corpse is discovered, such as in the Posey case, entomologists look at the stages of insect activity. Blowflies and beetles feed directly on the corpse, and their stages of development over about two weeks help to indicate how long the person has been dead. Blowflies are the first to arrive, laying eggs immediately. Insects that feed on these flies – wasps and beetles – arrive next. Then come the spiders.

The adult insects should be collected and preserved in ethyl or isopropyl alcohol. Migrating insects are also studied, because, thanks to scientific measurements, their location and distance from the body can help to establish when they left.

Serology

Serology The analysis of body fluids like blood, semen, and saliva.

Serology is the analysis of serums, including blood, vomit, semen, saliva, sweat, and fecal matter. These samples can assist with identification (DNA), cause of death, or scene reconstruction. Collecting biological fluids involves precautions for preservation and investigator safety, so they use latex gloves, surgical masks, caps, booties, and full coverage paper or plastic gowns. Wet samples are dried, if possible, before being placed into evidence containers.

Most important to investigators at a scene is blood, which might be in liquid form, coagulated, or dried, and appear as a single drop, a series of drops and spatters, a wipe, a stain, or a pool. (We focus more specifically on blood spatter pattern analysis in Chapter 9.) A blood detection kit includes different chemicals with which to perform presumptive tests to determine if the substance is blood.

Once blood's presence is established, investigators use the precipitin test to determine whether it came from a human. Most screening uses color tests, based on the property of the heme portion of hemoglobin in red blood cells to catalyze the release of oxygen from hydrogen peroxide (Wonder, 2001). Chemicals have been used, such as o-tolidine, phenolphthalein (for the Kastle-Meyer test), and tetramethylbenzidine, and luminol, which reacts to make blood temporarily illuminate in the dark as a blue glow. However, luminol does react positively with substances other than blood, such as bleach, and can destroy some of the substance's properties. The Hexagon OBTI test allows for the immediate identification of a substance as human blood.

To collect blood evidence, one needs sterile water, sterile cotton swabs, storage containers, and glass vials. If the blood is dry, it can be scraped into a paper envelope. If it is wet, investigators collect it with a saturated cotton swab. This is air-dried and placed through a hole into the collection box to prevent it from touching anything.

Other serums besides blood, such as saliva or semen, might be collected for DNA analysis. In fact, the greatest number of crimes against persons in which DNA is used are sexual assaults, and victims are generally taken to a hospital. The analysis is performed with a sexual assault collection kit. Investigators should become familiar with these procedures and the contents of the kits, which include collection tools, evidence envelopes, and permission forms. They might need to explain to a traumatized victim what will be done.

Toxicology

Forensic **toxicology** is the detection of substances in human tissue that have a noxious or even a fatal effect (Fenton, 2003). Samples from autopsies are tested for a variety of drugs, environmental toxins, poisons, alcohol, and industrial chemicals, although no lab can test for all possible toxins. Examples of poisons that have been commonly used for murder include thallium, caffeine, aconitine, strychnine, arsenic, and cyanide.

Toxicology The section of the lab that tests tissues or products for contamination by drugs, poisons, and alcohol.

Chemists in the forensic lab dissolve the human tissues removed at autopsy in acidic or alkaline solutions and analyze them with high-pressure liquid or gas chromatography.

Summary

Death investigation is complicated. Investigators must know the death investigation laws and protocols in their state and county. Investigators will work with a coroner or medical examiner, as well as experts of subspecialties such as anthropology and entomology. The ME or pathologist will also include serological and toxicological analyses along with their autopsy findings on types of bodily trauma for cause and manner of death.

Exercise #6.1

A disarticulated foot turned up on the shore of Jedediah Island, British Columbia, in August 2007. Eventually, a dozen were found. Some theories featured a serial killer who cut off the feet of his victims and dumped them into the water. However, the feet had not been severed with any kind of tool. It remained a mystery.

1. What steps might a death investigator take to try to make sense of this phenomenon?

Exercise #6.2

In 1993, Glenn Turner, a police officer in Cobb County, Georgia, named his wife, Lynn Turner, as the beneficiary on his $150,000 life insurance policy. When Turner died soon after, his friends and family were astonished, but the medical examiner ruled that it was a natural death, related to an enlarged heart. Soon, Lynn moved in with Randy Thompson. He, too, purchased an expensive policy. Lynn overspent on their credit cards, running up bills. Randy moved out and Lynn went into debt. He continued to see her, but soon, he experienced serious vomiting. When he died, the cause was listed as an irregular heartbeat, due to clogged arteries. Lynn received $36,000 – far less than she had expected, because Randy had let his insurance policy lapse.

Glenn's mother contacted Randy's mother to compare notes. They brought their suspicions to Dr. Mark Koponen, deputy chief medical examiner of the Georgia Bureau of Investigation. Noticing calcium oxylate crystals in Randy's kidneys, Koponen sent samples to the crime lab. Nothing was found (Hayes, 2010).

1. Since the crime lab found nothing of concern, despite the fact that both healthy young men had died in oddly similar ways, what should the ME do next?

References

Baden, M., & Roach, M. (2001). *Dead reckoning: The new science of catching killers*. New York, NY: Simon & Schuster.

Bass, W., & Jefferson, J. (2003). *Death's acre: Inside the legendary forensic lab the Body Farm*. New York, NY: Putnam.

Benedict, J. (2003). *No bone unturned*. New York, NY: HarperCollins.

Dirkmaat, D. C., & Adovasio, J. M. (1997). The role of archaeology in the recovery and interpretation of human remains from outdoor forensic settings. In W. D. Haglund & M. H. Sorg (Eds.). *Forensic taphonomy: The postmortem fate of human remains* (pp. 39–64). Boca Raton, FL: CRC Press.

Fenton, J. J. (2003). Forensic toxicology. In S. H. James & J. Nordby (Eds.). *Forensic Science: An Introduction to scientific and investigative techniques*. (pp. 45–60). Boca Raton: FL: CRC Press.

Ferllini, R. (2002, 2012). *Silent witness: How forensic anthropology is used to solve the world's toughest crimes*. 2nd Ed., Buffalo, NY: Firefly.

Greenwood, V. (2016, July). How science is putting a new face on crime solving. *National Geographic*.

Hall, R. (2010). *Forensic entomology: The utility of arthropods in legal investigations*. Taylor & Francis Group, LLC. Retrieved from: http://www.esf.edufb/parry/expert testimony.pdf, pp. 460–475.

Haskell, N. Schoenly, K. G. & Hall, R. D. (2001). *Testing the reliability of animal models in research and training programs in forensic entomology, Part II, Final report*. Washington, DC: U. S. National Institute of Justice.

Hayes, A. (2010, September 15). Autopsy shows antifreeze killer's death was suicide. CNN.com. http://www.cnn.com/2010/CRIME/09/15/georgia.inmate.death/

Madea, B., ed. (2016). *Estimation of the time since death*. 3rd ed. Boca Raton, FL: CRC Press.

National Registry of Exonerations. (2014). Other Pennsylvania DNA exonerations. http://www.law.umich.edu/special/exoneration/pages/casedetail.aspx?caseid=4532

Nawrocka, M., Fratczak, K., & Matuszewski, S. (2016). Inter-rater reliability of Total Body Score – A scale for quantification of corpse decomposition. *Journal of Forensic Science, 61*(3), 798–802.

Ramsland, K., & Lysek, Z. (2008). *Murder in the Lehigh Valley*. Gettysburg, PA: Second Chance Press.

Randall, B. (1997). *Death investigation: The basics*. Tucson, AZ: Galen Press.

Rosier E, Loix S, Develter W, Van de Voorde W, Tytgat J, & Cuypers E. (2015). The search for a volatile human specific marker in the decomposition process. *PLoS ONE 10*(9): e0137341.

Sachs, J. S. (2001). *Corpse: Nature, forensics, and the struggle to pinpoint time of death*. New York, NY: Perseus.

Ubelaker, D. H. (1997). Taphonomic applications in forensic anthropology. In W. D. Haglund & M. H. Sorg (Eds.). *Forensic taphonomy: The postmortem fate of human remains* (pp. 77–90). Boca Raton, FL: CRC Press.

Wecht, C. (2003). *Mortal evidence.* New York: Prometheus Books.

Wecht, C & Kaufman, D. (2014) *Final exams.* Rule Publications.

Wonder. A. (2001). *Blood dynamics.* San Diego, CA: Academic Press.

Zugibe, F. & Carroll, D.L. (2005). *Dissecting death: Secrets of a medical examiner.* New York, NY: Broadway Books.

Chapter 7
Criminal Psychology 101

Half Zantop and his wife Susanne were professors at Dartmouth University. They were home in Etna, New Hampshire, on January 27, 2001, when someone knocked at the door. Two young men introduced themselves as students conducting a survey. Zantop invited them in. They proceeded to fatally stab the Zantops. After discovery of the scene, first responders arrived, followed by detectives (Lehr & Zuckoff, 2003).

Two empty knife sheaths on the floor suggested two attackers, but the weapons were missing. Two boot prints turned up from a hiking boot that matched no boots in the home. Trooper Charles West traced the SEAL 2000 commando-type knives to a company in Washington State. After searching dealer lists, West found the sale of two SEAL 2000 knives to sixteen-year-old Jim Parker, who lived near Etna.

Police visited Parker and took his fingerprints. They also fingerprinted his close friend James Tulloch, 17, who owned the right type of hiking boots. When investigators confiscated the boots, the young men fled. They were caught in Indiana. Parker cut a deal, identifying Tulloch as the mastermind. Tulloch believed he had a "divine intellect" and could outwit police. His aim had been to commit the "perfect murder" while acquiring money to establish a new life in Australia. Tulloch pleaded guilty and received a life sentence.

It is hard to imagine teenagers viewing murder as a way to improve their own lives. However, the disciplines of criminology and criminal psychology arose to make sense of such thinking and to identify categories of offenders in terms of how they develop and how dangerous they might become. Definitions of crime and criminals vary from culture to culture, but all cultures arrest and punish those who violate social rules.

This chapter features an area of psychology that addresses the types of criminal minds and mental states that investigators might deal with during an investigation and arrest.

Many departments have devised training programs to teach police officers about mental illness, especially for handling critical incidents. A confrontation with a mentally unstable person used to end in violence more often than it does now. Educating first responders and investigators has made a difference (Goode, 2016), because most officers otherwise act from social stereotypes. If they know little, they believe that bizarre behavior will explode into violence. The trainings educate them in psychological syndromes, medications, and mental states, as well as best ways to handle a confrontation, an arrest, and an interrogation. They learn that the mentally ill are not necessarily aggressive.

Forensic Psychology

Forensic psychology (or psychiatry) addresses psychological issues in the investigative and legal system (Arrigo & Shipley, 2005). While most practitioners are clinicians who perform mental state assessments, this discipline involves a range of activities in civil and criminal arenas. Forensic psychologists might consult, evaluate mental states, assess threats of violence, determine fitness for duty, evaluate the psychological impact of mistreatment, or develop specialized knowledge of forensic-relevant areas. Relevant research areas include criminal development, cognition and perception (especially memory), eyewitness accuracy, criminal behavior, the detection of deception, threat prediction, and false confessions.

Actus reus Latin term that refers to the physical act or omission required for conviction of a crime; the person must have conscious physical control.

For the court, forensic psychologists might be hired (by an attorney or the court) to evaluate a person's present psychological state for competency to participate in the legal process. They might also evaluate defendants' mental states at the time at which they committed an offense (the MSO). In addition, psychologists might assist attorneys on jury selection or evaluate degree of emotional damage (Welner & Ramsland, 2005).

The legal system recognizes that criminal responsibility is linked to two factors: *actus reus*, or evidence that the accused can and did engage in the act, and *mens rea*, the mental state required to have intended to commit the act and to appreciate its legal or moral consequences. The standard for determining criminal responsibility varies by state, but in the context of a trial, insanity is strictly a legal concept, overlapping but not the same as a psychotic mental illness: individuals can be psychotic and also be judged sane if they understood the wrongful nature of their act. Even lacking a specific mental illness, in some jurisdictions a defendant can also be judged temporarily insane or suffering from a diminished *mens rea*.

Mens rea The mental state that accompanies a forbidden act; required for conviction.

To make an MSO determination, clinicians examine the defendant's actions, circumstances, and perceptions leading up to the offense and coordinate these findings with police reports. The MSO evaluation might appraise the motive behind a crime, even if motive will not be part of a legal case, because a lack of a rational motive supports impaired appreciation of wrongfulness or ability to conform one's conduct to the law.

Psychologists also participate in forensic work in other contexts, such as working in a prison, psychiatric hospital, or police department. Mental health experts might also be present in emergency service fields, or perhaps consult on mass disaster response or hostage negotiations.

Clinicians, psychologists, psychiatrists, and criminologists who have used their training and skills to probe the minds of the most extreme murderers have retrieved important information about motives, predatory preparation, pre- and post-crime behavior, fatal fantasies, compartmentalized personalities, and mental disorders.

Criminogenic Factors

Criminology, an area of sociology, is the scientific study of the nature, causes, prediction, and management of people who commit crimes. This involves individual case analysis and social trend analysis, overlapping with the concerns of forensic psychology.

Criminology The study of crime from a sociological perspective.

What questions about the criminal mind do investigators need to have answered? First, is there evidence at a crime scene that reveals the offender's mental state? This can help narrow the pool of suspects and offer leads. Questions also loom about the offender's danger to others (including police) and propensity to strike again in the future.

The U.S. Sentencing Commission (2016) published the results of a study of more than 25,000 federal offenders who were released from prison in 2005. Older offenders and those with more education, it turned out, were less likely to do something criminal again. Yet nearly half were rearrested within five years. When offenders outside the federal system are added to the pool, the recidivism figure rose to 77 percent. Inmates who failed to finish high school had a higher probability of re-arrest. If offenders were under the age of 21, their re-arrest rate hovered near 70 percent. Because those who were likely to recidivate would do so within two years, it makes sense that society should invest in reentry programs and greater supervision during that vulnerable time period, especially for offenders who used guns to commit their crimes.

Almost every scholarly field concerned with human behavior has offered at least one theory about the causes of crime. Some theories focus on character disorders and mental illnesses, while others examine situational factors or they group crime into certain types of categories. Below is a sample:

1. Sociological: a social or cultural force or circumstance, such as poverty and lack of opportunity, causes crime. Those who are members of an affected group are more vulnerable to becoming offenders.

2. Biological: some factor arising from the body causes crime, such as a genetic predisposition or brain damage.

3. Psychological: certain personality types or traits are more likely to cause criminality than others. Dr. Stanton E. Samenow (2004), for example, insists that the criminal's way of thinking derives from "errors of logic."

4. Mixed: Most mental health professionals believe that crime arises from a complex balance of factors. Niehoff (1999), a neuroscientist, states that physiology and environment both contribute, with a unique blend attached to each individual.

Investigative concerns with an offender's criminal trajectory are most urgent at the crime scene and in court. Investigators should become familiar with certain types of mental illness and personality disorder.

Diagnostic Codes

Mental health practitioners rely on coded manuals for diagnosis and treatment, such as the *International Classification of Diseases* (ICD-10) or *The Diagnostic and Statistical Manual of Mental Disorders* (DSM-V). These manuals contain standardized information about mental illness, providing common reference points for professionals (O'Donohue, Fowler, & Lillienfeld, 2007). Those disorders that affect a person's MSO or competency include the following:

1. Personality Disorders
   An estimated 20 to 30 percent of the general population has at least one of the ten defined **personality disorders**. Grouped into three thematic clusters, these disorders are enduring maladaptive patterns of perceiving and relating to the environment in a way that hinders adaptive functioning. Cluster A features the paranoid, schizoid, and schizotypal disorders. Cluster B includes antisocial, narcissistic, borderline, and histrionic, while C focuses on avoidant, dependent, and non-delusional obsessive-compulsive.
   Although people with schizoid (loners) or schizotypal (odd and eccentric) disorders participate in crime, those personality disorders that most often occupy

Personality disorders
Enduring patterns of thought and behavior that are maladaptive, causing impairment and distress. For criminal proceedings, the most common are Antisocial, Borderline, Narcissistic, Paranoid, and Schizoid.

forensic mental health specialists are found in Cluster B. Narcissistic personality disorder involves a pattern of grandiosity and need for admiration. Like the young men in the Dartmouth murders above, they feel immune to the laws that govern "lesser" individuals. Some display a perplexing resilience, narcissistic immunity or "Teflon narcissism." They have a talent for rebounding from setbacks, because they're so certain of their invulnerability.

The Cluster B condition most prevalent in prisons is antisocial personality disorder. People with antisocial personality disorder are defiant of social norms, deceptive and manipulative, and frequently break the law. They show aggression and exploit others.

More volatile are those with borderline personality disorder. They exhibit poor impulse control, an unstable self-image, extreme emotions, and sometimes self-mutilation, such as cutting. If they sense a person leaving a relationship or failing to deliver something they want, they can become criminally punitive.

Cluster C disorders rarely show up in criminal activity unless the person also has other psychological conditions.

2. Psychotic Disorders

The most prevalent psychotic disorder, schizophrenia, is marked by confusion of thinking and speech, usually delusional and often paranoid. Some sufferers of this condition develop violent tendencies, although there is a misperception that this condition is inherently violent. With paranoid features, voices may command a person to kill or take his own life, hold someone hostage, commit property damage, or stalk someone.

Bipolar affective or manic-depressive disorder can have dramatic mood swings that border on delusional. In the manic phase, they might become violent, especially if someone tries to hinder their goals.

Some disorders become conditions of temporary insanity, such as extreme emotional disturbance. Substance abuse can also trigger psychotic delusions that cause bizarre behavior that resembles extreme forms of **psychosis**.

Psychosis A major mental disorder in which a person's ability to think, respond, communicate, recall, and interpret reality is impaired. The person shows inappropriate mood, poor impulse control, and delusions. Often confused with insanity, which is a legal term, and psychopathy, which is a character disorder.

Rape

Rape can be difficult to classify, because the offenders and victims represent a variety of ages, races, and occupations. However, rape by a stranger lacks the complex factors of current or prior relationships, and one of three motivators has been identified: anger, power, and sadism (Ramsland & McGrain, 2010).

Stranger rape can result from frustration and hostility, so symbolic victims are targeted. In other cases, forced sexual contact seems to offer a sense of power and control. The most dangerous is the sadist, who wants to hurt people to arouse himself, especially through torture. He might kidnap and imprison a victim, male or female, for prolonged sessions.

No single variable predicts future or serial rapists, but they often express misogynist beliefs, such as that women are inferior or have specific roles. They are often hyper-masculine. They solve their problems with aggression. Someone who begs for release makes them feel tough. They persistently seek sexual outlets, as if their prowess defines them, and they tend to be difficult to get along with.

Extreme Offenders: Motives and Mechanisms

After immediate concerns about safety and scene preservation are addressed during an investigation, questions center on motive and mental state. Since the nineteenth century, "alienists," anthropologists, and criminologists have tried to understand the acts of criminal offenders. In 1809, Philippe Pinel was the first professional to define the remorseless behavior of a **psychopath**. Such offenders were more brutal and more likely to repeat their crimes, but showed no "mania" that might explain their lack of control.

Psychopathy Personality disorder defined by long-term unsocialized criminal behavior by a person who feels no guilt or remorse and is not inclined to stop; usually diagnosed with the PCL-R.

In 1941, Dr. Hervey Cleckley published *The Mask of Sanity*, to lay out the traits of a psychopath, including deception, manipulativeness, narcissism, and a lack of empathy (Hare, 1994). He defined it as a character disorder. Now, neuroscientists study diagnosed psychopaths with brain scans to try to determine if something in their neurological make-up can explain their acts and attitudes. This could assist with treatment, to which psychopaths have been highly resistant.

Dr. Robert Hare (1994), a Canadian prison psychologist, created the primary diagnostic instrument used today, the Psychopathy Checklist-Revised (PCL-R). Hare believes that among the most devastating features of psychopathy are a callous disregard for the rights of others and a propensity for predatory violence.

Crimes involving psychopathic offenders leave distinct scenes. Clarifying this distinction can assist law enforcement in linking serial cases, so the FBI's Behavioral Analysis Unit (BAU) worked with Hare to view crime scene behavior via characteristics of psychopathy (O'Toole, 2007). According to their reports, identifying a homicide series is easier in rapidly developing cases with low-risk victims, but in general, psychopathic crime scenes reveal whether an offender tends toward being a manipulative charmer, callous killer, impulsive thrill-killer, or an experienced offender.

Dr. Kent Kiehl (2015) is at the forefront of the emerging neuroscience research on psychopaths. He is a professor of psychology at the University of New Mexico and Director of the Clinical Cognitive Neuroscience program at the Mind Research Network in Albuquerque, New Mexico.

Figure 29. Mind Research Network

Source: Katherine Ramsland

With neuropsychologist Elsa Ermer, Kiehl set up a program to explore the suspected neurological deficits of psychopaths. If they think differently, as they seem to, then it is reasonable to hypothesize that they have different brain structures.

Ermer and Kiehl used the PCL-R to identify incarcerated psychopaths and placed them inside an MRI scanner to record their brain structure and its function during specific tasks. In one study, the inmates responded to a target sound while ignoring standard and random non-target sounds. As a group, the psychopaths exhibited unusual brainwave patterns when detecting the target sound. This supported earlier findings that psychopaths over-focus on items that grab their attention. This could mean that they can ignore other input, including cues that they are at risk. Kiehl's metaphor is apt: psychopaths are like passengers who get on a train and cannot disembark until it arrives at where it is going.

Not all psychopaths are violent or even criminal, but when they do become violent, they are more predatory, self-serving, and calculated. Their coldblooded crimes excite them, more for their skill and power than for the crime itself. Psychopathic serial killers often have an edge of sadism and can operate in a compartmentalized manner, passing as normal to their associates while developing their darker acts.

Serial killers like Ted Bundy come to mind. He once aspired to become the governor of Washington State, and many who knew him believed he might succeed. However, his secret life as a serial killer derailed him. Just before his execution in 1989, he confessed to raping and killing at least 30 young women. He was a clever predator, moving from state to state, even escaping twice from prison, to carry on his crimes.

Bettmann/Contributor

Figure 30. Ted Bundy

Dr. Al Carlisle, a prison psychologist, evaluated Bundy after his arrest in Utah in 1975. He spent over twenty hours on psychological assessments. He found Bundy to be charming while also smoldering with anger. When Carlisle asked Bundy's friends and relatives about him, they described Bundy as intelligent, achievement-oriented, savvy, and loyal. Carlisle (1999) proposes that the ability to seem normal while also killing develops through three stages: The offender fantasizes about scenarios that make him feel powerful. He accommodates unacceptable impulses that offer arousal and excitement. To indulge, he dissociates from his normal existence, and this habit ultimately yields a compartmentalized existence. Bundy and others like him would relegate different self-images to specific mental frames. To keep them apart, he develops psychological barriers. Gradually, fantasy melds with reality, and the offender acts out.

Team Offenders

Around twenty percent of serial killers operate on teams, and this can be one of the most challenging crimes for investigators to decipher. Many killing teams follow a common pattern: A dominant person directs someone with an unstable personality or deficient IQ, who becomes a "compliant accomplice." The dominant person isolates the partner(s), making them dependent, before chiseling away at their sense of morality.

Most teams involve just two offenders, but some are nearly definable as gangs. About one-third are male/female couples. Criminologist Eric W. Hickey analyzed trends for over 500 serial killers (2013). "Without exception," he states, "every group of offenders had one person who psychologically maintained control." That person looks for someone who is insecure, exploiting dependency, youth, lack of education, and lack of ability to think fully about consequences.

Former FBI Special Agent Robert Hazelwood conducted a study with Dr. Janet Warren, a professor of clinical psychiatric medicine (2002). They exhaustively interviewed twenty wives or girlfriends of sadistic sexual predators. Four of these women had seen or participated in one or more acts of murder. They were middleclass woman with a background of physical or sexual abuse. Their male partners had used a series of steps: 1) Identify a vulnerable person, 2) Seduce her while 3) isolating her and eroding her boundaries and sexual norms. Already fragile, these women became dependent on their partner for their sense of self-worth and life direction. Some grew afraid for their own lives. Some adopted distancing mechanisms, such as dissociation or just looking away when violence occurred. Generally, they had to agree to do something that scared or disgusted them.

Hickey's analysis indicates that it is rare for the female to take the lead, but it does happen. In Pennsylvania in 2013, Miranda Barbour, 19, instigated a murder with her new husband Elytte, who was eager to experience something exciting with her. According to him, she had said she knew how to kill. They used a Craigslist ad to lure Troy LaFerrara into their SUV. Elytte hid in the backseat as Miranda drove to the designated site. Once LeFerrara got in, Elytte used a cord around the victim's neck to incapacitate him while Miranda repeatedly stabbed him. They dumped his body, cleaned their car, and went to a strip club to celebrate.

Cyber-criminology

Many crimes today are committed on the Internet, especially those that target children, so there is a category of cyber-predator that engages investigative attention (Wolak, Finklehor, Mitchell, & Ybarra, 2008). Chapter 11 focuses on digital forensics, but we examine the psychological angle of these predators here. Online, predators can achieve a faster sense of intimacy than in person, especially if they're unattractive, because they can be invisible or use a fake photo. They also have more time to learn about their prey. Using deceptive information as bait, they develop a relationship prior to any visual interactions; kids who meet them already view them as friends or mentors.

Predators look for certain types of behaviors: kids who freely post personal information about themselves and their whereabouts, post provocative photos, use vulgar language, visit erotic sites, give out phone numbers, talk about feeling lonely or alienated, skip school, and come from broken families. These kids are vulnerable.

Investigators who specialize in Internet predation offer a series of red flags for parents to know, such as their child being secretive about their Internet activity, receiving gifts from a stranger, and behaving aggressively.

Threat Interventions

Elliot Rodger used a YouTube channel to air his grievances. The twenty-two-year-old resident of Isla Vista, CA, was angry that he could not attract pretty sorority girls, so he ranted about making them "pay." On May 23, 2014, Rodger launched an act of coercive suicide: taking others with him before he died.

He fatally stabbed his two male housemates and a friend of theirs, then uploaded his final video to YouTube and emailed an angry manifesto to several people. His plan was to get invited into the Alpha Phi sorority house at the University of California at Santa Barbara. Once inside, he would shoot or stab every young woman there. When no one answered the door, Rodger went on a rampage outside, fatally shooting two female students before driving his BMW down the road. He shot into a shop, killing another man. His rampage ended when he crashed his car and shot himself. He had killed six altogether and hurt fourteen. Later scrutiny of this case showed that there had been a chance for police intervention.

On April 30, 2014, Rodger's concerned parents had requested a welfare check. Officers visited, but found nothing amiss. Rodger spoke with them amiably. They did not – and were not required to – search his apartment. Had they done so, they would have seen his weapons. On this day, Rodger did not meet the criteria for being a danger to self or others.

Three weeks later, Rodger emailed a lengthy autobiographical manuscript, "My Twisted World," to several people that revealed his lack of self-esteem and desperate need for status by being with a certain type of woman. He had been in therapy since he was eight, had been bullied, and had difficulty socializing. In college, he had committed minor acts of aggression. His videos attested to his revenge fantasies. Then he purchased guns. He planned an attacked, which was thwarted. Rodger's therapist alerted Rodger's mother to a YouTube video in which Rodger claimed that the day of retribution was at hand. She called her ex-husband and the Isla Vista police. However, it was too late (Beekman, 2014).

Investigators might find themselves doing such a risk of future danger evaluation, because they are the first responders to many events involving mentally unstable people. Generally, this means making a quick judgment of state of mind. It can be tricky to know just how great a risk an individual (or group) might be, especially when they are careful. There must be a balance between recognizing when threats are just venting and when they are rehearsals for a violent scenario, such as the massacre in Orlando in 2016 that killed 50 people at a nightclub. There must also be more awareness among law enforcement of the predatory planner of violence versus a delusional psychotic individual. The standards used today failed to accommodate the danger from terrorists or mass shooters with a suicidal agenda.

Mass homicides and a surge of workplace violence in the 1980s prompted focused research into methods of identifying and preventing such catastrophes. Employees who threaten others are referred for an assessment of whether they are likely to become dangerous, and under what circumstances. Since then, psychological tools have been developed to determine such conditions as impulsivity, paranoia, and anger. Character and mental disorders are examined, along with all pertinent records (Conroy & Murrie, 2008).

One risk assessment instrument is the Self-assessment of Reported Violence Inventory, based on the importance of learning offenders' thoughts and feelings before, during, and after a violent act. Any unwillingness or inability to evoke memories of what they experienced during a violent act suggests a poor prognosis for self-control. A useful item is a questionnaire that examines their attitudes about weapons.

The Psychopathy Checklist-Revised (PCL-R) turned out to be an accurate predictor of violent recidivism (Hare, 1998). Psychopaths were found to be more likely to commit violence, use a weapon, commit a variety of crimes, and become aggressive than other offenders. If released on parole, they were more likely to commit another crime.

Monahan and his colleagues (2001, 2005) undertook significant research on risk evaluation. They state that the research must meet certain criteria, such as segregating the risk into distinct areas for different types of evaluation. The Research Network on Mental Health and the Law of the MacArthur Foundation also examined the relationship between mental disorder and violent behavior, identifying 134 risk factors across four primary domains:

- Dispositional (e.g., demographics, personality, cognitive)
- Historical (various histories and records)
- Contextual (e.g., social support, stressors, means for violence)
- Clinical (e.g., diagnosis, present functioning, substance abuse)

Relevant factors within these domains were field-tested, associated in prior research with violent acts, affirmed by experienced clinicians, and grounded in established theory. Those factors found to be most potent for violence included being male, having a record of aggression, abuse during childhood, a substance-abusing parent, a disadvantaged neighborhood, psychopathic traits, command hallucinations, anger issues, and violent fantasies. Substance abuse in such individuals heightened their risk to commit future violence. Looking at so many factors is a complex and time-consuming approach, so professionals have devised the Classification of Violence Risk (COVR) software to assist the process. The National Institute of Mental Health validated it (Monahan, Steadman, Robbins, Appelbaum, Banks, et al, 2005).

In general, when threats are vague, implausible, indirect or inconsistent, with no specific targets, it raises no red flags. The risk level rises with specific details and with evidence of planning. A medium-level risk threat could be carried out, but indicators of the place and time are vague, or the target is clear but the subject has no means to carry out the plan. When preparatory steps are clear and an angry individual has access to weapons, the threat level rises – especially with a specific target and date in mind. If they have experienced or they anticipate a major life stressor, the threat level rises. In their minds, they have nothing to lose.

For medium to high threat level, among the specific traits or behaviors that should raise alarms include:

- A time-consuming preoccupation with themes of violence
- Attention to violent incidents or people in the news
- Low frustration tolerance
- Significant recent stressors
- Collecting injustices (lists of names or targets)
- Blame against specific others
- Sudden withdrawal
- Absent support system
- Incidents that reveal simmering rage
- Intolerance, rigidity, suspiciousness, and paranoia
- Increased substance abuse
- Mental instability that involves aggression
- Collecting weapons

While no country, company, school, or person can ever be entirely free from risk from someone who intends them harm, there are ways to diminish the danger. Among them for investigators is education about mental illness and instability.

Threat assessment
The procedure for determining how likely it is that a certain person or group might become violent in the future.

The more sophisticated the technology becomes, the easier it is to make predictions. PredPol uses algorithms to target locations with higher probabilities for crime, for example. Computer databases that collect crime reports, gun purchases, family disputes, and hundreds of other data points can merge the data into a **threat assessment**. Probability analysis through software programs such as Palantir can even identify individuals who are likely to commit future crimes.

While officers raced to an emergency call about a man in Fresno, California, for example, who had threatened his ex-girlfriend, a police operator consulted "Beware," a software that scored the suspect's potential for violence (Jouvenal, 2016). The program scoured hundreds of available data points, including arrest reports, property records, commercial databases, deep Web searches and the man's social-media posts.

The subject's threat level was red. He had gang associations and a firearms conviction. The police sent a negotiator. When he surrendered, officers found his gun. The software has provided critical information for fast decisions in potential mass shootings, terrorist acts, or suicide gestures.

However, these threat-scoring programs border on violations of privacy. To be able to make accurate predictions, a lot of personal data is needed. Yet to collect that data without identifying someone as a threat is quite difficult. Someone like Elliot Rodger would not come up as an obvious threat unless police had access to quite a lot of personal data, such as gun purchases, social media postings, and clinical records. Even his YouTube rantings, while disturbing, do not support police intervention. Models for computerized information about anyone and everyone are driving emotional debates across the country, and yet police departments are quietly putting such data collection and analysis systems in place. High-tech policing is here to stay.

Police cameras are set up in strategic areas, officers wear body cameras, drones are sent out on data-collecting missions, cellphone data is collected, and law enforcement systems tap into traffic cameras and other surveillance systems. In addition, psychiatric, military, and medical records are digitized. If gunshots are fired, a system called ShotSpotter can triangulate the location using microphones strung around the city. Other programs sift through social media sites for illicit activity. The largest project is the FBI's Next Generation Identification project, which is creating a trove of fingerprints, iris scans, and data from facial recognition software and other sources that aid local departments in identifying suspects. Cell site simulators, which mimic a cellphone tower and scoop up data on all cellphones in an area, have been instrumental in finding kidnappers, fugitives, and people who are suicidal, law enforcement officials report (Next Generation Identification, n.d.).

Threat-scoring software seems particularly invasive, because when an incident is tied to an address, searches return the names of residents and look for their publicly available data to generate a color-coded threat level. Yet it is not clear how the software maker introduced the specific calculations, in terms of determining which factors weigh more than others. Even so, awareness of such things as whether someone at a specific address suffers from depression or has been posting threats on Facebook can help officers to stay safe. Either way, there are benefits and tradeoffs.

Perhaps greater transparency about how the threat scores are calculated would minimize concerns. It might also show weaknesses in the system that need to be rectified, such as an ability to distinguish between genuine threats on social media and role-playing, for example (something therapists must be able to do).

For any threat evaluation, the factors to consider (whether with software or simple judgment) are whether the person has acute or chronic stress measured against stress *buffers*, such as close family, access to healthcare, a stable job, and problem-solving skills. Any officer who had checked Elliot Rodger's YouTube channel would have seen obvious signs that he had lost his sense of perspective and was angry and ready to act in a punitive manner. His goals were lofty and probably unattainable, his complaints were unlikely to be addressed, and he did not have appropriate skills for absorbing frustration.

In Chapter 8, we will see a suicide evaluation tool that might also be useful with people in danger of committing coercive suicide (i.e., taking others with them). Those who know these people are often not surprised at their violence.

Some mass murder fantasies are victim-specific, but others involve a symbolic target, such as a location or an employee in a specific occupation that has drawn their anger (Kelleher, 1997). Generally, they try to hide their agenda, but those officers who are versed in the signs of a suicidal mind can use these skills in some cases to avert mass murder. In light of all the recent mass shootings, it might be time to train officials in better evaluation methods. A brief conversation, such as the one the officers had with Elliot Rodger, is no way to assess a person's potential for danger.

Officers, or a team of risk evaluators, can also look at their online presence, if they have Facebook or other social media accounts. Quite often, they will describe their anger, anxiety, depression, and dabbling in self-destruction. This is called leakage. Many people who later committed a mass shooting had revealed their plan or potential for it in their social media posts or other writings (e.g., Adam Lanza, Seung Hui Cho, and Omar Mateen).

With many such incidents, there is no opportunity for evaluation; but whenever there is, officers need to have been taught and be able to use tools for making assessments that are based on clinical data. At the central symposium of the 2014 International Chiefs of Police conference, administrators declared that officers must learn more about the nature of mental illness and how to handle such people better. A lesson in suicidology should be part of their training. We will say more about this discipline in the next chapter.

Summary

Although criminology goes into more detail about offenders than investigators need to know, it pays to have a working knowledge about personality disorders and mental illnesses. Behavior at a crime scene can suggest investigative directions. In addition, investigators who might be faced with offenders still at crime scenes benefit from knowing more about what they are confronting. This includes anything from a psychotic break to a vengeful shooter to a manipulative, charming psychopath.

Exercise #7.1

In 1993, over a period of 18 months, a beloved elementary school teacher, Joanne Chambers, complained of receiving hate mail and death threats. The content of the letters showed that whoever was doing this knew a lot about her movements. There were other distasteful incidents, such as feces smeared on her chair, items stolen from her desk, her own face pasted into porn images and sent to parents, and a doll sent to the school with a razor blade across its throat. Letters went to parents of students accusing Chambers of lewd acts with children.

Suspicion fell on another teacher, Paula N., who was caught on video taking a mug from Chambers' desk. Paula said that Chambers had asked her to do so. Yet, she failed a polygraph when asked if she knew about the threatening letters. (Chambers passed a polygraph.) Prosecutors formed a theory that Paula was jealous of Chambers' popularity. Then Chambers told police that Paula had run her off the road. Paula was arrested.

She insisted that none of what she was accused of doing was true. She spent $100,000 in her own defense, and won, because DNA proved that she had not licked the stamps on the letters. Nothing tied her to the incidents, aside from Chambers' report. However, DNA did point to Chambers. Damages were awarded to Paula.

1. How might investigators have erred in this case?
2. What does the case suggest for investigators?

Exercise #7.2

In 2002, Chrissie Long, age thirteen, went missing. Her aunt was raising her, since her parents had been negligent, and to assist her with a difficult transition, she bought Chrissie a computer. It was not long before Chrissie began to spend all of her spare time online. She even locked her door. She entered chat rooms, using the name Long2Hot4U. Her aunt saw it but ignored her misgivings, believing that it was just something cute for a 13-year-old. Chrissie was an honor student and a cheerleader. There seemed to be no reason to worry. Chrissie repeatedly reassured her aunt that she was always with friends. In fact, she was meeting adult men offline for sexual encounters.

A search of Chrissie's computer revealed several sexually explicit emails with men named Carlos and Saul dos Reis, a married twenty-four-year-old. Both were questioned, but insisted they did not know where Chrissie was.

1. What should detectives do in such a situation?
2. How can they determine if either man is lying?

References

American Psychiatric Association. (2013). *The diagnostic and statistical manual of mental disorders,* Fifth ed. Washington, D.C.

Arrigo, B., & Shipley, S. (2005). *Introduction to forensic psychology* (2nd ed.). New York: Elsevier.

Beekman, D. (2014, May 26). Elliot Rodger wrote manifesto on his hate for women and his vindictive scheme prior to deadly rampage. *New York Daily News.*

Carlisle, A. C. (1993). The divided self: Toward an understanding of the dark side of the serial killer. *American Journal of Criminal Justice, 17*(2): 23–36.

Conroy, M. A., & Murrie, D. C. (2008). *Forensic assessment of violence risk.* Hoboken, NJ: Wiley.

Goode, E. (2016, April 26). For police, a playbook for conflicts involving mental illness. *New York Times.*

Hare, R. D. (1993). *Without conscience: Inside the world of the psychopath.* New York: Pocket.

Hare, R. D. & Logan, M. H. (2009). Criminal psychopathy: An introduction for police. In Michel St-Yves and Michel Tanguay (Eds). *The psychology of criminal investigations: The search for the truth.* Cowansville, QC: Editions Yvon Blais.

Hare, R. D. (1998) Psychopaths and their nature: Implications for the mental health and criminal justice systems. In Millon, T. et al. (eds.). *Psychopathy: Antisocial criminal, and violent behavior* (pp. 188–214). New York, NY: Guilford Press.

Hickey, Eric W. (2013) *Serial murderers and their victims,* 6th ed. Belmont, CA: Wadsworth.

Jacketti, M. (2015, September 25). Scandalous past gives school board pause on hire. *Standard-Speaker.* http://standardspeaker.com/news/scandalous-past-gives-school-board-pause-on-hire-1.1948096

Jouvenal, J. (2016, January 10). The new way police are surveilling you: Calculating your threat score. *Washington Post.*

Kelleher, M. (1997). *Flash point: The American mass murderer.* Westport, CT: Praeger.

Kiehl, K. (2014). *The psychopath whisperer*. New York, NY: Crown.

Lehr, D. & Zuckoff, M. (2003). *Judgment ridge: The true story behind the Dartmouth murders*. New York, NY: HarperCollins.

Monahan, J, Steadman, H., Robbins, P., Appelbaum, P., Banks, S., Grisso, T., Heilbrun, K., Mulvey, E., Roth, L., & Silver, E. (2005). An actuarial model of violence risk assessment for persons with mental disorders. *Psychiatric Services, 56,* 810-815.

Monahan, John, Steadman, H., Silver E. Appelbaum, P., Robbins, P., Mulvey E., Roth, L. Grisso, T. & Banks, S. (2001). *Rethinking risk assessment: The MacArthur study of mental disorder and violence*. New York, NY: Oxford University Press.

Next Generation Identification. (n.d.). https://www.fbi.gov/services/cjis/fingerprints-and-other-biometrics/ngi

Niehoff, D. (1999). *The biology of violence: How understanding the brain, behavior, and environment can break the vicious circle of aggression*. New York, NY: Free Press.

O'Donohue, W. T., Fowler, K. A., & Lillienfeld, S. O. (2007). *Personality disorders toward the DSM-V*. Thousand Oaks, CA: Sage.

O'Toole, M. E. (2007). Psychopathy as a behavior classification system for violent and serial crime scenes. In H. Hervé and J. C. Yuille (Eds.).*The psychopath: Theory, research, and practice* (pp. 301–325). Mahwah, NJ: Lawrence Erlbaum and Associates.

Ramsland, K. (2011). *The mind of a murderer: Privileged access to the demons that drive extreme violence*. Westport, CT: Praeger.

Ramsland, K., & McGrain, P. (2010). *Inside the minds of sexual predators*. Westport, CT: Praeger.

Sentencing Commission. (2016) Recidivism among federal offenders: A comprehensive overview. http://www.ussc.gov/research-and-publications/research-publications/2016/recidivism-among-federal-offenders-comprehensive-overview

Welner, M., & Ramsland, K. (2005). Behavioral science and the law. In C. H. Wecht & J. T. Rago (Eds.), *Forensic science and law: Investigative applications in criminal, civil and family justice* (pp. 475–493). Sarasota, FL: CRC Press.

Wolak, J., Finklehor, D., Mitchell, K., & Ybarra, M. (2008). Online 'predators' and their victims: Myths, realities, and implications for prevention and treatment, *American Psychologist, 63*(2).

Chapter 8
Behavioral Evidence

Learning Objectives

- ❖ Understand the psychological angles of death investigations.
- ❖ Learn the basic information for suicidology.
- ❖ Describe how the FBI developed and uses behavioral profiling.
- ❖ Examine the sub-discipline of geographical profiling.
- ❖ Recognize the value of linguistic analysis.

Key Words

Behavioral Analysis Unit, behavioral profile, equivocal death, geographical profiling, linguistic analysis, NASH categories, psychological autopsy, signature crime, suicidology

Lt. Charles Joseph Gliniewicz, a "cops' cop" and an Army veteran, was known locally as GI Joe. The father of four and an officer for three decades, he headed the Explorer Post 300 group in Fox Lake, Illinois. At 52, he made plans to retire. But on September 1, 2015, just before 8:00 AM, Gliniewicz called for backup. He gave his location at an abandoned cement plant and said he was pursuing three men.

Help quickly arrived but too late. They heard a single gunshot before they discovered Gliniewicz, fifty yards from his cruiser, with a fatal wound to his chest. His bulletproof vest had stopped one bullet but failed to stop a second from his own .40-caliber service revolver, angled downward. The weapon, found later in tall grass two feet away, had been fired twice.

On a surveillance video, officers spotted three men in the area who fit the description. However, all had alibis. No other suspects were located.

The news of this homicide shocked cops and residents alike. They mourned the loss of this hero, cut down in the line of duty. Leads came in and people were swabbed for DNA.

Authorities brought in K-9 units, helicopters, and teams with night-vision equipment. Hundreds of officers and volunteers scoured the woods and swamp. Even federal agents joined the search. Gliniewicz' funeral, covered by media, attracted thousands. Government buildings flew flags at half-mast. The incident seemed like a terrible tragedy: An officer murdered just before he was set to wrap up three decades of meritorious service and retire with honor.

However, County Coroner Thomas Rudd could not rule out an accidental death. It appeared that Gliniewicz could have shot himself. Some officers – especially the first responders – had also considered the incident a suicide. Their voices were ignored. But there were irregularities that prompted an investigation of the decedent himself.

The FBI discovered that "GI Joe" had a dark side. For seven years, he had presented the image of a clean-cut hero who cared about kids while simultaneously embezzling thousands of dollars from the Explorers' funds. Just before his death, a new administrator was set to audit his books. Deleted text messages from Gliniewicz' phone revealed that he had considered framing this official or putting a hit on her.

An unbiased analysis of the evidence showed that Gliniewicz had killed himself but had staged his death as a homicide, possibly to protect his family, his reputation, and his legacy.

One suspicious behavioral inconsistency was that Gliniewicz had been at the cement plant for twenty minutes before he called the dispatcher and only casually had requested backup ten minutes after his first call. He had used the time to delete hundreds of text messages. There was no evidence that anyone else was in the area, and the three men who matched his vague description had been entering a diner that Gliniewicz had passed. Also, the first responders thought Gliniewicz' hand looked as if it had just fired a gun.

Other behavioral factors were that Gliniewicz was adept at staging mock scenes, including "officer down." The same area he used for this was where he had died. His self-inflicted wound, which had missed his heart, had allowed him time to toss his gun. He had already placed his baton and pepper spray to appear as if dropped during a struggle. Finally, his employee file was full of complaints about harassment, physical threats, and ethical violations (Constable and Filas, 2015).

In November, the official call was suicide staged as a homicide. Gliniewicz had been corrupt. Authorities had initially downplayed the possibility of a suicide, and their bias that favored the hero story had cost the county a lot of money.

Death scenes tell a story. Sometimes a death incident turns out to be a crime, but it might also be a suicide, a natural death, or an accident. The truth might be found with a combination of physical and behavioral clues. This includes behavioral patterns that link one crime to another, as with serial murder, arson, or rape, or behaviors that reveal a psychological aberration. To be proficient with behavioral analysis requires in-depth education. The more one assesses motive, the greater the need for understanding behavioral evidence. Human beings are capable of a lot of strange behaviors!

In some types of investigations, knowledge of specific behaviors, such as those covered in Chapter 7, can provide or affirm leads. In the case above, some people said that Gliniewicz was too narcissistic to have killed himself. However, their understanding is shallow. Narcissists have a deep need for power and control. If Gliniewicz had felt trapped, a staged homicide would seem like an ego-saver. He had created such scenes numerous times, so he would believe in his ability to control how people would regard him after his death. In his own mind, he remained the pseudo-hero he had presented for so many years. Despite the need to erase himself, he retained his narcissistic sense of superiority at fooling his fellow officers and his community. In his planning fantasies, he would take satisfaction in getting away with his crimes. For this narcissist with no other way out, preserving his reputation and remaining in control trumped preserving his life.

Psychological autopsy Methods used to determine the state of mind of a person where the scene of a suicide is ambiguous and therefore questionable; also to make a determination about manner of death.

The postmortem analysis of mental state is called a **psychological autopsy**. It is one of the investigative methods discussed below that depend on the ability to recognize and interpret behavioral evidence. Human behavior is difficult to measure without margins of error, which can at times be significant. No matter what we know through experience and research, someone can always surprise us.

Psychological Investigations

Cases in which the manner of death remains unclear as to whether it might have been natural, accidental, a homicide, or a suicide (the NASH classifications) are called equivocal. A full psychological autopsy might assist the investigator in resolving the unanswered questions. This tool, first developed during the 1950s, helps to reveal the decedent's state of mind prior to death. It is used primarily to affirm a suicide, but it can also support other manners of death. The results might be used to aid in criminal cases, settle estate issues, or resolve insurance claims (Shneidman 1981; Ebert, 1986.).

Suicidology The discipline of studying suicide to lean about cause, treatment, and prevention.

Psychological autopsy is built from the little-known field of **suicidology**. It is related to victimology, which lays the foundation for all analysis of behavior that centers on a victim. The better one knows a person, the more likely it is that one can evaluate his or her state of mind. Yet such investigations are inherently full of ambiguity and bias, and are thus prone to the influence of notions about an incident that are formed too fast. Investigators must use factors from the death scene as well as from the decedent's life to provide a reasonable explanation for the death. As with any crime scene, it is important to adopt an objective approach when investigating death incidents.

Between ten and twenty percent of deaths in the United States are either equivocal or erroneously labeled. Sheleg & Ehrlich (2006) found numerous cases of supposed suicide that were clearly autoerotic accidents. We also find death investigators who assume that the presence of a suicide note confirms a suicide, but some notes are part of a staged suicide and some notes are merely written messages that are erroneously believed to be expressive of a suicidal state of mind. Due to these errors, we cannot definitively state how much error might exist in death statistics, especially in jurisdictions lacking resources and education about unusual death events.

The method of psychological autopsy began during the late 1950s when the Los Angeles medical examiner, Theodore Curphey, had to make determinations about an overwhelming number of drug-related deaths. Some were clearly accidental overdoses, but others might have been natural or suicidal. Curphey heard about the Los Angeles Suicide Prevention Center (LASPC) and invited Edwin S. Shneidman and his co-directors, Norman Faberow and Robert Litman, to assist him (Selkin, 1994). He gave them access to his cases. Shneidman and Faberow (1957) published *Clues to Suicide*, identifying three types of important raw material for evaluating a death event as a suicide: psychiatric case histories, psychological test results, and suicide notes. Their research formed the basis for the discipline of suicidology, which is the scientific study of suicide. Today, the American Association of Suicidology carries on this research, building extensive databases. All investigators should become familiar with it.

There is a great deal to be learned from postmortem research. For example, although common sense holds that those people intent on suicide, if thwarted, will find another place, a study of 515 people who'd been blocked from jumping off San Francisco's Golden Gate Bridge revealed that fewer than 5% had gone on to kill themselves in another way. They even stated that they had changed their minds. This demonstrates that actual facts can contradict cultural notions. Several common myths about suicide tend to bias investigative observation, so improved education can influence how deaths are evaluated (Joiner, 2010).

In 2016, the *New York Times* ran a story about the spike in suicides from an annual average of 30,000 to over 40,000 (Tavernise, 2016). Suicide currently holds steady as the tenth leading cause of death in the United States. Suicides spike during the spring, with Monday the day most often chosen. More than half of suicidal people used firearms, and males take their lives at nearly four times the rate of women (78%), even though three times more women make the attempt. Contrary to popular belief, 80% gave observable signals. Over 60% who threaten to kill themselves do actually attempt or complete the act (Center for Disease Control, 2015).

Figure 31. Suicide Note

Source: Katherine Ramsland

Psychological consultants examine numerous factors to make the proper determination of suicide. A psychological autopsy collects extensive biographical information about a decedent to assess behavior, feelings, stress factors, recent events, and the status of employment and relationships (Ebert, 1987). This is a full victimology. Investigators study the death scene and all relevant documentation; conduct extensive interviews with friends and relatives; and evaluate the subject's medical history and evidence of recent stressors. They also note recent changes in the decedent's will or life insurance policies, seeking signals for what Shneidman (1994) calls a "psychache," or pain so great and seemingly without relief that the person feels trapped and sees death as the only way out.

At times, the results will be clear, while at other times the decedent's ante-mortem state of mind cannot be accurately judged. A behavioral analysis seeks to crystallize the psychological factors and decrease the ambiguity.

Investigators who are unfamiliar with cases of autoerotic fatalities (AEF) might confuse an accidental death with a suicide (Shelig & Erlich, 2006). Often, but not always, AEFs have obvious features, such as sexual paraphernalia and pornography. Although most AEF victims are adolescent males, there are exceptions. Some investigators erroneously think that the practice always involves hanging, so the lack of a hanging mechanism misleads them. There are other methods, such as "cocooning," in which a person uses plastic sheeting or zippered bags to restrict airflow during masturbation.

Even those who accept the value of a full behavioral analysis realize that they cannot predict every possible human behavior or trait from what they see at a scene. Yet botched investigations have shown that the less that investigators know about behavior, the more they will rely on gut-level notions and superficial stereotypes. It pays to be educated, especially when behaviors are considered bizarre.

For investigators who have spent time studying depression and desperation, a suicide assessment mnemonic can be helpful: "IS PATH WARM?" (Berman, 2006):

Ideation – active suicidal thoughts or images; a reported desire to die

Substance abuse – excessive use of alcohol or drugs

Purposelessness – sees little sense in continuing, listless

Anxiety – agitation, sleep disorders

Trapped – feels as if there is no way out of a situation

Hopelessness – negative sense of self and the future

Withdrawal – isolation, not responding to significant others

Anger – rage, revenge, sense of need to punish

Recklessness – acting restlessly, risky behaviors

Mood swings – dramatic shifts in mood and affect

Each letter corresponds to a risk factor noticed in many cases within months prior to a suicide attempt or completion. If a number of these items show up when evaluating someone, the risk for suicide is medium to high. These indicators are also used to decide whether a person's death is consistent with suicide.

In the case of Gliniewicz, for example, he felt trapped, hopeless, anxious, and angry. Apart from his criminal behavior, he was not at high risk for suicide, but his need to control what people thought of him and his awareness that the investigation was closing in would put him at greater risk.

Besides psychological autopsies, the other most common investigative method that involves psycho-logical awareness and calculation is **behavioral profil-ing**. Associated with the FBI's **Behavioral Analysis Unit**

Behavioral profiling   See Criminal Profiling.

Behavioral Analysis Unit (BAU)   The investigative part of the National Center for the Analysis of Violent Crime, specific to threat and terrorism, crimes against adults, and crimes against children; formerly the Behavioral Science Unit.

(formerly the Behavioral Science Unit), psychologists and psychiatrists can also offer consulting assistance with this method.

Behavioral Profiling

Austrian officials had linked several prostitute murders in Prague and two Austrian cities during the early 1990s that had distinct behaviors in common. The victims were strangled with an item of their own clothing, left in wooded areas, and covered with leaves and twigs. They still had their jewelry. Officials had developed a solid suspect with a criminal past and reason to believe he had killed three prostitutes in the United States. The suspect had been arrested, but the physical evidence was minimal. Ernst Geiger from the Austrian Federal Police hoped to strengthen the case with behavioral evidence. He contacted Special Agent Gregg McCrary (2003) at the FBI to find out about the technique of linkage analysis. McCrary invited Geiger's team to try the computerized Violent Crime Apprehension Program (ViCAP).

Without naming the suspect, Geiger's team brought his credit card receipts from hotels, restaurants, and rental car agencies. They could place him in all of the right locations and they had a witness statement that confirmed his presence. They also had three unsolved murders in Los Angeles during the time their suspect had visited there, and some hairs and fibers that were forensically significant.

McCrary placed the crime descriptions and records in a succession, from the first known crime to the last, to look for escalation or a change in the *modus operandi* (MO). He filled out the detailed ViCAP forms for each murder to enter them into the database, which at the time held the details of 10,000–12,000 solved and unsolved homicides.

"We had a similar victimology and manner of disposal," he writes. "Most of these women had been prostitutes and were left outside, with branches or foliage placed over them. We had no semen left on or in [most of] those bodies. The cause of death for those on which we could tell was strangulation, but some bodies were too decomposed to make a determination. Most had restraint bruises on their arms and wrists. No one had seen them getting into a car, so this offender had been careful. There was an absence of any indication of sexual assault. The trace evidence was next to none as well, and he appeared to have a calculated MO. He was smart and he was organized" (McCrary & Ramsland, 2003, pp. 250–51).

McCrary used fifteen cross-referenced criteria for the search, which linked the eleven suspected incidents and another homicide in California. In this one, the killer had been convicted.

Geiger now offered the activity timeline of his suspect, Jack Unterweger, and compared his MO from a murder for which he had been convicted years earlier. It added up. In addition, the Los Angeles Crime Lab criminalist linked the complicated knot used for ligatures on their three victims to the pantyhose knots on the European victims, as a behavioral signature. On several factors, the behavioral analysis was strong. McCrary traveled to Austria to testify, and Jack Unterweger was convicted for nine murders, including those in Los Angeles.

It was a satisfying experience for McCrary, whose practice of martial arts has given him insight into anticipating criminal behavior. During his 25-year career with the FBI, he became part of the Behavioral Science Unit. After retiring, he served as a senior analyst for the Threat Assessment Group. McCrary has investigated and consulted on thousands of cases throughout the United States, Canada, Central America, Europe, and Asia. He currently trains law enforcement agencies internationally, provides expert testimony in court, and offers expert analyses for news organizations. A contributing author to the FBI's *Crime Classification Manual*, McCrary also published a book of his cases, *The Unknown Darkness: Profiling the Predators Among Us*. His work was highlighted in the Emmy-nominated PBS documentary, *The Mind of Serial Killer*.

The FBI's criminal investigative analysis support for local law enforcement includes criminal profiling, and McCrary explains how profiling is used to evaluate behavioral evidence and link serial crimes, as well as to discern motive and the dimensions of an offender's personality. A behavioral profile is an educated attempt to provide investigative agencies with clear parameters about the type of person who has committed a certain crime or series of crimes (McCrary & Ramsland, 2003; Douglas, 1996).

Victimology comes first. Complete background on the victim or linked victims creates the foundation for a profile. Victims' risk factors are identified, as well as any potential past or present relationship with offenders. Where victims were first contacted, abducted, attacked, and/or killed determines the degree of risk taken by both, as does age and occupation. Among low-risk victims are those who live quiet lives and are killed or raped at home. High-risk victims include prostitutes, exotic dancers, and substance abusers. The key issue is to learn why a particular person was targeted. Then the profiler might be able to determine how the victim was approached and whether there was resistance.

Profiling starts with a detailed timeline of the victim's known movements up until the time of the crime. This can involve going through emails, letters, social media postings, journals, phone and texting records, statements to acquaintances, employment records, health records, and memberships in groups and clubs. Other sources include the victim's mental health history, criminal record, and evidence of substance abuse.

Focus on a potential suspect (Unknown subject, or UNSUB) comes next, as they did with Unterweger. The profiling process assesses whether the person is predatory vs. opportunistic, and organized or possibly mentally ill. They determine if the offender(s) used a vehicle, had criminal experience, pays attention to news about the investigation, or is acting out a sexual fantasy. One offender, for example, surgically removed the victim's eyes. Many others have posed their victims in some manner.

"In trials," says McCrary, "I often educate judges and juries about what profiling is and isn't. It's one tool among many. It's crime scene analysis and interpretation, based on behavioral consistency. A profile can emerge from the investigative process, but that's not what it's all about. People can get blinders about that. We refer to it as criminal investigative analysis. We start with an actual crime and an event, and then work backward to talk about the characteristics and traits of that particular individual who might have done that crime. It's not a template against which to compare people; it's not generic. It's a specific profile based only on a case" (personal interview, 2001).

The more uniqueness the behavior shows, the better, because the signature or personality quirk helps to link incidents to a common source. Unterweger's was the complex knot and the use of victim underwear for strangulation. Signatures that show criminal addiction might also predict future incidents. Some are tied to dates, for example, or moon phases. Those offenders who show sexual oddities are likely to keep committing this same crime.

Profiling estimates the MO, race, age, sex, marital status, educational level, employment status, and other factors. Profilers are trained in psychological theories that are informed about delusions, offender thought patterns, and character disorders. They also need to know about statistical data, such as the age range into which offenders for specific types of crimes – rape, bombing, arson, murder – generally fall.

As mentioned, profiling is not limited to the FBI. Police officers from all over the country train at the FBI's National Academy (NA), and can network with other NA graduates. In addition, private psychologists associated with police departments who gain experience with investigative practices can assist to develop profiles. However, people with no training have tried to claim expertise, and their efforts can mislead.

"One of the issues with profiling," says McCrary, "is professionalism. Anyone can raise their hand and declare themselves to be profilers. There are no board exams or licensing requirements. Maybe we'll have standards some day, but now you get a lot of quacks running around selling their product. From the Bureau point of view, you must first have years of investigative experience. Then you come into the unit, and it's a two-year process of work and studying before someone can stand on their own. The only place to get experience with a crime scene is in law enforcement. It's like any other area of expertise: To be good at it, you need to be in it every day."

McCrary has worked closely with another expert who developed an approach to profiling that focuses on detailed geographical analysis.

Geographic Intelligence Analysis

In a neighborhood in Lafayette, Louisiana, a man raped several young women in their homes or in homes where they were babysitting. He had an odd MO: he made them clean up afterward, held his flashlight up over his shoulder, and warned them that he would know if they reported the incident. This was his behavioral signature. The victims reported him, anyway. Police learned that the rapist was a stocky, white male who wore a hat, scratchy gloves, and a bandana as a mask.

No leads proved useful, so they invited Dr. Kim Rossmo to use a software program that he had developed for geographical profiling. It is an investigative support technique or information management system for serial violent crimes, assisting to show with a high degree of probability where the offender might work or reside. The assumption, based on research, is that serial offenders tend to start within their comfort zones (Rossmo, 2000).

In Lafayette, Rossmo visited the scenes and realized that one could easily see from outside what was going on inside: each house had no curtains. The rapist could see a woman alone. Rossmo plotted the incident locations on a map to locate the offender's "zone of familiarity," a two-mile radius.

A tip identified a police officer, Ernest Randy Comeaux. Investigators discovered that during the period when the rapes had occurred, Comeaux had resided in the targeted area. He was also engaged to a rape crisis center volunteer, so he had inside information. A DNA sample tied him to the rapes, and he was arrested and convicted.

Geographical profiling is valuable whenever several linked offenses can be tied to a tight geographical area. (Used for loosely related incidents, it has proven a poor indicator.) Among the factors that the software uses for calculations are victim selection locations, incident locations, likely travel routes, and body dumpsites. This information reveals an offender's range and degree of mobility, their likely method of transportation, and their psychological perception of barriers, such as rivers and state lines.

Rossmo's software is called Criminal Geographic Targeting (CGT). With a minimum of five incidents, the program makes calculations and produces a topographic map. This shows a "jeopardy surface," or offender's base of operation. It is superimposed on a map. The more crime sites identified, the higher the program's predictive power (Grierson, 2003; Rossmo, 2000). Central to this approach is a psychological notion: perceived distance can be different from actual distance. Some people think 50 miles is far; others view it as an easy trek. The perceived distance suggests traits about the behavior and offers predictions about future violence. As offenders grow bolder or shift their MO, their maps can change.

Linguistic Analysis

Attributional or linguistic analysis for investigative purposes involves analyzing the content and style of a questioned document for source identification. The questioned document will either show characteristics of a fake or it will be compared with what the suspected source typically writes. It might also affirm or undermine the finding of a manner of death as suicide. Linguistic analysis is another form of behavioral analysis, but it can also fall under the heading of pattern analysis. The assumption is that no two people use language identically and this signature uniqueness can be detected across documents that they author.

Civil or criminal cases might involve ransom notes, forged wills, suicide notes, threats, alleged confessions, plagiarized documents, patent disputes, social media messages, blog posts, and contract issues (Chaski, 2005; Leonard, 2005). "A forensic linguist," writes Leonard, "is morally and professionally bound to describe the language situation the way it is, rather than to slant the conclusions to one side or the other" (p. 1448).

Investigators must know such things as who is believed to have authored a note, what can be learned about this person, and whether the questioned sample is authentic (Chaski, 2006). Syntax is the unconscious manner in which a person combines words to create phrases and sentences, which then grow into habits or a specific style. Questioned items that involve writing are statistically analyzed for distinct syntactic patterns. "Idiolect" refers to the language system of a specific speaker (Leonard, 2005). Linguists sometimes look for a common idiolect among known and questioned samples. Grammars describe the patterns that are available to a language user, as well as those that are not (Chaski, 2006).

Authorship attribution uses three main approaches: stylistics, stylometry, and syntactic analysis. Dr. Carole Chaski is associated with the latter. She is president of ALIAS Technology LLC and founder of the Institute of Linguistic Evidence (ILE), a nonprofit agency founded in 1998 that supports research on the validity and reliability of language-based author identification. ALIAS stands for Automated Linguistic Identification of Authorship System. ILE was the first scientific research organization to devote its resources to testing new methods in forensic linguistics and improving the science that backed its approach. The ultimate goal is to provide reliable tools for investigators and attorneys, based in linguistic theory and standard analytical techniques. ALIAS Technology LLC provides software.

The research agenda at ILE involves four cornerstones:

1. Author identification
2. Text similarity
3. Text typing
4. Linguistic profiling

"Linguistics is closely related to cognitive psychology," says Chaski (personal interview, 2014), "which deals with questions about language structure, language processing, and language acquisition, and to sociology, which is about dialects, the history of languages, and subcultures." At an intimate workshop of experts at her Delaware estate in 2014, Chaski explained how she makes a detailed analysis of linguistic structure to compare with what a suspect generally writes and/or reads. The pattern of unique differences, along with repetition of those traits in other writings, provides internal evidence that links someone to a questioned document.

With unknown subjects, when linguistic profiling may help an investigation, forensic linguists search text databases to locate those that contain similar language habits, such as specific phrasing. The analysis can help establish the writer's age, sex, ethnicity, educational background, and ideology. It can even assist with threat assessment and can sometimes establish a geographical location. The key items used are vocabulary, grammar, spelling, syntax, and punctuation habits, as these can be associated with sociological characteristics.

Chaski is known for her work on what has been called "the keyboard dilemma," i.e., the difficulty with identifying authorship when documents are written with a keyboard to which multiple users have access. How does one narrow down to an individual? This problem has increased exponentially with shared computers and digital devices in homes and offices. Chaski uses a cross-validated syntactic approach, wherein she analyzes a questioned document for syntactic patterns – the unconscious way in which a person automatically combines parts of speech. Chaski's software counts and categorizes these patterns statistically. She is aware of the need to meet current court standards, such as those discussed in Chapter 4, and she strives to be diligent.

"As one of the social sciences," Chaski states, "linguistics is learned and taught within the normal scientific paradigm which the *Daubert* ruling espouses. Any science is built on the idea that human error and bias must be constantly guarded against through clear and repeatable procedures and multiple replications with similar findings. Science makes predictions based on known patterns. These predictions are only as good as they seem to be when tests show that they are correct at a certain rate in certain conditions, over and over again. Further, any science recognizes its own limitations. The most developed sciences have gathered enough replications to provide error rates. The only forensic linguistic method that I know has passed the scrutiny of *Daubert* is the syntactic analysis method for author identification, which I have been developing and validating since 1992."

Chaski's method of syntactic analysis derives from generative grammar, and she utilizes a standard statistical test. "After I had cases in which my conclusion was validated by the suspect confessing on the witness stand," she says, "I sought research funding to pursue validation studies independent of any litigation. I won a research fellowship at the U.S. DOJ's National Institute of Justice, where I stayed for three years. I created a database of known authors' writing samples so that I could run experiments. I also tested hundreds of linguistic variables in these experiments. I tested several different statistical procedures. The current validation tests show that the method called SynAID assigns documents to the correct author 95% of the time."

Chaski's recommendations are as follows: The collected samples should have been written within three years of the questioned document. Known exemplars are the primary source, but if needed, ask a suspected author to write more. Although they might purposely alter their writing, there might be no alternative. The procedure is to seat them at a table in a room without distraction, and avoid dictating. The standard method for obtaining handwriting exemplars is:

1. Do not show the subject the questioned document
2. Do not dictate punctuation or word spelling
3. Use materials similar to the document
4. Dictate text samples that match part of the document
5. Repeat the dictation at least three times
6. Ask the subject to sign and date the text
7. Have an objective witness observe

This procedure can be adapted for gathering linguistic exemplars. Chaski recommends the following steps for this process:

1. Do not show the subject the questioned document
2. Ask the subject to write as much as possible on each of ten different topics, where one of them is similar in theme to the questioned document. These ten topics should include themes that will invoke different styles (e.g., emotional, business, narrative, essay, letters, emails, even texting).
3. The author can use any medium: handwriting, typing, or an electronic device that is similar to the medium of the questioned document
4. Ask the subject to sign and date the text
5. Have an objective witness observe, preferably also writing at the same time on the same topics

In an early case, Chaski was asked to determine if a note left on a computer disk, unsigned, was a suicide note for a deceased individual who was found dead in bed. His roommate had called 9-1-1. The decedent had died from a mixture of drugs, including Lidocaine. Yet no needle was present near the body. The 9-1-1 caller, with a medical background, had access to Lidocaine. An investigation turned up an altercation, as well as false statements from the roommate. Chaski applied her software analysis program to the note and to writing samples from both the decedent and the roommate. She reduced the note to the words and rebuilt the phrases from scratch, linguistically, and the software produced a numerical profile of each document to which to apply her statistical method. Key syntactical items, such as an excessive use of conjunctions to form long sentences and the complex formation of adverbs, were more closely matched to the roommate's linguistic habits. They eliminated the decedent. The note's contents, which had caused the decedent's family great distress, were meaningless, and, in fact, deceptive. The roommate was arrested, and during his trial, he admitted to writing the suicide note after accidentally injecting the decedent with medication to ease a migraine headache (Chaski, 2005).

In 2012, an American computer engineer was found hanging from the bathroom door in his Singapore apartment. His parents insisted that he had not committed suicide, as investigators had determined. Five typewritten suicide notes were located. Chaski was one of two experts to separately examine the notes. One expert determined that the decedent had been raised in a different culture from whoever had written the notes. Chaski used software that she has tailored for authenticating suicide notes (SNARE), finding that the notes were not classifiable as authentic. Unfortunately, the Singapore police destroyed the noose and towel, which had contained unknown DNA from two other people (LaRosa, 2014).

ILE publishes a journal, *LESLI: Linguistic Evidence in Security, Law, and Intelligence,* to provide resources and research updates and to warn about improper methodology. Chaski also trains investigators in her suicide note authentication software.

Summary

Behavioral evidence for death investigation centers on victimology, primarily for state of mind prior to death but also on behavioral consistency. Psychological autopsies focus on support for a finding of suicide, while behavioral profiling features detailed analyses of specific crime scene behavior. Linguistic analysis can support other behavioral findings.

Exercise #8.1

On the morning of June 2, 2007, a resident on Linden Street in San Francisco called 9-1-1 to report blood in the sidewalk outside an apartment. Within seven minutes, police arrived. The first responders noted that the drops had a rounded appearance. This suggests someone bled on the porch, which was several steps above street level. Inside, in the midst of a lot of blood, was a body with three stab wounds to the neck and torso. Due to locked doors, the responding detective decided that he was looking at a suicide.

The two-story apartment dwelling has four units and the decedent lived in the lower right apartment dwelling, which shared a contiguous wall with an adjacent apartment. Inside, at the kitchen sink were vertical blood drops, which indicated that someone had stood there. A wine bottle lay on the floor, and a plate of partially eaten peas and rice sat on the counter. A sharp knife, rinsed, was in the sink. There was also a cheese plate with a dull knife. A bloody mark on the counter appeared consistent with someone's palm. The bloodstains on the kitchen floor showed some pooling, consistent with someone bleeding in place, and then walking slowly away. There were blood drops on the doorsill and the edge of the front door. There were large splashes of blood in the living room, and smeared blood was found on the inside of the door above the deadbolt and dripping blood beneath it.

Bloody footprints consistent with the decedent's shoes, which had bloodstained soles, led through the hallway, from the living room to the kitchen and back to the living room. There was blood on the front stoop, but no footprints. On a cinderblock wall of the adjacent building, at the foot of the steps were small droplets of blood spatter, which resembled cast-off.

The apartment lights were off, including the kitchen light switch, which showed a bloody swipe consistent with a downward motion. A light switch in the hallway also had blood drips and swipe marks consistent with a downward motion. The bloody shoe prints, which matched the decedent's shoes, show bi-directionality to and from the kitchen. There were blood drops on top of several shoe prints.

The resident, Hugues de la Plaza, lay dead in a massive amount of blood, pooled, wiped, and spattered. The television was overturned and there was a broken wine glass beneath the couch. The adjacent coffee table had a laptop; both had blood on them. A cell phone next to the laptop bore no blood. Blood on CD and DVD cases was consistent with someone standing above them while bleeding. A notepad adjacent to the cell phone contained a note, "Learn as if you were to live forever, Live as if you were to die tomorrow." The computer was dormant but active, and set to a pornographic website.

When the decedent was moved, paramedics discovered his broken wristwatch beneath him. No weapon was evident near the decedent, but both knives were collected from the kitchen. A few strands of pulled hair were found in the decedent's left hand.

Antonio Casillas, the lead homicide investigator, arrived two hours after the initial call. He noted that the dripping blood in the hallway and kitchen indicated someone walking, not running. There had been no calls to 9-1-1, although the cell phone was on a table near the decedent. His team learned from the immediately adjacent neighbor, who shared a wall between apartments, that he had heard a loud thud during the early morning hours. He also heard the front door to the decedent's apartment slam three times and the sound of someone running down the stairs. Casillas asked about de la Plaza's frame of mind, and this neighbor had the impression he believed this was a suicide (Eskenazi, 2009). During the subsequent crime scene reconstruction, the neighbor's report was eliminated.

1. What is the immediate problem with this investigation?
2. What should be the first order of business for this investigation?

Exercise #8.2(profiling)

An active 87-year-old woman had not been seen in several days in her quiet, gated community. A neighbor found her in a chair, stabbed to death. Detectives found a phone cord, cut, and a Nike shoe print visible in the dust. Beneath the body was a bloody phone. It seemed likely that the killer had known how to get into the secure community, as well as into the house. There was no evidence of a break-in. The victim had been stabbed eleven times and manually strangled.

Two more elderly women were fatally attacked in the area – one bludgeoned with an iron, the other stabbed – and an antiques dealer was attacked by a customer, strangled, and left for dead.

1. How might this scene be analyzed for a behavioral profile?
2. What are the key behaviors of interest?

References

Berman, A. (2006, July/August). Risk assessment treatment planning and management of the at-risk-for-suicide client: The how-to aspects of assessing suicide risk and formulating treatment plans. *Family Therapy Magazine, 5*(4), 7–10.

Center for Disease Control. (2015). Suicide: Facts at a glance. http://www.cdc.gov/violenceprevention/pdf/suicide-datasheet-a.pdf

Chaski, C.E. (2005). Who's at the keyboard? Recent results in authorship attribution. *International Journal of Digital Evidence, 4*:1.

Chaski, C. (2006). Forensic linguistics, authorship attribution, and admissibility. In C. H. Wecht & J. T. Rago (Eds.). *Forensic science and law: Investigative applications in criminal, civil, and family justice* (pp. 505–522). Boca Raton, FL: CRC Press.

Constable, B. & Felis, L. (2015, November 23). Special report: Gliniewicz' final hours as he staged his 'hero' cop death. *Daily Herald*. http://www.dailyherald.com/article/20151122/news/151129722/

Douglas, J. (1995). *Mind hunter*. New York: Scribner.

Ebert. B. (1987). Guide to conducting a psychological autopsy. *Professional Psychology Research and Practice, 18(1), 52–56*.

Eskenazi, J. (2009, February 26). Father of Hugues de la Plaza says SFPD now considers case a murder – two years later. *San Francisco Weekly*.

Ferenc, M. (2009, February 11). Review of death scene/autopsy findings of Mr. Hugues de la Plaza. SFPD case 070-557-605.

Grierson, B. (2003, March 21). The hound of the data points. *Popular Science*.

Hinkel, D. (2016, Jan. 5). Cop at scene considered suicide in Gliniewicz death, documents show. *The Chicago Tribune*.

Joiner, T. (2010). *Myths about suicide*. Cambridge, MA: Harvard University Press.

LaRosa, P. (2014, September 2). Experts: Engineer found dead didn't write suicide notes. *CBS News*. http://www.cbsnews.com/news/experts-engineer-found-dead-didnt-write-suicide-notes-2/

Leonard, R. A. (2005/2006). Forensic linguistics: Applying the scientific principles of language analysis to issues of the law. *International Journal of the Humanities, 3*, 1447–1450.

McCrary, G. & Ramsland, K. (2003). *The unknown darkness: Profiling the predators among us*. New York, NY: Morrow.

Rossmo, K. (2000). *Geographic profiling*. Baton Rouge, FL: CRC Press.

Selkin, J. (1994). Psychological autopsy: Scientific psychohistory or clinical intuition? *American Psychologist, 49(1)*, 74–75.

Shelig, S. & Erlich, E. (2006). *Autoerotic asphyxiation: Forensic, medical and social aspects*. Tucson, AZ: Wheatmark.

Shneidman, E. S. (1981). The psychological autopsy. *Suicide and Life Threatening Behavior, 11*(4), 325–340.

Shneidman, E. S. (1993). *Suicide as psychache: A clinical approach to self-destructive behavior*. New Jersey: Jason Aronson.

Shneidman, E. S. & Faberow, N., eds, (1957). *Clues to suicide*. New York, NY: McGraw-Hill.

Tavernise, S. (2016, April 22). U. S. suicide rate surges to a 30-year high. *New York Times*, pp. A1, A15.

Chapter 9
Patterns, Impressions, and ID

Learning Objectives

❖ Learn how forensic artists make victim identifications.
❖ Discover resources for identifying or locating missing persons.
❖ Follow a fingerprint examiner's steps for taking and reading prints.
❖ Study how blood spatter pattern analysis is interpreted.

Key Words

Blood spatter pattern analysis, class evidence, Doe Network, DNA phenotype, fingerprints, forensic art, latent print, minutiae, NamUs, visible print

Just before Christmas in 1987, construction workers in Venice, California, dug a hole and struck a human femur. Coroner's deputies discovered that concrete that had once been poured into the hole had partially encased an upper torso and head, which outlined the hands and facial features of a female. Investigators found no form of identification with the body. Fragments of a soft pack of L&M brand cigarettes were removed from the grave (Citron 1988).

The bones, along with the concrete pieces that had formed around the face before it decomposed, were sent to forensic anthropologist Judy Suchey. She positioned the remains to determine the woman's stature, ancestry, and approximate age. She also looked for evidence of trauma. Knife nicks on several bones supported a finding of homicide. Police researched the homeowners over a fifteen-year span, while a police artist used the hardened cement to make a plaster cast and a sketch.

Hercules Butler had owned the property during the 1970s. A neighbor recalled that he had poured the concrete. The cigarette brand was also linked to him. Police located him, but Butler had sustained brain damage and could not answer questions. One of his relatives recognized the police sketch as "Adrienne." Eventually, investigators learned her last name, Piriano. She had once lived with Butler, but had disappeared.

From a job application, police got Piriano's fingerprints. Latent print examiners poured rubber silicone into the concrete mold. When it dried, it revealed a clear ridge pattern that confirmed the decedent's identity. Circumstances suggested the Butler had killed Piriano. He was arrested but was found not competent to be tried (Boyer, 1988).

Reading impressions is part of the science of pattern evidence. When coupled with careful investigation, it has solved many cases and identified victims for whom no typical identification exists. Today, they might have done DNA phenotyping, which can produce facial composite predictions from the genetic markers (Greenwood, 2016). This method shows eye and natural hair color, geographic ancestry, and a possible facial shape. Researchers look for tiny variations, single nucleotide polymorphisms, which are associated with facial features, including details about earlobes and a tendency to freckle. The DNA phenotype can be used with extensive databases for confirmation of these associations, with which they can reverse engineer a Jane or John Doe's appearance. This will not necessarily identify an individual but it can be effective for excluding people.

Basic pattern evidence is part of most crime investigations. Often, it requires specialized trainings for interpretation and comparisons. Even with specialists, sometimes it still does not qualify as solid evidence. For example, as discussed in Chapter 4, bite mark and handwriting analysis have come under serious scrutiny for reliability claims. Among the pattern evidence that does prove useful are fingerprints, tire tread impressions, shoe or footprints, tool marks, and bloodstain patterns.

Facial ID

The Doe Network is a volunteer organization that attempts to assist law enforcement with the identification of found bodies. Its mission is to give names to the nameless. The network offers a website that provides information for potential matches with missing people and has a number of people who devote their time and resources to scouring records. Although it is tedious, solitary work, there are opportunities for interaction among these people. A subculture exists via websites, conferences, and caring civilians who align with a single purpose (Halbur, 2014).

It is estimated that there are 40,000 unidentified sets of human remains, with up to 4,000 added each year. In 2007, the National Institute of Justice's (NIJ) National Missing and Unidentified Persons System (NamUs, NamUs.gov) became a uniform national centralized repository and resource center for missing persons and unidentified decedent records. It offers a free system that can be searched online by medical examiners, coroners, law enforcement officials, and the general public from all over the country in hopes of resolving these cases. Included are databases for missing, unidentified, and unclaimed persons. Whenever a new profile is added, the system automatically updates and performs cross-matching comparisons. NamUs also provides free DNA services for unidentified human remains, along with some anthropology and odontology assistance.

The NamUs best practice advice for using its AFIS and CAFIS (permanent repository) fingerprint unit lists the following:

1. Scan fingerprint images at 500 dots per inch (dpi).
2. Scan or photograph all fingerprint images in a 1:1 scale.
3. 10-print fingerprint cards will produce the most comprehensive search results.

In the case of a skeletonized John or Jane Doe, a forensic anthropologist or artist can offer a facial reconstruction (Spaun, 2016). There does exist a scientific working group for training in, and the improvement of, facial identification, and we now have automated face recognition systems that use algorithms for this purpose. Still, some people, known in the London police force as "super recognizers," can beat the computer (Keefe, 2016). After the 2011 London riots, the Met gathered two hundred thousand hours of CCTV footage. Computer systems for facial-recognition identified only one rioter, while super-recognizer Gary Collins, an officer, successfully identified nearly two hundred. Best practices hold that reviewers must be trained to compare faces from multiple images and perspectives to a single individual. The next step is that agencies should use only those experts trained in the nuances of facial comparison. This discipline begins with the basics of facial appearance and biometric morphological analysis.

Frank Bender, now deceased, developed methods for identifying John and Jane Does through several forms of art. His Philadelphia-based art studio was housed in a former meat shop. Bender got his start as a sketch artist and photographer. Then in 1976, he was invited to the local morgue to enhance his knowledge of human anatomy. He saw the body of an unidentified woman, shot in the head, known only by a number, 5233. It seemed she might remain unknown indefinitely. Bender believed he could use his artistic skills to show what she would look like (Ramsland, 2002).

The pathologist, Dr. Halbert Fillinger, Jr., invited Bender to try to recreate her face, so he took facial measurements. Because he was a commercial photographer at the time, he understood lighting conditions. He created a 3-D sculpture and photographed it. Fillinger placed the images in the newspaper. This led to the identification of a 62-year-old woman, as well as the arrest and conviction of her killer.

Before starting a project, Bender would gather as much visual information as possible about the subject. He looked at clothing found with a body and studied the pathology reports. Only then would he focus on the skull, which he often defleshed himself. He noted asymmetries and unique features. Then he consulted standard skin-thickness charts that other artists and anthropologists have devised.

One facial sculpture technique involves casting a skull. Then, holes are drilled in strategic places for inserting thin pegs for laying out skin and muscle depth. With modeling clay, the artist builds up muscles and features around the nose, mouth, cheeks, and eyes. The neck is developed next, along with the ears (Taylor, 2001). Individual features are created from educated guesses about idiosyncrasies; eyebrows and skin textures humanize the face. Glasses, jewelry, or items of clothing found with the remains are used before adding a wig and prosthetic eyes. Photographs and/or drawings are made for use on posters and in the newspaper.

At one scene, police found a single lens from a pair of glasses, so Bender used them to look at frames that he believed would work with the victim's face. He selected a pair and put them on the sculpture. The police were able to identify her. From his experience, it is easy to derive advice for investigators: Find an artist who would be willing to work on human remains (some will jump at the opportunity). Because they're creative, they might offer intriguing innovations that no investigator has considered.

Take this case. In 1999, human remains floated to shore on a Wisconsin river. The face of the female victim had been skinned, so she proved difficult to identify, and there were no associated missing person reports. Because an artist's rendering required defleshing the skull, authorities decided against this technique, fearing destruction of potential evidence.

Six months later, detectives heard about experts at the Milwaukee School of Engineering's Rapid Prototyping Center. The Center offered a technique that could develop a three-dimensional model without damaging the original. The police asked for assistance. The technicians did successive CT scans of the murder victim's head, using thousands of thin layers of paper. They got a three-dimensional image that assisted a forensic artist to create a sculpture and poster image ("Fingerprints," 2000). The former wife of Peter Kupaza of Baraboo saw one of the posters. She called police to report that Mwivano Kupaza, age twenty-five, had gone missing at the time the remains turned up. She had been living with a relative, Peter Kupaza. He was arrested and charged. A search of his home turned up items belonging to the missing woman. A background check indicated that Kupaza had raped Mwivano two years before she disappeared. She became pregnant, and he forced her to get an abortion. A cadaver dog search in Kupaza's apartment turned up traces of blood, which analysis linked to the remains. Kupaza was convicted.

Unique Identifiers

The first trial that involved fingerprint evidence for criminal identification occurred in Argentina in 1892. A book about fingerprints for crime investigation by Sir Francis Galton had been published, wherein he described three primary features that yielded 60,000 fingerprint classes. Galton had worked with Scotland Yard's Edward Henry, who had devised a classification system based on five pattern types and established the Fingerprint Office. Assistant Commissioner Melville Macnaghten from Scotland Yard's Criminal Investigation Department had a case with a thumbprint left on a cashbox in the dwelling where the thieves had murdered two people. Macnaghten established the value of fingerprint identification when he matched the thumbprint to a primary suspect (Beavan, 2001). Investigators in other countries paid attention. The fingerprint method soon replaced former approaches to identification.

During an appeal in 1911, the Illinois Supreme Court examined whether finger-print methods were sound. An intruder had entered Clarence Hiller's home and shot him. Thomas Jennings, armed and wearing bloodstained clothing, was apprehended. The cartridges from his revolver were like those found in Hiller's residence. Investigators said that four fingerprints left in fresh paint near a window used for the home invasion matched Jennings. A jury had convicted him of murder. In the appeal, Jennings' attorney was challenging the admissibility of fingerprint methodology. No U.S. court had yet set a standard for scientific evaluation. (This would occur a decade later, in 1923.) The appellate court set a precedent: the methodology was considered to be sound.

Figure 32. Fingerprinting items

Source: Katherine Ramsland

In 1915, the International Association of Identification (IAI) was founded. Nine years later, the FBI set up its national depository of fingerprint records, taking custody of over 800,000 fingerprint files from prisons. In 1975, the agency established a computer database, the Automated Fingerprint Identification System (AFIS). Nevertheless, fingerprint analysis has come under scrutiny, in part because it was used in court before scientific standards were established, and some standards have changed, as mentioned in Chapter 4.

Andy Kehm instructs the fingerprint workshop for local police departments in the Northeast Forensic Training Center. He is a retired Detective/Sergeant and Supervisor of the Bethlehem Police Department's Forensic Services Unit, the A.F.I.S./I.A.F.I.S. Operator/ Coordinator, and currently the chief deputy coroner in Pennsylvania's Lehigh County. He claims to enjoy the daily chaos of death investigations. He has completed multiple training courses in processing and reconstructing crime scenes, as well as in fingerprint comparison. He also learned on the job what to look for, how to process prints, and how to deal with the inevitable complications. Kehm has experimented with various powders and different surfaces, and understands the most common types of mistakes investigators can make.

In the classroom/lab is a U-shaped blue table with ten sinks, each of which has a curved, longneck faucet. In front of the table are long rows of plastic containers filled with supplies. Around the room, one can see microscopes, bowls, gloves, tape, scales, rags, and paper towels. A Sirchie® fingerprint chart hangs on a wall illustrating the standard patterns, and nearby is a chart that demonstrates how to do latent print processing. Yet nothing replaces hands-on training.

The workshop, intended for new officers, begins with the basics. The examination of fingerprints is known more technically as dactyloscopy and is based on the fact that the smooth, hairless surfaces of the hands and soles of the feet are covered with patterns of raised friction, or papillary, ridges. These patterns are considered so unique that they can serve for individual identification, because these skin friction ridges, formed in the inner layers of the dermis in a developing fetus, remain the same throughout life (short of intentional alteration).

Present on top of these ridges are miniscule sweat pores that exude perspiration, which combines with amino acids and adheres along the ridges. Electronic fingerprint systems that scan the fingers of a suspect and store the information digitally are now in use (FBI, n.d.), but knowing how to use fingerprint powders and lift cards is still important.

© Larysa Ray/Shutterstock.com

Figure 33. Fingerprints

To start, the fingers are numbered one through ten, starting from the right thumb. The left thumb is number 6. The fingerprints are coded on a ten-print card, along with descriptions of any extra, missing, or uniquely scarred fingers. If it is not possible to take a print of a specific finger or thumb, a notation is made about it in the block on the card for that print. The FBI methods list deformed fingers, missing fingers (due to injury that prevents recording a print), amputated fingers or tips, scarred fingertips, and those worn down from ageing or some type of work. "Milking the finger," which involves rubbing the fingers in a downward motion from palm to fingertip, can raise ridges that are worn or thin. Extra fingers, while described, are not recorded as prints (FBI, n.d.).

The recommended height for the fingerprinting device (ten-print cards or Live-Scan) is approximately thirty-nine inches from the floor, so as to capture the lower portion of the first joint and all of the ridge detail. The steps for rolling a print are as follows:

1. Fingers must be clean and dry. If necessary, wipe with an alcohol swab and then dry them. If fingerprinting roughened fingertips, or a mummified corpse, use lotion to soften them.

2. The subject should stand in front of and at a forearm's length from the finger-printing device.

3. To get the print, grasp the individual's right hand at the base of the thumb, and tuck the fingers under.

4. With ink-and-paper, roll the finger or thumb on an ink plate or pad. Make sure the entire fingerprint pattern area is evenly covered, from one edge of the nail to the other. The ink should be sufficient for a clear print that shows the patterns and can be photographed.

5. Place one side of the finger on the fingerprint card or device and steadily roll it toward the other side. Get an impression of the print from the tip to the first joint. Thumbs should be rolled toward and the fingers away from the center of the subject's body.

6. Follow this procedure with each finger and thumb.

At the bottom of the card or on the device, the subject's four right-hand fingers are pressed together at a 45-degree angle. Repeat this procedure for the left hand. Print both thumbs at the same time in the plain impression thumb blocks.

Prints left in readable mediums are called "visible" or patent prints; latent prints are invisible, except under certain alternative light conditions and with certain procedures, such as Superglue fuming; plastic prints are left in soft but pliable surfaces. Once the developed latent print is photographed and preserved, it can be used to try to identify its source. Generally, this means either comparing it with a specific suspect or entering it into a computerized database, such as AFIS.

To make a match, an unknown print is examined against prints that have been identified as belonging to a certain person. The examiner looks for unique minutiae for comparison, and on any given fingertip there can be as many as three hundred. Characteristics that make fingerprints unique are called minutiae, and identification via fingerprints relies on the detection of their patterns and a comparison of their relative positions on a reference print.

Initially, prints were developed primarily from nonporous surfaces using a soft brush with fine, gray-black dusting powder, a practice which is still used today. Kehm demonstrated this with basic black powder, although he also showed a variety of other colors. These colored powders were developed to contrast with surface colors, and some powders or dyes glow under alternative light sources. Fluorescent reagents, which react with amines from body secretions, yield fluorescent patterns, which can be useful on multi-colored surfaces. The method works best with fresh prints, before the oils dry. The excess powder is blown off, leaving a clear impression from the powder that adheres. The print can then be photographed, or lifted with a tape and placed onto a card.

Fingerprints must be stabilized, because they're fragile. Gloves should be worn for collecting this evidence. Chemical sprays allow technicians to lift fingerprints on surfaces as rough as semi-smooth bricks or as slick as vinyl. Since traditional powder techniques can potentially obliterate fingerprints and fail to pick up older prints, this technology is a significant improvement. The spray contains iodine-benzoflavone or ruthenium tetroxide as alternatives to dry powders, and can treat large areas much faster than powders can. It does not replace the powder, but it expands the type and quantity of surface that can be analyzed. These sprays require protective garments while lifting and special equipment for cleaning the crime scene afterward.

Kehm points out that factors to consider with fingerprints are their quality, their degree of pressure, the duration of time they have been on a surface, the type of surface, and the potential for pressure distortion. "If you have a unique item or surface," Kehm says, "practice on something similar, so as not to corrupt the surface with miscalculation" (personal interview, 2016). He also warns that one can over-powder a print and thereby smudge it beyond usefulness. "Powder adheres to fatty surfaces and to water," he says. "If your brush hits water, it will smear across the print." You can use fingerprints either for identification or for elimination (e.g., people who were legitimately at a scene).

For identification or comparison, Kehm describes three levels of friction ridge detail. Level 1 involves pattern types: fingerprint patterns can be divided into eight basic types, via specific features: Plain arches are ridges that run across the fingertip and curve upward in the middle, while tented arches show a spike. Loops, which flow inward and then recurve in the direction of origin, have a delta-shaped divergence and are either radial (toward the thumb) or ulnar (toward little finger). Whorls are oval formations, often making a spiral or circular pattern around a central point. Patterns that have two or more deltas will probably be a whorl. There are plain whorls, central pocket loop whorls, double loop whorls, and accidentals.

Level 2 involves the finer points in the configurations: bifurcations, dots, and ridge endings. Level 3 focuses on pores and ridge shapes. There are several basic ridge characteristics: the ending (dead-end with no connection), the bifurcation (forked ridge), and the island (enclosed ridges) or dot (isolated point), and these may form composites such as double bifurcations, ridge crossings, or bridges. These are used as the basis for comparison, and some areas of the print yield more points in a given space than others.

Examiners compare where the ridges start and end on a finger, where they split, and where they join, as well as where unique minutiae are located. An identification is made when the examiner decides that the degree of similarity between two prints is sufficient to conclude that the suspect print and the exemplar both came from the same person. Currently in the United States there is no established minimum of points of identification. "Point minimums," says Kehm, "are mostly viewed as a form of a quality control measure rather than standards. The four elements that must be met for an identification to occur are: a) latent fingerprint and a known impression, b) ridge formations, c) in sequence, d) having sufficient uniqueness." Some jurisdictions require a minimum of eight, some twelve, others more. An identification is more complex than just number of points of comparison: fewer points but more unique might be as good as many points. It takes only one dissimilar point to nix an identification.

With computerized systems, the analysis involves digital imagery. Against a database of millions, a computer compares an unknown print and selects a short list with closely matching coordinates. A human examiner performs the comparisons and potential final identification. No statistics exist on false fingerprint matches, but false matches have been made in some high profile cases. Three FBI examiners were certain that American attorney Brandon Mayfield had been part of a terrorist bombing of a train in Madrid in 2004 that killed 191 people. All were wrong (FBI, 2004).

"The error rate when following the Analysis, Comparison, Evaluation and Verification (ACE-V) methodology," says Kehm, "is zero." The best practice with ACE-V requires a minimum of a second examiner to verify an identification, and this procedure should be blind. "Keep an open mind," he says. "Be careful of bias. Get someone with no vested interest to verify, if possible."

Kehm gives advice about which fingerprint lift tape to use, as some work better than others. "It depends on surface convolutions," he says. Once the print is powdered and the powder carefully brushed off with a fiberglass brush, the investigator applies lift tape and places the print onto a special card for preservation. "Use a measurement device next to the print and use a marker to assign a number, or an arrow for orienting the latent fingerprint. The mid-range and close-up photos should be taken at a 90-degree angle. To avoid creasing, pull tape in continuous smooth motion to avoid crease. Use a credit card to smooth it into the index card, to remove air bubbles."

If a print is found on a dirty window, Kehm advises processing and lifting it twice. "This method will result in a lighter print, but it will be freer of dirt." Yet even prints of poor quality hold some value. "A poor print might still be swabbed for DNA," says Kehm. The most important thing, he adds, is to "document everything. It can all fall apart in court if you don't document correctly."

Shoes, Tires, Tools

Shoe and tire impressions can be visible, plastic, or latent. Latent impressions are difficult to spot, but they can be developed with powders or chemicals. For both, extensive and searchable make/model/manufacturer databases exist. Impressions require casting in plaster or dental stone, but they must first be measured and photographed, in case the casting process inadvertently damages some part of the pattern. The impressions might also be sprayed with a chemical fixative. In the presence of a series of prints at a scene, the distances between them must be measured, along with any apparent patterns (Suboch, 2016).

A special dam placed around a shoe or tire print keeps casting materials like dental stone contained. It should be mixed to a thick consistency and poured around the edges to let the material run on its own toward the center rather than poured directly onto the impression. It must set before being removed.

Figure 34. Shoeprint impression cast

Source: Katherine Ramsland

With tires, investigators look for the type and class, the manufacturer or seller, the type of vehicle that uses such tires, the direction of travel from the scene (possibly), whether more than one vehicle was involved or the vehicle has more than one type of tire, and characteristics unique to the manufacturing process. They will also document wear patterns/defects in a particular tire, as this could become crucial evidence.

Figure 35. Tire tread impression cast

Source: Katherine Ramsland

Print impressions are class evidence, which means they can identify a general source but not a specific one. Still, this can be narrowed down to where a specific brand was sold. If a shoe or tire is rare, it is also less generic. Wear patterns and other details individualize print characteristics, which make it easier to match a suspect shoe, once found. With shoeprints or footprints, investigators can learn how many potential suspects might be involved, whether they were walking or running, and possibly their point of entry and/or exit.

Weapons, too, can make impressions if they leave unusual patterns. Comparisons are made between impressions left on a body and some specific implement (e.g., a hammer, a fireplace poker). Most such wounds derive from blunt trauma, where there are contusions, lacerations, and abrasions. Making an actual match to a weapon, however, means finding one with blood, tissue, or hair attached, or some part of the weapon broken off at the scene. Unique tools are better evidence, such as a letter opener with a special symbol, laid in the victim's blood. Investigators might also found out if the implement penetrated bone and left a distinctive mark.

Tools are often used to pry open doors or windows, break locks, damage property, and open locked areas or safes. Single tool marks occur when the tool strikes once; multiple marks are the result of the tool being used several times in the same place. They might leave impressions on softer material or striations.

Unless they have a distinguishing feature, such as a chip in a blade, tool marks offer only class evidence. However, they can develop a wear pattern if used repeatedly. To make a comparison, the tool mark is microscopically compared against a suspected tool. The more points of similarity that show up, the greater is the consistency.

Blood Patterns

During the early morning hours of December 9, 2001, Michael Peterson called 9-1-1 from his Durham, North Carolina home. His wife Kathleen, he said, lay at the bottom of the steps. Paramedics found the forty-eight-year-old woman collapsed inside the well of a stairway, surrounded by walls covered in sprays of blood. She was deceased. An autopsy showed seven scalp lacerations on the back of the decedent's head, as well as facial bruises. The manner of death was blunt force trauma to the head, inconsistent with a fall. Peterson was arrested. Attorney David Rudolf hired a team of criminalists, including a blood spatter expert and a biomechanics engineer.

Oddly, Peterson was associated with another woman who had taken a fatal fall down some stairs in 1985. DA Jim Hardin, Jr. exhumed the body of Elizabeth Ratliff, a former friend of Peterson and his first wife. A maid had found her, but Peterson had walked her home the night before from a social gathering. Her death appeared to be from a stroke. The North Carolina pathologist who re-autopsied Ratliff concluded that blunt force had killed her.

At Peterson's trial, Hardin theorized that Peterson had battered his wife to death with a fireplace blow poke, in order to get insurance money to pay off debts. Later, Hardin changed the motive: Kathleen had discovered her husband's attempt to arrange a homosexual liaison and had fought with him.

The defense team claimed that Kathleen's head injuries and the blood spatter patterns were more consistent with a fall than a beating. A night of drinking had disabled her. She had climbed the stairs in flimsy sandals, blacked out from hypoxia, fallen and struck her head. As she tried to get up, she slipped in blood and hit her head again on the stairs. Some of the spatter was from coughing, wheezing, and shaking her blood-drenched hair.

At trial, this case came down to the blood spatter patterns. Key factors in the reconstruction were the amount and placement of over 4,000 spatters, along with skull lacerations. Also at issue was whether Peterson had failed to call for help immediately. His story failed to match some of the facts. Duane Deaver, a blood spatter expert from the North Carolina Bureau of Investigation, described his simulation experiments, showing from three patterns that Peterson had bludgeoned his wife: possible cast-off, blood found high on the door molding, and eight drops of blood inside Peterson's shorts. These items suggested that Peterson had been close to Kathleen when she was hit.

Dr. Jan Leetsma, a forensic neuropathologist for the defense, stated that the speed of the fall and the angle of the decedent's head could have caused the death. The skull lacked any fractures, so it was unlikely that a blow from a weapon had caused the injuries. Dr. Henry Lee (See Chapter 1) followed with a demonstration of how Kathleen's continuous coughing could have left the blood spatter on the wall. In addition, a blow poke used in a confined space should have left some telling damage.

Tim Palmbach, Director of the Forensic Science Program at the University of New Haven and instructor in the Henry Lee Institute of Forensic Science, was a criminalist on the defense team. He had worked for the Connecticut Department of Public Safety, retiring as a major in charge of the Division of Scientific Services, and has been an expert witness throughout the United States.

"Through several defense experts, a plausible theory of a death attributed to a fall down the stairs was established," he said (personal interview, 2004, 2016). "However, much of what transpired within that stairwell remained a mystery. We were there to show that the prosecution's team had not done a good job with their crime scene analysis and to show that the evidence was inconsistent with their narrative about the blow poke. Technically speaking, what we demonstrated should have worked for reasonable doubt. The blood was such a complicated series of patterns that it could only be explained by a complicated series of events. Because of what happened subsequent to the trial, this case has now become pivotal for the community of blood spatter pattern analysts in terms of what should be done scientifically.

"One of the main areas of the scene was the north wall, the bottom of the stairwell. That's where the vast majority of the spatter evidence was. I estimated there were some 14,000 blood droplets between one and three millimeters in size. Out of that number, approximately 4,000 were on that one wall. It had a mixture of blood stain patterns, contact transfer patterns, swipe patterns, void patterns, wipe patterns, spatter patterns, and even an overlay of what I believe was the luminol enhancement reagent, although they [the investigators] denied they used it there. So while you had all of this on one wall, their expert [Duane Deaver] attempted only a very limited reconstruction. He said, 'I'm going to take a small selection of drops from that wall, string them, project them, and show you what the two impact sites are.'

"But our point was that he had selected just thirty-seven out of 4,000 droplets. We wanted to know how he was confident that his selection was a representation of the entire picture. If more than three thousand and nine hundred droplets didn't coincide with that picture, why didn't this mean something? As we looked at the convoluted patterns of blood, the lack of correct type of cast-offs, the dynamics and limitations of the width of the stairwell, and their [the prosecution's] faulty theory of the forty-inch blow poke, it was unequivocally clear that there was no possible way that it happened as a blunt-force beating death."

Palmbach's team was able to demonstrate that the work done by Deaver had no scientific credibility. Yet on October 10, 2003, the jury convicted Michael Peterson of first-degree murder. He received life in prison without parole. The case was not over.

In August 2010, an investigation resulted in finding the prosecution's witness, Duane Deaver, guilty of fraud and poor work on at least 34 cases. Deaver was found to have grossly exaggerated his ability to analyze blood patterns and to conduct professional research. He claimed he had been involved in 500 cases of blood spatter pattern analysis and had investigated 15 cases involving accidental falls. In fact, he had investigated no cases involving falls and had been involved in only 54 cases involving blood spatter pattern analysis, generating just 36 reports. He had also shown bias in favor of the prosecution. Deaver was fired for falsifying his credentials and withholding information.

An independent audit determined that agents at the state crime lab had manipulated and withheld results from hundreds of tests that confirmed the presence of blood. Deaver was found to have repeatedly aided prosecutors in obtaining convictions and had misrepresented his credentials in at least 34 cases. The state's bloodstain unit was disbanded and placed under investigation (Rudolf, 2012).

On July 16, 2013, a North Carolina appeals court affirmed Peterson's appeal for a new trial, stating that Deaver was the state's central expert and had played "a determinative role" in the jury's conviction. However, a new trial would prove difficult, since the evidence had not been properly preserved and the prosecution's original experiments had no basis in science. To completely reconstruct the blow poke theory, given the lack of solid crime scene work years ago, will be difficult, if not impossible. The case stands as a good example of why blood spatter pattern analysis should establish scientific standards, train experts in them, and hold all experts accountable for the methods they use for interpretation.

Blood pattern analysis (BPA) requires specialized knowledge (Suboch, 2016). It is best for inexperienced investigators to leave this to experts, but all investigators should have a basic sense of how blood behaves on different surfaces and under diverse conditions. What follows is a simple overview, which should not replace hands-on expert training in this area.

BPA involves the use of the shape, distribution patterns, size, and location of bloodstains to explain physical events that caused them. Blood pattern analysis plays an important role in the reconstruction of many crime scenes, because the types of bloodstains indicate how blood was projected from a body (living or dead), according to several factors:

1. Type of injury
2. The order in which wounds were made
3. Whose blood (victim and suspect) is present
4. The type of weapon used
5. Whether and where the victim was moving during infliction of injury
6. Whether the victim was moved after infliction of injury
7. The relative location of the victim and suspect
8. The number of suspects
9. How far the blood drops fell before hitting a surface
10. Potential scene alteration

Human blood has physical properties that make it predictable when subjected to external forces. A lot of research has been performed in this area. Blood spatter can be traced back to its point of origin by considering such factors as the surface it hits, the angle, and the distance it traveled. This is often done with complicated trigonometry or software. Hence, there is a need for experienced investigators with training in this area. Those who arrive at a scene might be looking at passive patterns, back spatter, forward spatter, blood dripping into blood, spurt patterns, cast-off, flow, puddles, saturation into a surface, wipes, swipes, transfer, and possible cleanup. All must be photographed carefully and documented.

Figure 36. Blood patterns

Source: Katherine Ramsland

Bloodstain patterns help investigators understand the victim/suspect positions and movements. The proportions of the drops can reveal the energy that disbursed them. The shape of the stain can illustrate the direction in which it was traveling and the angle at which it struck a surface. Several stains in one area enable investigators to form a three-dimensional recreation of the area of origin, possibly using the stringing method to approximate the trajectory and locate convergence (Suboch, 2016; Wonder, 2001). A flexible rule of thumb for interpreting blood patterns on a generally smooth surface might include:

1. If blood falls about a foot at a 45-degree angle, the stain tends to be circular.
2. If drops fall straight down, the edges may be crenellated (star-shaped).
3. A height of six feet or more can produce small spurts.
4. If there are many drops but no large ones, impact happened.
5. If the source was in motion, the drops resemble exclamation marks. The smallest size blob shows the direction of motion.
6. Splashes with long tails come from blood flying through the air and hitting a surface at an angle of 30% or less.
7. Smears left by pressing a bleeding object against a surface leave a transfer pattern.

8. Trails may take the form of smears when a bleeding body is dragged, or droplets when someone wounded walks or is carried for some distance.

9. Cast-off patterns reveal the positioning and the possible size of the assailant, as well as whether he or she was right- or left-handed.

10. Arterial spurting can give the position, movement, and seriousness of the injury, while "shadows" – the absence of blood where one expects it – suggest movement or the removal of objects and possible staging of the scene.

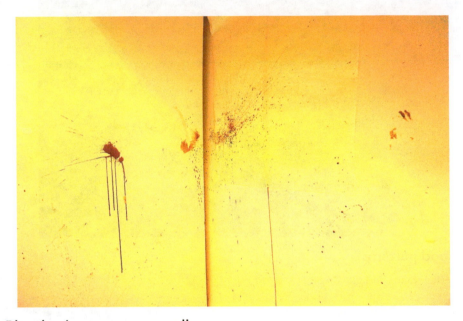

Figure 37. Bloodstain patterns on wall

Source: Katherine Ramsland

All investigators should take at least a basic course in blood spatter, but in-depth courses can run a full 40-hour week, and even go into advanced education, such as learning how to read bloodstains on fabrics, or how to photograph bloodstains under various conditions, inside and outside. This is an intricate skill, but not yet a science, and no investigator should make claims of certainty about bloodstain patterns. However, the consistency of how fluid in motion behaves provides credibility, if the investigator is versed in this area of physics. No one should overstate credentials, because oversight about claims made in court is now more vigilant.

Accrediting

The Forensic Science Education Programs Accreditation Commission (FEPAC) encourages universities that offer forensic science degrees to develop and implement pattern evidence degree programs for any and all areas of pattern interpretation. There has been a "paradigm shift" in the education and training of pattern evidence disciplines, due in part to the 2009 National Academy of Sciences (NAS) report described in Chapter 4. The report criticized many areas of forensic science, particularly the areas of pattern and impression evidence. The result is an increase in demand for research and education, especially in the scientific method.

"Forensic science examiners need additional training in the principles, practices, and contexts of scientific methodology," the report states, "as well as in the distinctive features of their specialty… It is crucially important to improve undergraduate and graduate forensic science programs. The legitimization of practices in the forensic science disciplines must be based on established scientific knowledge, principles, and practices, which are best learned through formal education. Apprenticeship has a secondary role" (p. 238).

Few programs dedicate courses to pattern evidence-based disciplines, so the many new examiners rely almost exclusively on knowledge passed down from examiner to examiner via on-the-job training. This means that the same perspective from which errors arise continues to be practiced. It also impedes innovation, because we often find the philosophy of "if it ain't broke, don't fix it" as a foundation of such mentoring. It can be daunting for new officers to try to improve on "tried-and-true" methods. Even when research fully supports a new or improved approach, minimal progress is made in moving the knowledge and technology out of the lab and into the field. Older officers often prefer experience and subjective analysis for making visual comparisons. See Chapter 2 for reasons why.

FEPAC encourages a change in this approach, posting the following statement on its website in 2016: "This change involves forensic professionals, educators, and researchers joining forces with physicists, engineers, and computer scientists to create and implement university curriculums in pattern evidence. Such a change will better prepare graduates for pattern evidence positions in the workplace as well as accelerate the evolution of the pattern evidence disciplines."

Summary

Pattern evidence interpretation looks deceptively simple. However, only intensive training and practice can make one an expert. Those who overstate their credentials undermine justice, get themselves into trouble, and sometimes have widespread negative consequences, including putting innocent people behind bars and letting guilty ones go free. A lot of evidence involves pattern analysis, and some disciplines are more advanced in their training and testing than others. All investigators will need to know about interpreting fingerprints, shoeprints, blood spatter, and tool marks. All are common to crime scene reconstruction, crime solving, and identification of victims and offenders.

Exercise #9.1

Bill Mowbray was found dead in his bed. He had been shot. He had an insurance payout of $1.8 million, which made his wife, Susie, a suspect. She claimed that he had been depressed over financial difficulties and had threatened to kill himself. He also had a past suicide attempt. A blood pattern expert testified at her trial that there was no blood spatter on his right hand or arm, as there would be if the wound was self-inflicted, and that blood spatter on her nightgown proved that she had been near her husband when he was shot. Nine years later, in 1998, she was acquitted at another trial, because prosecutors had suppressed blood interpretation evidence that contradicted the report they had used ("After 9 years," 1998). What other interpretation might there be?

Exercise #9.2

Concetta "Penney" Serra drove into a parking structure one morning. She did not know she was being followed. A man stabbed her repeatedly, and chased her as she ran. Penney died in a stairwell. She was barefoot. Her attacker left several clues: a thumbprint in blood on a Kleenex box; a 300-foot-long trail of blood; blood on the car door handle, gas pedal, carpet, steering shaft, tissue, tissue box, and driver's side floor, as well as on interior and exterior trim; a colored rag similar to those used by mechanics; and a blood-stained white envelope. Penney was found on level 10, but her car was on level 8 and her bloodstained keys were on level 7, along with a bloodstained white handkerchief that bore traces of car paint. Another blood trail was found going to level 5. A blood-stained ticket turned up with the parking attendant, who said he had taken it from a man with a foreign accent with an injured left hand. Several witnesses from levels 5, 6, and 8 had seen a thin man with long, dark hair chasing a young woman. Penney's blood was present in only the area where she had been stabbed in the stairwell. This incident occurred before DNA analysis was discovered. The case went cold.

What types of pattern evidence are available and how does each piece function in the investigation?

References

After 9 years in prison, woman is acquitted in husband's death. (1998, January 24). *New York Times.*

Beavan, C. (2001). *Fingerprints.* New York, NY: Hyperion.

Boyer, E. (1988, June 28). Paraplegic seized in '74 killing of woman. *The Los Angeles Times.*

Bross, D. (2015). Ex-FBI agent faults Fairbanks police interrogation tactics. *Alaska Public Media.* http://www.alaskapublic.org/2015/10/22/ex-fbi-agent-faults-fairbanks-police-interrogation-tactics/

Capuzzo, M. (2010). *The murder room: The heirs of Sherlock Holmes gather to solve the world's most perplexing cases.* New York, NY: Penguin.

Citron, A. (1988, January 8). Foul play suspected in death of woman whose skeleton was found. *The Los Angeles Times.*

Citron, A. (1988, April 23). Slain woman's identity pulled from a Venice of another era. *The Los Angeles Times.*

Federal Bureau of Investigation. (n.d.). Recording legible fingerprints. https://www.fbi.gov/about-us/cjis/fingerprints_biometrics/recording-legible-fingerprints

Federal Bureau of Identification. (2004). Statement on Brandon Mayfield case. https://archives
.fbi.gov/archives/news/pressrel/press-releases/statement-on-brandon-mayfield-case

Fingerprints lead to victim's identification. (2000, February 3). *Beloit Daily News.* http://www
.beloitdailynews.com/beloit-daily-news---thursday-february/article_08aecffe-b248-5f4c-
afb4-fb95810b87bd.html

Greenberg, M. (2014, November 25). 5 types of pattern evidence all investigators should know.
PoliceOne.com. https://www.policeone.com/investigations/articles/7835023-5-types-of-pattern-
evidence-all-investigators-should-know/

Greenwood, V. (2016, July). How science is putting a new face on crime solving. *National
Geographic.*

Halbur, D. (2014). Skeleton crew: How amateur sleuths are solving America's coldest cases.
New York: Simon & Schuster.

Keefe, P. R. (2016, August 22). The detectives who never forget a face. *The New Yorker.*

http://www.newyorker.com/magazine/2016/08/22/londons-super-recognizer-police-force

Lee, H. and R. E. Gaensslen. (2001). *Advances in fingerprint technology, 2nd Ed.* Boca Raton,
FL: CRC Press.

McDannel, M. (2016, January 3). False confessions and the lessons of the Fairbanks Four. *Alaska
Dispatch News.*

National Academy of Sciences, *Strengthening forensic science in the United States: A path forward*
(2009) https://www.ncjrs.gov/pdffiles1/nij/grants/228091.pdf.

Ramsland, K. (2002, February). Recomposer of the decomposed: Frank Bender. *Crime Library.*

Rudolf, J. (2012, May 14). North Carolina State Bureau of Investigation scandal grows with
new evidence of fraud. *Huffington Post.* http://www.huffingtonpost.com/2012/05/14/north-
carolina-state-bureau-of-investigation-duane-deaver_n_1516328.html

Spaun, N. (2016, Summer). Forensic face comparison training. *Evidence Technology,* 24–25.

Suboch, G. (2016). *Real-world crime scene investigation.* Boca Raton, FL: CRC Press.

Taylor, K. T. (2001). *Forensic art and illustration.* Boca Raton: FL: CRC Press.

Wonder, A. Y. (2001). *Blood dynamics.* San Diego, CA: Academic Press.

Chapter 10
Enhancements

Learning Objectives

❖ Discover how visual and audio enhancements assist investigations.
❖ Recognize the importance of handling enhancements carefully.
❖ Understand how enhancements can be manipulated.
❖ Learn the way hair and fiber analysis require enhancement.

Key Words

Acoustic analysis, audio enhancement, digital enhancement, hair analysis, fiber analysis

Dannie Ray Horner took sexual photos of kids to exchange with email pen pals. He ensured that his face was never in them, but his hands were another story. In three photos involving the sexual abuse of a one-year-old boy – a live victim that police could identify – someone's fingers were visible. Digital forensics experts in the Sarasota County Sheriff's Office's Intelligence Unit in Florida used the high-resolution digital images from a Samsung Galaxy Note 3 cellphone in 2015 to isolate the fingers and enhance the print details (digital enhancement). Metadata linked the prints to the camera. The AFIS Unit analyzed five images. Because Horner was an artist, his prints were stained with paint, which distinctly defined the ridges. One image of the left middle finger, inverted with Adobe Photoshop, was of sufficient quality to compare against Horner's prints. Two more images were matched to his left thumb. A second examiner independently verified these identifications.

The evidence was used at trial and seemed to play a significant role in helping to convict Horner. He was found guilty of 26 charges, including the possession and transmission of child pornography, molestation, and sexual battery. (McHenry & Gorn, 2016)

Forensic enhancement involves images, video, and audio that provide a real-time account of an incident. This includes surveillance videos, hidden cameras, smartphone cameras, tape recordings, and any other device that records sounds and images. Often, these artifacts are poor-to-medium quality, so experts can use software to repair, recover, and enhance them. The most common procedure is to clarify recordings or images to see small details or hear background.

To perform any enhancement described below, examiners first identify the portion they need by observing or listening. They first must grasp the big picture. They will make a working copy before doing any filtering, so that an original remains available and uncorrupted. They will change no recorded data, which means making careful enhancements.

The Scientific Working Group on Digital Evidence and the Scientific Working Group on Imaging Technology publish guidelines for best practice in each field to ensure quality and integrity. Investigators should consult these to see updates.

Images and Video

Investigators must follow special procedures with digital imaging, especially during enhancement, because the images and recordings must be a true and accurate copy of the subject being photographed or videotaped (Witzke, 2016). Digital cameras use a different technology from traditional film cameras, and someone skilled with photography software can easily alter it. Defense attorneys can successfully challenge testimony unless the investigator understands the processes of maintaining image integrity and the detection of alteration.

With digital photography, the JPEG Format Analysis algorithm uses information from meta-tags. They contain information about matrices, code tables, and other parameters. The tag content, availability, and sequence depend on the image and the device used to capture it. They also depend on the software. These tags show shooting conditions, ambient light levels, shutter settings, exposure compensation, and information about the camera. If a JPEG file has been edited and saved, certain compression artifacts appear. Maintaining the data in image files is required for all photos intended for use as evidence.

The investigators for the murder of Travis Alexander in Arizona in 2008 discovered a digital camera in the washing machine (Martinez, 2016). It had been put through a wash cycle, with bleach, but they were able to develop the time-stamped deleted images. Once these images were enhanced for detail, they could see that the killer, former girlfriend Jodi Arias, had inadvertently snapped three shots that implicated her. Her striped pants and foot were in one shot, and the person with the camera had then dragged the bleeding body down the hall. On this camera were several photos of Arias and Alexander in sexual poses and positions during that same afternoon. When he took a shower later that day, she attacked him with a knife and chased him down the hall, slitting his throat. She dragged him back to the bathroom and shot him in the head and stuffed him into the shower stall. The photos, along with other items, made a powerful case against Arias and she was convicted of first-degree murder.

Enhancement must be done carefully. Photos can be manipulated by changing exposure, using a specific lens, or taking a photograph from certain angles. The accuracy of every image depends on reliable image capture, so it becomes important to use the highest possible resolution. Low quality images cannot be improved even with the best software enhancements.

A common practice for alteration is cloning, or lifting part of an image to transplant to another area (e.g., to cover over something), or using software to remove or blur part of an image.

Figure 38. Cloned and enhanced photo; colors sharpened, dried peppers cloned to cover a fire extinguisher, and wall cloned to eliminate dark spots

Source: Katherine Ramsland

To detect this manipulation, an analyst identifies image blocks that have artificial qualities. (Even the naïve eye can sometimes spot them.) Fraud analysts implement algorithms based on a statistical analysis of the image information and they can readily detect most alterations of JPEG files. They might also examine the camera's grid of light sensors. Of the millions available, several are usually flawed, and these flaws produce a slight discoloration that repeats across photos. Patterns of unusual discolorations that show up in photos taken by the same camera should match. If not, this suggests an alteration. Digital images are also time-stamped.

Enhancing a video recording uses filters to adjust brightness and contrast, enhance color and detail, and reduce distortion. In addition, investigators might adjust the playback speed or stop it altogether in order to more fully view specific frames. Techniques include sharpening, stabilizing, masking, and isolating distinct images from multiplex systems.

Some systems have not switched over to digital recording, so investigators might learn from earlier cases. When Wanda Mason was shot to death in a convenience store in Lansing, MI, in 1998, the surveillance machine was a VCR, and the recording was unstable because the tape was old and had been used before. A blurred image of a dark-skinned man was seen, as well as an image of his car outside, but even when police had a suspect in Ronald Allen, they had trouble proving his ID with the tape. They turned to Veridian Corporation, which used mathematical algorithms for reconstructing images to make them viewable. It reduced background distortion in order to enhance just the essential data. Allen's mugshot was used for a photo skull superimposition to see if the shape of his skull was consistent with the images from the tape. It was. Along with ballistics evidence that proved his gun was the murder weapon, the enhancement helped to build a solid case (Video diary, 2001).

Audio

A 9-1-1 dispatcher listens to a woman tell him that her son just shot himself in the head. In the background, the tape picks up other voices. The woman gives her address and says that her son has been depressed because he's in debt and can't find a job. She ignores the dispatcher's request to see if her son is still breathing. By the time help arrives, the young man is dead.

Because the 9-1-1 caller was uncooperative on key items, the tape was analyzed with software. One voice was heard exclaiming that he did not shoot himself, and the other voice was from someone trying to quiet him. Sample recordings were available from the woman's son and her live-in boyfriend. The voice that insisted he did not shoot himself was consistent with the son's, and the other voice was consistent with the boyfriend's. This audio enhancement and comparison gave investigators solid evidence for further investigation.

The above example is from the discipline of "speaker recognition and identification." Speech or noise recognition expertise deals in acoustic evidence and involves training in linguistic analysis, human voice anatomy, phonetic distinctions, and even physics.

Post-World War II, senior Bell Labs employee Lawrence G. Kersta, a physicist, recognized that qualities unique to an individual's voice can be processed and charted on a visual graph. The size and shape of the vocal cavity, tongue, and nasal cavities contribute to the uniqueness, as well as how speakers coordinate their lips, tongue, and soft palate. Short of an accident or illness involving the vocal chords, these habits remain stable across the person's lifetime. Kersta's work led to the development of a sound spectrograph.

As a sound is produced, such as someone speaking, those harmonics nearest the vocal column's resonant frequency increase in amplitude. The spectrograph converts them into a graphic display, a voiceprint. Degrees of darkness within each region on the graph illustrate increased or decreased volume intensity.

For forensic purposes, comparisons are made between questioned samples, like the background voices on the 9-1-1 call, and known samples, such as the actual recordings of individuals suspected to be the source of the background voices (the son and boyfriend). When sufficient similarity exists, there is a high probability that the questioned and known samples originate from the same source.

When nine-year-old Jessica Knott disappeared in Altamonte, FL, an anonymous call came to 9-1-1 dispatchers directing them to the body. The girl had been strangled.

However, the payphone recording was full of static, so it provided no leads. A hair and fiber analyst used an FBI dog hair database to narrow fur removed from the body to a specific breed, a Shar-Pei. When Jessica's mother listened to the tape, she recalled a neighbor with a Shar-Pei talking to kids in the neighborhood. The techniques that NASA used to clean up communications from space were applied to the recording, removing enough background noise for a comparison when James Crow, Jr. was brought in. The probability of a match was around 90%. Crow initially said he was innocent, but an abundance of evidence pressured him to plead no contest and accept a sentence of 40 years (Stutzman, 1998).

Techniques for enhancement of audio include frequency equalization to make speech intelligible and compression, or reducing files, to boost faint sounds. Speech enhancement involves using a filter to eliminate interference, such as background noise, in order to clarify or amplify the questioned speech or sound. Background noises can then be isolated and subjected to the process of identification. If a suspect is developed, as with the call above, this person's voice can be recorded and compared to the questioned sample. The skills involved in aural and visual voice interpretation include critical and sensitive listening, an ability to check for tape tampering, experience reading magnetic tapes, and an ability to operate the spectrograph equipment.

To verify the authenticity of a recording, and check on potential alteration, examiners can listen for sudden shifts in background noise, tone or volume, or look for an unnatural waveform or fluctuations in electrical frequencies. If the recording medium is magnetic tape, the splicing mechanism is usually detectable by visual observation.

Besides voices, other types of sounds might also be key factors in a forensic investigation. Philip Van Praag and Robert Joling (2008) used acoustic analysis to find new evidence in the assassination of Senator Robert F. Kennedy on June 5, 1968, at the Ambassador Hotel in California. Known assassin Sirhan Sirhan did take several shots at Kennedy, but the new theory indicates that Sirhan had at least one accomplice and did not make the fatal wound.

Kennedy was hit four times. Three bullets entered his body, including one into his brain; one lodged in a shoulder pad on his suit. Five other people were wounded. Kennedy was taken to a hospital, where he died. Sirhan, a Palestinian refugee, admitted he had shot Kennedy for a political purpose. Yet Sirhan had been in front of Kennedy, while the autopsy indicated that the bullets had hit Kennedy from behind, at close range. Sirhan had only eight bullets in his revolver, but between wounded people and bullet holes in walls, more than eight bullets were discharged.

A journalist recording Kennedy's appearance captured the incident, so a tape was available for analysis, albeit from 1968. Joling and van Praag applied their analysis to this recording and claimed to have counted thirteen distinct shots. Two pairs of double shots occurred so close in time it was impossible for a single shooter to have gotten them off. Five shots had unusual frequency anomaly. This suggested more than one type of gun, pointed from a different angle. Although other sound engineers disputed this interpretation, none could explain how a man in front of Kennedy could have shot him from behind.

In a more recent controversial case in February 2012, a 9-1-1 call came in to a Florida dispatcher from George Zimmerman. He reported a young black man walking suspiciously through his neighborhood. He followed the stranger and got into a struggle, which ended with the young man, Trayvon Martin, shot dead. A voice was recorded during their altercation calling for help. Zimmerman claimed it was him, fighting for his life. Yet people who knew Martin said the voice was Martin. Various experts argued over this issue, with defense experts claiming that there was insufficient audio to make a definitive determination (Di Maio, 2016). In the end, the judge ruled that the prosecution's audio experts could not testify because their methods of comparing a screaming voice to normal voice were not provably reliable or based in science.

This did not stop news media from hiring experts to address the issue (George Zimmerman trial, 2013; Rogers, 2016). They came to differing conclusions. None listened independent of the context. Their inability to form a consensus only validated the judge's decision.

In the end, forensic pathologist Vincent Di Maio affirmed the evidence that Zimmerman had shot Martin at close range, which was consistent with Zimmerman's account of what had happened. The muzzle of Zimmerman's gun, Di Maio found, was pressed against the fabric of Martin's hoodie. The jury apparently accepted this version, as they acquitted Zimmerman (Di Maio, 2016).

Speech is a behavioral phenomenon. It requires interpretation. Speaker recognition seeks better footing as a science, because past methods have involved too much subjective analysis, even with a visual graph charted out. Although the spectrograph transformed voices into images, it remained up to examiners to declare the degree of similarity between questioned and known samples. Automated systems that measure frequency components of speech and eliminate subject bias are now being tested (Rogers, 2016). They have been used in banks for voice recognition, but these conditions are artificial. More tests are being designed to capture real-world conditions.

Speech analysts recognize that the same individual can sound quite different in different circumstances. They must focus on factors other than content, because bias toward a specific story ("Zimmerman is a trigger-happy racist" versus "Martin was an understandably threatening figure") can influence their interpretation. In addition, the method must be demonstrated to be suitable for its intended purpose (Schwartz, 2016).

To identify best practices, NIST has carried out Speaker Recognition Evaluations. The research community in audio forensics attempts to reproduce and perform validity testing on a variety of sources of variability in such things as recording process, noise levels, compression schemes, and audio coding. Extrinsic factors are associated with the recording and intrinsic factors with the speaker. To date, more effort has been expended on extrinsic than intrinsic factors (e.g., inebriation, illness, fatigue, and emotional arousal). Among the barriers for the latter is the difficulty of matching patterns between emotional states, as well as getting high quality recordings. At this time, the forensic community agrees that, given the difficulty of controlling for quality and comparison samples, more research is needed (Schwartz, 2016). The goal is to reduce the number of compromising factors.

Enhancement Use

Enhanced sounds or images can have a variety of purposes. They can be matched against real objects, such as faces, voices, or items of clothing, for example. They can undermine or corroborate a narrative. For example, a suspect claims that she drove in a specific direction, but the surveillance video undercuts her story. Or, a suspect can be identified.

Eleven-year-old Carlie Brucia was abducted from behind a car wash in 2004, and surveillance video caught the crime on tape. The suspect was an adult male wearing a short-sleeved dark gray work uniform and possibly driving a yellow Buick station wagon (recorded separately). Enhancement brought out the man's tattoos, nametag, unusual gait, and facial features. In an effort to identify this man and perhaps save the girl, the tape was made public. An acquaintance of the man, as well as several witnesses, pointed police toward Joseph Smith (Eckhart, 2004). A relative who told police that Smith had confessed to the rape and murder of the girl assisted them to find her body. It was too late to save her, but Smith was arrested and later convicted.

Given the increased presence of security cameras, traffic cameras, and people using cellphone recorders, it is possible that multiple mediums have recorded a specific event. The bombing of the Boston Marathon offers a good example. Investigators need to think of possibilities and gather all sources to compare from various angles before proceeding.

Hair and Fibers

Cross transfers of fiber often occur in cases in which there is person-to-person contact, and investigators hope that fiber that will be traceable back to the offender can be found at the crime scene, as well as vice versa. In the case above of Jessica Knott, hair from a dog and fibers from Crow's car and house helped to build a case against him. Success in solving the crime often hinges on the ability to narrow the sources for the type of fiber found. However, fibers are not unique, so they cannot pinpoint an offender in any definitive manner. Other factors must be involved, such as something unique that sets the fibers apart, such as a stain. Thus, microscopic enhancement might yield important individualizing characteristics. The same can be said for hair. Microscopic analysis can distinguish animal from human hair, and can even distinguish different breeds of dogs. However, an ability to make a match from hair strands to specific individuals has been overstated.

Natural fibers come from plants (cotton) or animals (wool). Synthetic fibers include rayon, acetate, and polyester, made from polymers. Generally, crime

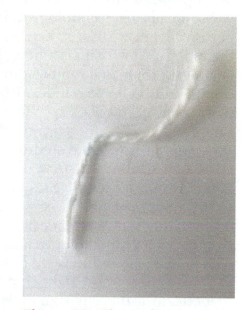

Figure 39. Fiber enhancement

Source: Katherine Ramsland

lab analysts receive a limited number of fibers from a scene or suspect. Those from a scene or victim can be structurally compared against fibers from a suspect or suspect source (vehicle or residence).

The type of enhancement will depend on the tool used. A compound microscope uses light reflected from the surface of a fiber and magnified through a series of lenses. A comparison microscope (two compound microscopes joined by an optical bridge) offers more precise identification. A phase-contrast microscope reveals a fiber's structure, and electron microscopes pass beams through samples to acquire a high-resolution magnification or reflect electrons off the sample's surface.

The first step in fiber analysis is to compare color and diameter. If there is agreement, then the analysis can analyze dyes with chromatography, which uses solvents to separate the chemical constituents. Under a microscope, the analyst looks for lengthwise striations or unique shapes on a fiber's surface. Only if the fibers can be individualized due to wear or some other effect are they valuable as unique evidence.

Hair specimens are also understood in forensic research as "class characteristic", unless the hair strands have been pulled out in such a way as to retain the skin tag that offers DNA. Although hair samples can be used to exclude a suspect, as with a Negroid hair excluding white perpetrators, they can only be considered as contributing evidence.

In homicide cases, hair is picked up at the scene and/or collected from suspects from several different parts of the body. Because different hair strands on the same person can show many variations, the larger the sample for analysis, the better. A sample of strands that have no DNA capability ranges from 20 to 50 pieces. Hair analysis can identify hair as human or animal, and can pinpoint characteristics of race. It can also determine if the hair has been dyed, cut in a certain way, or pulled out, and where on the body it grew.

Forensic hair analysis has been overstated for matches, as mentioned in Chapter 4, but it proves useful for other forensic purposes (Armitage & Rogers, 2016). The goal is to use sophisticated technology to infer characteristics that tell a story about an unknown person, victim or suspect. Keratin, the primary component of hair, contains amino acids, the ratio of which differs among individuals. Certain forensic techniques can develop a chemical profile that can be compared to databases for such items as age, sex, region of origin, and body mass index. Isotopic analysis of hair can offer clues about where the person has been over a specific period of time (based on hair growth). If water or soil samples that affect food growth differ significantly from one region to another, this can show up in the hair, as can drugs or poison ingested.

Robert Curley, 32, grew ill in August 1991, entering the hospital in Wilkes-Barre, Pennsylvania, for tests. He stayed just over a month before he died. After several attempts to diagnose his ailment, he was tested for heavy metal poisoning. Curley had elevated levels of thallium. His worksite was eliminated as the source, especially because the levels were so high the pathologist found that Curley had been deliberately poisoned. Curley's wife, Joann, showed elevated but not toxic levels.

Investigators asked the independent toxicology lab, National Medical Services, to perform a thorough analysis of Curley's tissues, especially his hair. The analysts conducted a segmental analysis with atomic absorption spectrophotometry on the hair shafts to devise a timeline of thallium exposure. They were able to plot more than 300 days prior to his death. They located periods of systematic ingestion, with a massive spike on this graph just before his death. Whenever he was away from home, according to biographical data, Curley's thallium levels dropped. They rose only while he was hospitalized, during a time when his wife visited. Investigators pressured Joann Curley. In 1997, she confessed to having killed her husband with rat poison to get his life insurance payout.

Summary

A variety of items might have to be enhanced during an investigation. Care should be taken to retain their integrity, especially with sophisticated techniques that could possibly change characteristics and elicit challenges from defense attorneys.

Exercise #10.1

A female model claimed that a photographer had posted nude "revenge photos" on the Internet, showing her posing in his car in various pornographic ways that depicted consent. The photos showed parts of the car dashboard and the woman. She admitted being in a rental car with him once, but had not posed at all on the day he claimed. He turned the 35-millimeter photos over to investigators, along with a consent form, signed by her. The film had been double-exposed and water damaged, so it was difficult to determine if these were the same photos. The photographer allowed them to search his office. They collected more photos of other models, a car rental form for the time period in question, and camera equipment.

What forensic procedures should they perform?

Exercise #10.2

When Skylar Neese went missing in July 2012, a neighborhood surveillance video showed a blurred image of the girl running toward a four-door silver sedan. She got in. Her behavior suggested that she knew who was picking her up. No enhancement showed the license plate number or helped with make and model. Some gossip from Skylar's friends suggested that she might have snuck out to go to a party. Police knew the likely location. They also knew that two of her closest friends had admitted to joy riding and dropping her off just before she disappeared. One of them drove a car similar to the video image, but she insisted that it was not her car. Still, their behavior was odd. One seemed quite nervous, the other stone-cold. They also gave conflicting stories.

What can investigators do next?

References

Armitage, H., & Rogers, N. (2016, March 11). How hair can reveal a history. *Science, 351*(6278), 1134.

Di Maio, V., & Franscell, R. (2016). *Morgue: A life in death.* New York, NY: St. Martin's Press.

Deutsch, G., & Valiente, A. (2014, July 16). From best friends to killers: Teens murder friend because 'they didn't like her.' ABC 20/20. http://abcnews.go.com/US/best-friends-killers-teens-murder-friend-didnt/story?id=24573749

Ekhart, R. (2004, February 7). Florida girl abducted in video is found dead. *New York Times.* http://www.nytimes.com/2004/02/07/us/florida-girl-abducted-video-found-dead-mechanic-with-criminal-record-charged.html?_r=0

George Zimmerman trial: Audio experts not allowed to testify on 911 calls, judge rules. Associated Press, June 22, 2013.

Joling, R., & Van Praag, P. (2008). *An open and shut case.* U. S.: JV & Co.

Martinez, J. (2016). *Conviction: The untold story of putting Jodi Arias behind bars.* New York, NY: William Morrow.

McHenry, J. & Gor, M. (2016, February). Fingerprint forensics. *Law and Order, 64*(2), 52–53.

Rogers, N. (2016, March 11). Whose voice is that? *Science, 351*(6278), 1140.

Schwartz, R. (2016, Spring). Your voice is evidence. *Evidence Technology Magazine,* 38–39.

Stutzman, R. (1998, June 6). Altamonte girl's killer gets deal. *Orlando Sentinel.*

Witzke, D. (2016, Spring). Making informed judgments using digital images. *Evidence Technology Magazine,* 6–8.

Video diary. (2001, January 9). *Forensic files* [television episode] 5(18). Medstar Television.

Chapter 11
Digital Investigations

Learning Objectives

- ❖ Learn how digital examiners handle devices and preserve digital evidence.
- ❖ Discover all potential sources for evidentiary data.
- ❖ Be able to describe how to recover digital data from various devices.
- ❖ Understand the requirements of a digital forensics lab set-up.
- ❖ Acquire information about crime mapping systems.

Key Words

Cloud forensics, crime mapping, digital forensics, encryption, Faraday bag, horizontal analysis, iOS system, steganography, streaming data, time of access

Dr. James Aune sent a text and then jumped to his death from a six-story parking garage on the morning of January 8, 2013. It came as a shock to many. Aune, a fifty-nine-year-old communications professor at A&M University in Texas, had a wife and two sons.

Digital forensics
Investigations involving digital data and devices.

Digital forensics solved the mystery and revealed a complicated back-story rooted in the fraud and fakery rampant on the Internet. It seems likely that if Aune had understood how he was being played, he might not have jumped.

The text message Aune sent said, "Killing myself now and you will be prosecuted for blackmail." He sent it to Daniel Duplaisir in Louisiana, a con man who had threatened to expose Aune to the university for having an explicit online relationship with Duplaisir's underage daughter.

Digital analysis pieced together the entire story. Aune believed he had met a girl online who was willing to send him graphic photos of herself. He did the same. Soon, her father (Duplaisir) intervened, telling Aune that he had damaged the girl and she needed money for therapy. In reality, Duplaisir had created a false profile with his daughter's photo on MocoSpace.com. He would send interested men, Aune among them, graphic photos. Acquiring their cellphone numbers, he would pose as an outraged father to extort money.

From the cash-strapped Aune, Duplaisir demanded $5,000. Aune gave him a partial payment. Duplaisir kept harassing him. If the money did not come, he said, he would get the police involved and also post Aune's nude photos on the Internet. He gave Aune three hours to pay. Aune elected instead to end his life.

Aune's wife had known that something was wrong and Aune had finally confessed to her about his sex addiction and the trouble he was in. She had seen through the plot and forbidden him from paying. But he had felt cornered. He could not bear the thought of professional shame.

Investigators arrested Duplaisir for extortion, using the digital evidence as proof. In November 2013, he was convicted and sentenced to a year in federal prison.

Digital evidence is information of probative value that is stored in digital form (Pollitt, 2006). It can be hidden in layers of information and is easily altered or corrupted. Nearly every crime today has a digital component. It might be found on a hard drive, a USB stick, a DVD or CD, or memory cards. It might be in records on a cellphone, GPS, tablet, or game system. Such evidence is often the key that develops a lead. In addition, digital evidence might be located on the "dark net" that people with special software and non-standard communication protocols can access, or within hidden apps.

As the world goes digital, offenders exploit weak security for easy access to data and to underground markets for illegal goods. Keeping up with digital crime involves constant training, increasingly sophisticated resources, and fully staffed labs. Digital forensics, a form of applied engineering, is no longer an afterthought, and enforcement is needed in both the public and private sectors. Today, digital forensics is a thriving discipline, with sophisticated databases and trained investigators. Still, even experts might overlook digital evidence in key sources. Devices grow more powerful every year, as well as more plentiful, with new methods of communication and storage. No area of forensics is evolving faster.

This chapter cannot cover all potential scenarios. It is offered as a quick guide for investigators who will handle digital devices.

Digital Basics

The first priority is to secure a scene and make it safe. Any device might be rigged to destroy evidence. Once a data source is secured, examiners can usually recover deleted data, decode encrypted files, and restore corrupted files, as well as determine which Web sites a person has visited to acquire information or make contacts.

If there is reason to believe a device has been part of a crime, it is important to preserve the evidence, but there must first be a legal basis for seizing the device (plain view, search warrant, or consent). The two primary dangers during evidence collection are data loss and data alteration. To be useful in court, the data cannot be changed.

Mobile workstation kits are available that hold specific tools for incident response. The tools used must be capable of collecting the needed data, *only* the needed data, and *all* of the needed data. In addition, the results they produce should be repeatable by other members of the same forensic community.

Officers should not try to access the device, because seizing and searching are two different processes, with different legal criteria. If the device is off, the officer should leave it off and take photos of its location and condition. If the device is on, officers should leave it on, unless they suspect remote access that could destroy evidence. If so, they should pull the plug or place the device in "airplane mode," which disables wireless connectivity. If the device does not have this mode, it can be placed in a Faraday bag or cage (a bag or case made of conductive material used to block electric fields).

Apple mobile devices, which run the iOS operating system, have their own protocols. Shutting down a device, especially an iOS device, locks encryption, stops background processes, and disables iCloud back-up (Zdziarski, 2014). These features cannot be re-enabled without a passcode. Also, the battery should not be allowed to drain. The device must maintain its authenticated state. Some tools offer live-capture of RAM. If the device is a computer, investigators should take a photo of the screen. They should follow proper shutdown procedures or go to battery power, taking care not to disturb possible fingerprints and DNA on the device and peripherals. Network hardware, such as a router, might point toward additional evidence. So might notes around a computer, offsite file storage, or removable media, such as CDs and thumb drives. (Thumb drives have many different forms; they can be quite small and some are hidden in items that look like toys.)

Figure 40. iPhone 6

Source: Katherine Ramsland

Apple uses strong encryption as a way to ensure its customers that their data is secure. Devices like iPhones are programmed to be wiped remotely via iCloud, and it can take just seconds to accomplish. (It is best to place an iPhone into airplane mode when seizing it.) iPhones and iPads contain the same processing components as a desktop: storage, memory units, and processing facilities. Data are stored on solid-state NAND chips, and the way data is moved around can result in dormant data that endures. Seizing an iPhone with the suspect's computer can help to gain access to the phone, but the two devices might sync, which must be avoided because it can destroy some evidence and add items that make searching for something specific much harder. The investigator can prevent the phone from turning off by going into Settings>General>Auto-Lock>Never. Because the device's memory is volatile, acquiring it should be done immediately with a reliable field acquisitions tool.

Data available on an iPhone can include many different items. Among them are encrypted passwords to websites, keyboard caches, screenshots of applications, deleted address book entries, browser history, Wi-Fi pairings, geo-locations of towers that show coordinates of where the device has been, text history, apps that hide other apps, voice-mails, and numbers for calls sent and received. It is hard for users to delete data alto-gether unless they know how to perform a complete wipe (Zdziarski, 2014).

Digital Data

Examiners should never work on original copies of evidence. It is usually necessary to duplicate a hard drive or create a forensic image, which preserves the integrity of the evidence. It can be imaged onto a dedicated forensic system, transferred to another com-puter, or imaged on the original system. The original evidence, which some examiners call a master copy, should be securely stored. If the media that holds suspected evidence is removable, the first option is best.

Stored as ones and zeroes, digital data is found in one of two forms: static (stored in a fairly permanent location, with an organizational system) or streaming (in motion from one device to another). Data communication protocols keep track of data being transferred. They contain the basic data, any addresses associated with it, and the transfer protocol (how it was created, stored, and manipulated). All changes to the data should be carefully documented. This includes the data recovery process, protocol deviations, and password changes.

Figure 41. Digital analysis device

Source: Katherine Ramsland

For those devices that cannot be imaged, some type of communication with the device must be established. This requires the use of proper tools. For iOS, sometimes Apple Backup systems or queries to "Siri" are used.

In older DOS computer systems, hard drives have multiple platters, or disks, for storing data, which are written in clusters. Large files might be broken up and spread around various clusters. Many newer computers are solid state, which means they have no moving mechanical components. They are more resistant to physical shocks and have less latency. Some web browsers create cache files, which also yield information to investigators with the right tools. They often show Internet searches, for example, or websites from which hacking tools were acquired (Stephenson 2003).

Performing an investigation requires a standardized process. However, as of this writing there is no set of international standards (Valjarevic & Venter, 2015), although models are being proposed. The FBI initiated a program, Automated Computer Examination System (ACES), for example, and the U. S. Department of Justice (2008) has published a guide for first responders that describes how to recognize and identify digital evidence, as well as how to handle, transport, and package it. There is also a basic section on examination and analysis.

Before any search commences on content, an evaluation must be made about whether privileged records are stored on the device (minister, attorney, psychiatrist, etc.). Specific investigative queries will depend on the alleged criminal context. Among them are unusual activity on accounts, how many people had access to the device, whether remote storage (such as cloud storage) is used, and how the device connects to the Internet. The most recent time of access should also be determined.

Criminals hide data with encryption (scrambling) or steganography (planted inside larger innocuous files, such as photos). This data can be used as direct or corroborative evidence. Some operate their computer remotely, so care must be taken to secure any device in which remote control is suspected. Evidence must be gathered within legal parameters and the anticipated cost should be in proportion to the incident. Federal Rules of Evidence apply, as do stipulations from *Frye* and *Daubert*, depending on the jurisdiction. For court, the tools used to gather the data must be probative and accepted as standard by the forensic informatics community; they must also be capable of producing replicable results, and the results must be relevant to the issue under consideration. The evidence should also make a positive impact on the outcome. Pre-planning is key, because mishandling can ruin the evidence irreparably. Thus, it is important to define the information system architecture and implement the appropriate procedures.

Digital Analysis

Examiners must determine what operating systems are present and define their goals. They look for the file storage system and the data itself. With dynamic data, such as Internet communications, original packets are collected from streams.

They must then be reassembled in proper order. The primary task is to identify the relevant data and separate it from the rest (which can be considerable). Examiners should formally document the plan, along with the rationale for a search and the choice of methodology. There should be a clear sequence for the tools chosen to recover the data, good reasons for selecting the relevant items, and a clear mechanism for matching keywords or codes. There should also be a plan for review and feedback.

Seizures might involve a single hard drive or an entire network of linked computers and devices. Once data are acquired, examiners decide which software to use for examination. The tools needed for analysis include a device for recovering intelligence, appropriate software for storage and analysis, nonmagnetic hand tools, proper cables, signal-blocking evidence bags, external hard drives, storage CDs and DVDs, write blockers, adapters, inventory logs, and a secure lab.

By 2000, commercial software had become available for forensic examiners. Among the software used today are EnCase, Cellebrite, X-Ways, and Forensic Toolkit. Open-source software is also available, giving free access to anyone with knowledge of how to use it. Among them are Autopsy, Helix, Paladin, and SANS Investigative Forensics Toolkit (SIFT). The National Institute of Science and Technology initiated validation testing on the software, while established digital labs began to achieve accredited status. Such software is used for disk imaging, data recovery, remote access, password recovery, restoring deleted files, and searching and sorting.

Examiners evaluate all data for probative value and then export forensically relevant results for preservation, reconstruction, and presentation. In our information-saturated society, this can be a time-consuming task.

Analysis involves not just looking at gathered information, but also performing a case comparison with similar cases (called a "horizontal analysis"). This can help to locate other experts who might assist with more complex cases. In addition, the analyst who gains experience might become a useful consultant to others. Networking is not just for computers; it is also for examiners.

The digital forensics laboratory must be sealed against outside wireless input. Different stations within this area are set up for duplicating hard drives and for examining different types of equipment. There must also be procedures for backing up data and for securely storing devices, especially those that hold evidence for a court case. Examiners must also have access to a separate stand-alone network.

As per the information from Chapter 2, all examiners must be careful to maintain context and not cherry-pick to support an investigative hypothesis. They should clearly document their plan, so they can demonstrate the process to other investigators, attorneys, or in court. To be admissible, computer data must be handled with proper protocol, with the information gathering method and chain of custody invulnerable to challenge. As a final step, examiners must be able to communicate the process and results to an attorney and possibly to a jury of lay people. Thus, they must understand what they are doing and be able to explain it in simple, objective terms.

Setting up a Digital Lab

In 2006, Detective David Petzold was killed while correcting a traffic hazard. A foundation in his name funded a laboratory for digital forensics. Detective Joe Pochron, Petzold's coworker in Pennsylvania's Lehigh County, saw demand growing for the investigation of digital crimes. They needed a local resource. However, there was little space in township offices. Pochron managed the entire workload with a single computer on a small desk. To find a better solution, he worked with the district attorney and a local university to set up the David M. Petzold Lab and he became its first director.

Lehigh County formed a Computer Crimes Task Force, which included ten officers from different police departments. First, however, the lab had to be designed and equipped.

Figure 42. Petzold Digital lab

Source: Katherine Ramsland

"I had to consider many different things," Pochron said, "and I grouped them under five basic concerns."

1. Security for evidence storage;
2. Cost of acquiring and updating the necessary tools, which included planning several years into the future and funding a forensic network;
3. Policy and procedure protocols, because a forensic lab on a university campus would have a unique set of circumstances;
4. Coordination of the county's information technology system with the campus information technology system (including distance education concerns); and
5. Lab maintenance and cleaning, which required supervising university staff.

The David M. Petzold Digital Forensics Laboratory opened on March 24, 2011, and was hailed as a state-of-the art hub for countywide digital forensics investigations. Within weeks, it was inundated with requests for processing computers, cell phones, global positioning systems, video game systems, security camera video, and other digital items.

"Digital forensics requires constant education and training," says Pochron. "The learning curve is so steep because it's constantly evolving. If you step out for two months, you'd be out of touch. It has so many sub disciplines. We're talking mobile devices, computers, video, audio, pieces of hardware, and file system techniques. There's a level of knowledge required for each area, but the hardware and software are constantly changing. For us, it's not just the *current* Windows or Apple operating system. We must also work with many older versions that people still use."

Besides the lab's scope, focus, storage, and security concerns, it is also important to decide how the lab will extract, export, and convert different types of data (Champagne, 2016). Although email files are not as much of an issue for criminal investigations as in the civil arena, the ability to export results to specific file types remains important.

Pochron cites the Casey Anthony digital testimony as "our OJ Simpson case." By this, he means that in the case, there was very public mishandling of evidence, which might have allowed a guilty person to go free.

As stated in Chapter 4, Casey Anthony was tried in 2011 for the murder of her infant daughter, Caylee Marie, in Florida in 2008. Prosecutors in this case had asked the Sheriff's Office to produce an Internet history of the HP computer from the Anthony home for June 16, 2008. They believed that Anthony was going to take the stand and claim that her frantic father had awakened her that morning while looking for the missing Caylee. The prosecutors believed that computer records would undermine her story, so they requested Internet history and user activity.

In response, lead sheriff's investigator Yuri Melich sent a spreadsheet that contained a small slice – less than 2 percent – of the computer's activity that day. They relied on only what the Internet Explorer (IE) browser offered, but in March Anthony had switched to the Mozilla Firefox browser. The spreadsheet included seventeen vague entries from the IE browser history and failed to list 1,247 entries from Firefox browser, including a search for "foolproof suffication" [sic]. Thus, prosecutors were unaware of more than 98 percent of the browser history records. To say the least, their timeline was incomplete.

Investigators did know that Anthony preferred Firefox, but they had trouble decoding it, sheriff's officials said. In 2008, in a deleted section of the Firefox records, they had found searches from March 2008 for "how to make chloroform," "neck breaking," and "death," but since no one had asked for a search on "suffocation," such records were never extracted as evidence.

Yet the defense expert had found them. Defense attorney Jose Baez would later write that he had braced for the prosecutor to sandbag him with the "suffication" search, but it never happened. Baez did not know until after the examiner's testimony that the evidence analysis had been poorly handled. A thorough search should have picked up the fact that Casey Anthony had logged in with her screen name just before the search for "suffication." She was provably the only one in the house at the time.

The sheriff's computer examiners had other problems as well. The times associated with the chloroform searches in March 9, 2008 were off by an hour, because the software they had used had not accounted for the change to daylight savings time. Also, the sheriff's independent computer consultant inaccurately testified that the browser had made 84 visits one day to a page that showed a recipe for making chloroform. The defense countered that this was inaccurate.

In the aftermath, analysts have explained the search issues. The software, NetAnalysis, was initially used to examine the data, which was later verified with a different tool, Cacheback. According to the trial testimony, the examiner had wanted the output to reflect the local time, so he had tried the second tool. When Cacheback failed to recover any records, he requested help from the developer, who corrected the issue. The software subsequently recovered 8,557 records.

Defense experts indicated that there were significant discrepancies between the tools. They asserted that the first tool was correct, but the second was not. Contrary to the incriminating notion of repetitive searches for a website about making chloroform, there was, in fact, just one Google search for the word.

This type of error in a high-profile case was bad for the field of digital forensics, which had posed as a technology so standardized that it was on the level of science.

"People were so impressed by the power of digital forensics to find these computer searches that seemed incriminating," says Pochron, "but then it turned out to be wrong. The [prosecution's] examiners not only misstated the number of searches, but they also missed Mozilla Firefox searches that were actually credible."

The Petzold Lab did a better job with a case close to home. Jamie Silvonek was 14 and her boyfriend, Caleb Barnes, was 20 when he allegedly stabbed Jamie's mother, Cheryl, to death in her car, buried the body, and shoved the car into a pond. The two were arrested and their cell phones confiscated for analysis. Jamie said she did not know where her mother was, but a series of text messages made it clear that she had wanted her parents dead. She seemed to have resented her mother's attempts to end her relationship with Caleb.

There was a hearing to decide whether Silvonek should be tried as a juvenile or an adult. A psychologist who spoke with her described her as a young girl in love, which had warped her sense of reality. Then, in February 2016, Silvonek accepted a plea deal that got her a sentence of 35 years to life in prison. "I'm a monster," she stated (Schroeder, 2016). She added she had been under no one's influence. "There's no mitigating factors. I wasn't under any influence." (Her sentence is currently under appeal.) The couple had discussed the murder for a week, which the text messages affirmed. Without the digital evidence, it would have been more difficult to prove that she had fully participated in the murder plan. Caleb Barnes was convicted in 2016 of first-degree murder.

Mobile Device Forensics

Many investigations involve searching through a mobile device for evidence. This category includes cellphones, game systems, tablets, MP3 players, and e-readers. Smartphone and digital tablet use now exceeds computer use. The advantage is that phones are generally personal, with single users who store information about themselves on their phones. Among possible evidentiary items, besides phone calls, are text messages, emails, Internet searches, videos, social media site visits, and photos. The phone can also show locations where and when it has been used, via a GPS. In some cases, a phone might be the sole source of evidence.

Figure 43. Mobile devices

Source: Katherine Ramsland

Tools are available that allow investigators to retrieve raw image files by accessing the device's internal memory. One tool will not cover all devices, not even for the same brand of phone, because there are different models. The tools might be able to extract only a fraction of the data actually on the device. Investigators must learn the limitations of the tools they select, as well as know about other tools that will surmount these limitations.

Acquiring the data is only part of the task. Investigators must also be able to carve and decipher data, including deleted data, times and dates associated with the data, and location information. Then they must convert the files into a readable format. They must know how file systems store data. This generally means undergoing training specific to various systems (with vendor-neutral courses being the best choice). Officers should also look for courses that offer "deep dive analysis" capabilities – how to manually carve and analyze files. Only if they know how to handle the data and explain the analysis will they be qualified as experts for court. At the very least, investigators need to know how best to handle a device while securing and delivering it to those with greater expertise in the lab (Mahalik, 2014).

Joe Walsh is a senior security consultant for an information security company where he is responsible for conducting forensic examinations of digital evidence, responding to computer security incidents, conducting security assessments, and performing penetration testing. Before moving to the private sector, he was a detective with the Criminal Investigation Division of the Delaware County District Attorney's Office in Pennsylvania.

As a member of the Internet Crimes Against Children (ICAC) task force and the Federal Bureau of Investigation Child Exploitation task force, he was responsible for conducting online undercover investigations and forensic examinations of digital evidence. He is recognized in court as an expert in these fields.

Walsh has received specialized training in JTAG and chip-off forensics (advanced methods of accessing data on electronic devices that are locked, physically damaged, or not supported by traditional forensic solutions). Walsh also holds several certifications, including the ISC(2) Certified Information Systems Security Professional (CISSP), CompTIA Advanced Security Practitioner (CASP), CompTIA Security+, EC-Council Certified Ethical Hacker (CEH), EnCase Certified Examiner (EnCE), and ISFCE Certified Computer Examiner (CCE).

Walsh cites Portio Research Ltd., which predicts there will be 8.5 billion mobile subscriptions by the end of 2016. Smartphones are portable computers. They can store so much data that many households now dispense with a desktop or laptop computer. "There are unique challenges involved in mobile forensics that are not usually involved in computer forensics," Walsh points out. "We find many different types of hardware and a large number of mobile operating systems, some with unique security features. We see many different manufacturers that have proprietary operating systems. This poses unique challenges for the digital examiner."

As with computers, there are several steps in mobile forensics: seizing, acquisition of data, and examination with analysis. Examiners must determine the make, model, and IMEI, MEID, or serial number, and define their goals. With mobile devices, they might locate data in the device, on a memory card, in the cloud, or in the cellular provider's records. The same evidence could be stored simultaneously on several devices (phone, computer, tablet).

Examiners must also be aware of intangible evidence. "This can be just as valuable as tangible evidence," says Walsh, "and sometimes more so." This might be found in email messages, social network profiles and communications, and cloud storage.

The type of data sought determines the type of analysis, as seen above in the Casey Anthony investigation. "This includes the call history," said Walsh, "an address book, email, web browsing history, social media activity, videos, and photos."

When faced with a locked device, examiners might forget the easiest way to access them: "Ask for the password," Walsh advises. Or it might be possible to see the suspect's fingerprint patterns when tapping in their passcode or swiping an unlock pattern. Apple devices, for example, have a 4-digit or 6-digit passcode. Repeated unlocking can leave a visible trace. In addition, even if the phone is locked, examiners "might be able to locate evidence on the microSD card." If they need to ascertain the phone's ownership, they might get useful fingerprints off the device.

Public Interest vs. Private

The FBI faced a situation with a cellphone after a mass murder incident on December 2, 2015. Syed Farook and his wife, Tashfeen Malik, launched an assault on the Inland Regional Center in San Bernardino, California. Fourteen people were fatally shot and twenty-two were wounded. As the tragic day unfolded, information revealed that the couple had a religious agenda. This had been a terrorist attack, possibly intended as the first of several, but the couple died in gunfire with police before they could escape (Lee, 2016).

The FBI collected items, including cellphones and computers. One was a locked iPhone made by the Apple Corporation. This posed a challenge. When Apple had introduced encryption into its iOS8 system, the company itself could no longer access locked iPhones that used this system. This was an intentional choice, so as to avoid ethical dilemmas.

The FBI asked Apple to provide a back door into the phone and to help with data analysis. Apple CEO Tim Cook provided information within legal limits and offered engineers to advise on the analysis. However, the FBI sought physical access to the phone's inner system, so Apple balked. This created an impasse.

In essence, the FBI wanted Apple to alter a System Information File (SIF), the software that runs the device. The FBI wanted a new SIF put on Farook's phone to prevent the phone from erasing itself, to automate the process for trying out passcodes, to remove the barrier that pops up when entering wrong passcodes, and to control the process without knowing how a solution was achieved. That is, no one in the FBI would possess information about the Apple system that could be released to the public. The SIF should work only on Farook's phone and only Apple would know how it was done.

Cook said that the FBI wanted Apple to reengineer its own system, to allow agents to bypass security features on a single recovered iPhone. Cook insisted that software of this nature would be able to unlock any other iPhones with a similar iOS, which would be an invasion of privacy. Even if the FBI agreed to this one-time use, there was no guarantee that it would comply, or that such requests would stop with a situation like this. Other law enforcement agencies also have iPhones associated with serious crimes to which they want similar access. Hence, broader implications had to be fully considered.

"You can't have a back door that's only for the good guys," Cook said (although Apple previously had offered such assistance).

However, some analysts say that one could introduce jailbreaking software to Farook's phone without weakening general iPhone security. To jailbreak, one forcibly removes restrictions within the software and puts new software in place. Apple could comply with the FBI's request with a customized iOS without dire consequences. It would be better, some said, to raise the restrictions on search warrants. Otherwise, Apple is put in the position of indirectly protecting a murderer and terrorist. Apple claimed it would be a burden to comply, and the Department of Justice viewed this response as a diversion.

Finally, the FBI hired a professional hacker to crack the phone. The effort was successful. The implication was that Apple had a software flaw, which allowed the hacker to create a piece of hardware that could get into the 4-digit security code without danger of erasing the phone's contents. This is a precedent-setting case in which a corporation challenged legal jurisdiction (Heisler, 2016).

Integrated Systems

Crime mapping is one of the most important technological advances in law enforcement today. It requires special software and a solid training plan. Visual data helps to see when and where crimes occur in specific geographical locations, especially those in clusters. Police departments gain a better grasp of how to allocate such resources as uniformed patrol officers or undercover surveillance units. Crime mapping software also generates important crime statistics for analysis and comparison with other jurisdictions and over defined time frames.

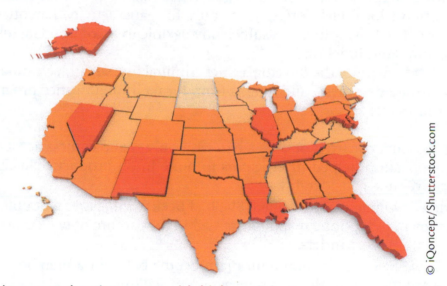

© iQoncept/Shutterstock.com

Figure 44. Crime map showing states with highest violent crime rates shaded dark; lowest shaded light

Crime is rising in smaller jurisdictions and local agencies must meet new challenges. District Attorney James B. Martin wanted to give his citizens the best investigative, tactical, and analytical tools. This meant developing an accessible and intuitive consolidated information hub.

The Lehigh County Regional Intelligence and Investigation Center (RIIC), governed by the Office of the District Attorney, serves agencies in Pennsylvania's Lehigh County. Conceived in 2006 after viewing methods and results at the Real Time Crime Center in New York City, the RIIC was launched in Lehigh County in 2013. This system quickly helped to solve a homicide.

The RIIC's secure collaborative online portal brings together county detectives and criminal intelligence analysts with a state-of-the-art information system to provide complex crime data analysis for investigative support. It offers a team workspace and 24/7 self-service to over 500 users. The RIIC can proactively identify leads, display crime patterns in graphs and charts, and analyze trends across the region.

"We have a chief criminal investigator and a part-time county detective," says director Julia Kocis (personal interview, 2016). "If the analysts need help, they're our consultants. The chief investigator also acts as a liaison between us and different police departments. We have a good rapport with the area detectives, but there can be an invisible wall at times between law enforcement and the civilian staff, so having an investigator who understands our mission can help to keep lines of communication open."

Primary data derives from public, police, and prison records from seventeen jurisdictions, the DA's office, and the county jail. The RIIC system also networks with the state police intelligence center (PaCIC) and the Pennsylvania Justice Network (JNET). The system integrates and analyzes this data for local, state, federal, and national intelligence, and provides a tactical search tool. Each agency also retains a separate space. Specialized databases support local task forces, specifically for gang activity, narcotics, auto theft, and sex crimes. The RIIC software is sufficiently flexible to accommodate future developments in features and functions.

The RIIC staff includes the director, a chief criminal investigator, criminal intelligence analysts, part-time detectives, and interns from local criminal justice programs. Among its success stories are:

- A gang shooting occurred outside a bar, with only vague witness accounts. The RIIC search application helped investigators to hone in on productive leads that cut the investigative time considerably.

- A murdered woman was identified. She had been a witness to a double homicide in another town. Cell phone mapping assisted in the capture of two suspects, who were charged with three murders.

- An extensive analysis of communication records between a man and his estranged wife assisted to support the wife's allegation of stalking.

- A Craigslist encounter that led to homicide offered cellphone data from both parties that showed routes traveled and documented conversations that supported a set-up by the person supposedly selling a car.

"We want investigators who haven't yet used the system to know how much time we can save them," says Kocis. "It can be considerable. We provide an intuitive interface, and we can train them here in our office or at their site. If they feel intimidated about the analysis, we can perform it for them. We give refresher trainings and update departments on new software. The chief decides who gets access to our search applications, because they're intended primarily for investigators and whoever needs the analytics. However, patrol officers have access to the daily blotter. In the future, we hope to open up more ways for patrol to use the resources."

They also hope to integrate more closely with the county digital lab, to develop applications using the cellphone data that they extract. "We want to store pieces in a database, so investigators can search information by name, phone number, search warrant number, or whatever they need. We're still walking through the legalities, in terms of privacy, e.g., how long we can keep this data in the system. So we need to work out data retention cycles and craft a clear policy.

"We also want to include data on human trafficking. For example, we want to keep track of the languages that victims speak, so we'll be able to get the translators we need. In addition, we want to gather information about the mental health and medical resources the victims might need. We can then work closely with area hospitals to coordinate assistance. We want to do more with Homeland Security. We hope to include more agencies and disciplines in the future in a coordinated effort."

Summary

The digital world is the new arena of crime and crime tracking. Digital evidence is information of probative value stored or transmitted in digital form. Digital forensics is the methodology for retrieving, preserving, and interpreting this data on various storage and transmittal devices. Procedures are becoming standardized even as methods are evolving to keep up with new developments in digital technology. This field will only grow, because Internet resources and new technologies offer new opportunities for criminals to look for victims and exploit vulnerabilities.

Exercise #11.1

Numerous homes had been burglarized after being listed on a popular Internet real estate site. Many were vacant. Copper pipes were removed. The owner of a scrap yard informed a state trooper that a man and woman were bringing copper to him on a regular basis. He provided a description of a vehicle driven by the female, along with the license plate number. This led police directly to a young woman, whose car contained a receipt for a scrap sale and a GPS unit, along with some copper piping and cutting tools. From the apartment of her male accomplice, police seized a cellphone and a laptop containing numerous addresses.

The GPS, laptop, and cellphone were taken to a digital forensics lab for processing. The unit recordings indicated that the car had been in the immediate area where burglaries had occurred. It turned out that over a six-month period, this couple had stolen copper and brass materials, which they sold at several local scrap yards. The total amount of stolen items and damage to the properties was over $200,000 from 75 homes in four counties.

What aspect of their MO would be useful in court as digital evidence?

Exercise #11.2

Sharon Guthrie seemed happy about a forthcoming wedding for one of her two daughters when she was found in her bathtub on May 14, 1999, having drowned. Four prescription pills were found in her system, one of which, Temazepam, was prescribed for her husband, Bill. The condition of the Temazepam pills indicated that she had taken them during the early morning hours. Bill thought his wife might have taken these pills accidentally while sleepwalking. The cause of death was listed as a Temazepam overdose.

When it turned out that Bill had a secret mistress and had filled his prescription at two different pharmacies the day before his wife died, investigators decided to check further. They also realized that Bill said he had dragged Sharon from the tub, and yet his clothing was dry. He said he had just come in from work, yet he wore no socks or shoes. Bill used a computer, so they looked through his email. He had recently searched for Temazepam, bathtub accidents, and sleeping pills.

When suspicion fell on Bill, he produced a typed, unsigned suicide note from Sharon that he said had been hidden in a liturgy book in the church. He said he had given it to his attorney in June but had not mentioned this to anyone. He told a daughter that he had told Sharon he wanted a divorce the night before she died, but Bill told investigators that he and his wife were getting along fine. The note was dated May 13, 1999 and addressed to a daughter, Suzanne: "I am sorry I ruined your wedding. Your dad told me about your concerns of my Interfering with Jenalu's and the possibility I might ruin hers. I won't be there, so Put your mind at ease. You will understand after the wedding is done. I love you all Mom." The note was not found on Bill's or the church's computer, but later, investigators learned about Bill's second computer. This one showed evidence that the note had been written on it in August 1999, although in parts, with some items taken from sermons. A second note was also found on the hard drive, dated August 11, with Sharon as the author. "I'm upset that you have had an affair and have not come clean with me," it stated, "I have thought of ending my life and you would have to face up to it. Believe me I known how to do it." Under questioning, Guthrie admitted he wrote it as a way to work through the emotional trauma of Sharon's death.

1. What aspects of this case raise red flags?
2. What else besides a computer search could investigators have done to gain evidence?

References

Casey, E. (2004). *Digital evidence and computer crime: Forensic science, computers and the Internet.* 2nd Ed. San Diego, CA: Academic Press.

Champagne, A. (2016, Spring). Planning a digital forensics lab. *Evidence Technology Magazine,* 16–19.

Cummings, R. (2008). Computer forensics. *Evidence Technology Magazine.*

Dubois, R. (March 27, 2013). The strange and sordid end of an A&M professor. *Texas Monthly.*

Heisler, Y. (2016, March 12). DOJ warns that it could compel Apple to turn over iOS source code. http://bgr.com/2016/03/13/apple-vs-fbi-compel-ios-source-code/

Lee, D. (2016, February 18). Apple vs. the FBI: A plain English guide. *BBC News.*

Mahalik, H. (2014, February 19). Achieving advanced smartphone and mobile device forensics. *Forensic Magazine.*

Marcella, A. & Menendez, D. (2008). *Cyber forensics: A field manual for collecting, examining and preserving evidence of computer crimes.* 2nd Ed. Boca Raton, FL: CRC Press.

National Institute of Justice. (2008). Electronic crime scene investigation: A guide for first responders. Washington, DC: U. S. Department of Justice. www.nij.gov/pubs-sum/199408.htm

Pollitt, M. (2006). Digital forensics. In C. H. Wecht & J. T. Rago (Eds.) *Forensic Science and Law: Investigative Applications in Criminal, Civil, and Family Justice* (pp. 495–503) Boca Raton, FL: CRC Press.

Schroeder, L. M. (2016, February 13). Jamie Silvonek: I was a monster. *Morning Call.*

State v. Guthrie. 21388 http://caselaw.findlaw.com/sd-supreme-court/1085831.html

Stephenson, P. (2003). Investigation of computer-related crime. In Stuart James and Jon Nordby, *Forensic science: An introduction to scientific and investigative techniques.* Boca Raton, FL: CRC Press. Pp. 469–486.

Valjarevic, A. & Venter, H. S. (2015). A comprehensive and harmonized digital forensic investigation process model. *Journal of Forensic Science,* 60(6): 1467–1487.

Zdziarski, J. (2014). Identifying back doors, attack points, and surveillance mechanisms in iOS devices. *Digital Investigation, 11*(1), 3–19. doi:10.1016/j.diin.2014.01.001

Chapter 12
Special Investigations

In 2005, a young man was found dead in the garage of his house in Italy. The body lay in a supine position near the front bumper of a car, wearing several layers of clothing. Blood covered the face and alcohol seeped from the mouth. It did not take investigators long to recognize that this person had been mentally unstable. He had covered the walls of the house with writing and drawings. One drawing was the head of Christ, with a thorny crown; another was a replica of Edvard Munch's "The Scream."

One passage described the death of a woman three years earlier and directed whoever found the note to a silicone-sealed wardrobe in a room on an upper floor. Inside was a female corpse in a sitting position. Although an ID card identified the man in the garage, DNA had to be collected and analyzed for the woman in the closet. Comparing this with DNA done on the man showed that the woman had been his mother.

Interviews with neighbors failed to turn up any reports that suggested overt mental illness. The woman's husband had died in 1997, so she and her son had moved to this house. They kept to themselves, aside from his regular trips to get the woman's pension check and prescription.

An autopsy on the man turned up no wounds, but coffee grounds in vomit were on his face and in his hair. A toxicological analysis found medications in his blood that corresponded with those found in the house. The mechanism of death was acute cardiac failure caused by gastric hemorrhage, which came about from an overdose of alcohol and psychotropic drugs. No traumatic injuries were found on the mummified woman. Toxicology picked up no evidence of drugs or poison.

To this point, the typical methods of investigation had been used, but a central mystery remained: what had happened here? The case resolution turned on behavioral analysis, specifically interpreting the writing on the walls. The principal question was whether the son had killed his mother or she had died naturally.

One wall text appeared to have been written in grief over the mother's death and in loving memory of her. "I absolutely couldn't accept that she wasn't there any more." Although this man was 33 when his mother died, he described his fear of growing up and living on his own. "Hence I decided to stay in this womb." He had taken care of the body, choosing clothes and making the decision to hide her in the closet – her "shrine" – so he would not have to face her decay. This way, nothing would separate them and he could speak to her daily.

The second text listed instructions, which suggested that he expected to die and wanted to ensure that his mother's remains were found and handled carefully. "My body, if the devil will catch me, will be in the room above the one of my mother." He mentioned earlier failed suicide attempts and ended with religious language and the belief that he would see Jesus.

The investigation used a "narratological analysis" of the wall writings. The first one showed the male decedent's inability to complete the developmental process into adulthood. Dependent on his mother, he could not accept her death. His subsequent writings showed depression, guilt, indignity and a sense of ruin, as his living conditions deteriorated. He had continued to live on his mother's pension, even after her death. He had also filled her medication prescription, which he had used more than once to try to overdose. He had used prayer as a rite of exorcism.

Although this man did fit the profile of an unstable son who might kill his mother, a full psychological autopsy supported a finding of natural death for the mother and a psychic collapse leading to suicide for the son. The case presented an opportunity for experts to describe the importance of a complex multidisciplinary approach for making sense of the scenario. Mummification had thwarted certain medico-legal procedures, but research from other cases helped. A psychological autopsy and narrative analysis, along with knowledge about psychological disorders, assisted in the ultimate case disposition (Ventura et al., 2013).

For investigators, the lesson is to focus on what appears to be a dead-end or where questions arise that might be answered with outside expertise. Then locate the necessary experts. For example, in 1992, the murder of Denise Johnson in Arizona seemed to have little useful evidence. She had been strangled, bound, and left near a cluster of palo verde trees. Although a pager belonging to Earl Bogan lay nearby, he had an alibi. His son, Mark, did not. However, Mark said he and Johnson had consensual sex before he dropped her off. She had stolen his father's pager. Mark's truck was seized, but investigators found no evidence that Johnson had been inside. However, they did discover scars on a palo verde tree near where Johnson had been found, and palo verde pods in the back of Mark's truck. This seemed too coincidental. Still, these items were class evidence at best.

Investigators discussed the case with a professor of molecular genetics, Dr. Timothy Helentjaris, to find out if the pods could be tested for DNA. Helentjaris used randomly amplified polymorphic DNA (RAPD) to compare the pods against trees in the general area and was able to match the pods from the truck to a specific tree – the one near Johnson' body that also bore a gash the same height of the truck's back bumper. The evidence suggested that Mark Bogan had murdered Johnson, inadvertently dropped the pager, backed his truck into the tree, and left Johnson lying there. He was convicted of first-degree murder, upheld on appeal (*Arizona v. Bogan*, 1995).

More recently, police asked computer science professor and biometrics expert Anil Jain at Michigan State University to assist them with a dilemma. A man was murdered and investigators believed that clues that could help them with a lead to a suspect were stored on the victim's phone. However, it was locked and needed fingerprint ID or a passcode. Police had a scan of the decedent's fingerprints from a prior arrest, which they gave to Jain. The lab recreated all ten digits as 3D replicas and then covered the plastic in a thin layer of metallic particles to ease scanner reading. Because it remains an open case, Jain could not provide details of what happened, but this is a good example of officers thinking outside the box to seek assistance from experts, who were cooperative (Eveleth, 2016). Jain stated, "We do it for the fun." Whether this collaboration will become a battle for the courts is another issue.

Besides approaching experts who might offer assistance, some cases also involve research and ingenuity. This is especially true for those investigators, whether officially on a police force or working privately, who take on cases that have long gone cold (cold cases). Solvability factors often hinge on available resources, as well as on a full victimology.

Arson Investigation

Two-year-old Cynthia Collins died in a fire on June 30, 1986, in her Ohio apartment. Her mother, Hope, was spending the night with her boyfriend. The fire spread quickly, killing the girl with smoke. Hope claimed she had left Cynthia in the care of a friend, Kenneth Richey. He denied any agreement to babysit and Hope had mentioned no babysitter to investigators. The state's fire marshal suspected arson. Richey was charged with arson, child endangerment, and the aggravated murder of Cynthia Collins. His alleged motive was that he was angry at a former girlfriend, who lived just below Hope's apartment.

Forensic analysis was conducted on an area of the apartment's carpet. Analysts said it had "pour patterns" and evidence of paint thinner. The smoke detectors had been manually disconnected and Richey allegedly had muttered to someone that the building "was going to burn." A witness said she heard Richey brag that he had set the fire. Richey had been diagnosed with a mental disorder and had a record of deception and immature behavior.

The prosecutor offered a plea deal of second-degree murder, which Richey refused. He faced a capital charge and possible death sentence. Based on the evidence, the jury convicted him. He went to death row.

After two decades, as the "science" of arson investigation was questioned, the evidence in Richey's case was reexamined. A new investigation turned up information that the evidentiary carpet piece had sat unprotected near a gas pump, and the gas chromatography used in the analysis had not been subjected to peer review. The defense expert was not qualified to refute the findings, and another expert found that the "pour patterns" were not patterns at all. The prosecution had also failed to recognize that fires often melt the frames of smoke detectors, so it could not be determined that they had been purposely dismantled. In addition, a thorough victimology would have found the child's history of fire starting in documents at the local fire company. Richey agreed to plead no contest in 2007 and was freed (Death row, 2012).

Figure 45. Arson exercise

Source: Katherine Ramsland

Arson is the willful or malicious burning of property for some improper or illegal purpose. Making a determination of arson must be based on trained expertise (Geberth, 2015). If the rate of burn is inconsistent with the type of combustibles, this can be suspicious. Also suspicious is the presence of a body, when further examination shows the person did not die in the fire. The arson investigator might see multiple points of the fire's origin, or no apparent cause, or might notice the odor of an accelerant. To complicate matters, the investigative procedures that some have labeled a science fall far short of these standards (Grann, 2009).

Arson investigators look for the cause of a fire, aware that arson is often committed for insurance fraud, thrill, revenge, or to conceal something like a robbery or murder.

They also know that many arsonists like to watch their handiwork and the way it affects others. All fires leave clues about the heat source that started them, and it is up to the interpreter to be knowledgeable about evidence collection and analysis. Accelerants generally start those fires that burn very hot, and they are used to spread a fire more rapidly than it would spread on its own. The most common are ignitable liquids like paint thinner, gasoline, and kerosene. Often, they leave a telltale odor.

These guidelines are general, not exact. Fire burns upward and outward, so the "seat" of a fire is most often found at its lowest point where damage is done. Since fires need fuel, investigators look for the source. Different fires have different appearances. Cooking oil, for example, causes a yellow flame with brownish smoke. Gasoline can have a yellow or white flame with dark smoke that looks black. Phosphorus has white smoke and flame, while burning wood and fabrics show reddish-yellow flames and gray or brown smoke.

Some fire patterns are predictable, so an arson scene can be reconstructed. An inverted "v" pattern points to a seat at the apex of the V, and the depth of charring shows the point of intensity. Hot spots on walls and floors cause spalling – chipping and splintering. Wood beams or floors tend to carbonize into a pattern that resembles alligator skin.

The collection of fire evidence requires sealable metal cans. For analysis, charred material might be placed into a glass flask with a few drops of carbon disulfide, which goes through a gas chromatograph for elemental analysis. The added solvent has a known peak on the graph, so any other manifestations indicate a substance to consider as an accelerant. Comparison samples, if available, should be put through analysis first, to separate out such items as fire retardant often placed on carpets, carpet treatment chemicals, and even the carpet's glue backing. Accelerants might be a petroleum distillate (kerosene, gasoline) or nonpetroleum accelerant, such as turpentine or alcohol.

Due to the number of past convictions based on arson analysis that have been questioned and found to be lacking in scientific methods, arson investigation and claims made from it must be undertaken with extreme caution (Grann, 2009).

Cold Case Investigations

On December 19, 1959, an intruder murdered Christine and Cliff Walker in their modest home in Osprey, FL, along with their two children, Jimmy, 3, and Debbie, 2. The family had been out shopping, with separate cars, and Christine had come home first, alone. Someone punched her, raped her, and shot her twice with a .22-caliber gun. As Cliff and the kids arrived half an hour later, Cliff and Jimmy were fatally shot at the door's threshold. Debbie was shot in the head, nonfatally, and drowned in the bathtub. A friend found this shocking massacre the following morning (Keglovits, McCrary, & Ramsland, 2013).

The physical evidence consisted of semen from the rape, .22 bullet casings, a bloody cowboy boot print, and a partial print (finger, thumb, or palm) on a bathroom faucet. In a shed a mile away, investigators found items of bloody clothing later linked to Cliff and Christine. The Walkers' framed marriage certificate, which had been hanging in the

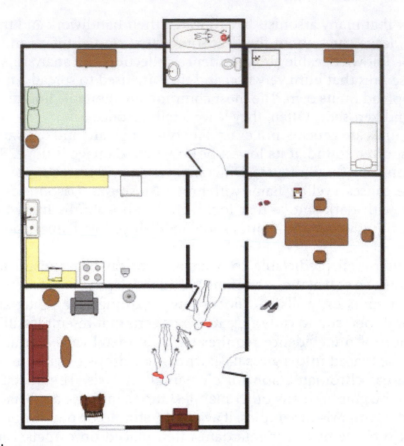

Figure 46. Walker scene

Source: Katherine Ramsland

living room, was missing, along with Christine's majorette uniform from high school, removed from a storage trunk.

Victimology at the time suggested that the crime was personal, aimed at Christine and possibly her daughter. When Christine came home, she had parked away from her usual spot, suggesting that a car was already there. She went into the house, which suggested she knew the person and was not afraid. The items taken from the house, and the treatment of the victims, pointed toward someone who was fixated on Christine and angry at Cliff.

In 2012, a Florida detective decided that two infamous drifters who had been in Florida at the time were responsible: Perry Smith and Dick Hickock, who had slaughtered the Herbert Clutter family in Holcomb, Kansas, the month before. Their tale became the basis for Truman Capote's famous narrative, *In Cold Blood*.

The detective's theory started with the suspects and inspired a double exhumation, which yielded no results. However, she might have spared her jurisdiction the expense had she started with a victimology.

This approach involves placing the victims along a risk continuum, from low to high, before even discussing whom they encountered prior to death. Investigators would

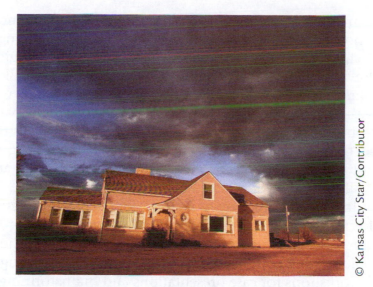

Figure 47. Clutter house in Kansas

conduct a comprehensive evaluation of the situational variables to determine what aspect of the victims' circumstances elevated their vulnerability to fatal assault. These variables are compared against datasets of known risk factors, such as volatile relationships, drug use, financial problems, and risky activities. The first task for victimology is to eliminate relatives, intimate partners, and known associates with grudges (as investigators attempted to do in 1959). The next phase includes focusing on neighbors, and distant associates and relatives. Last is the investigation of strangers. In addition, there might be links to similar crimes in the general area.

The original investigators for the Walker case were convinced that someone who knew the couple had killed them. Their home was isolated and they owned so little they would not have attracted burglars. There were rumors of Christine having an affair, so the treatment of the daughter should also be evaluated. It takes time to fill a bathtub, and she was a little girl. What was the point of drowning her? One theory held that the killer ran out of bullets, but this does not explain why he didn't just use the gun butt to bludgeon her. Instead, he (or they) focused on her for a longer death process. Christine, too, had been raped.

Numerous suspects were eliminated at the time with polygraphs, but some left town before they were thoroughly investigated. In 1963, for example, a rumor held that Christine was having an affair with her high school boyfriend, Curtis McCall, a man prone to angry outbursts who owned a .22-caliber gun. His polygraph was inconclusive and a later DNA test did not exclude him. In addition, there was a neighbor with whom Cliff had had an altercation. This man had no alibi and there is no information about a DNA analysis.

In cold case investigation, costs must be weighed against the probability of success, which depends on solvability factors. Among the best solvability factors are whether victims have been identified, informants still exist, reports and evidence are available, new techniques can be applied to evidence, witnesses are still alive, and new investigative leads have been noted. The detective could have exhumed the daughter to see if she was Cliff's child. This would have been less expensive and more logical. No behavioral links or physical evidence associated Smith and Hickock to the Walker case (Keglovits, McCrary, & Ramsland, 2013). Even the supposed eyewitness reports were tainted.

Cold case investigations should be selected for reinvestigation based on a hierarchy of solvability factors. Because the evidence in the Walker case is weak, the DNA degraded, and the expense considerable, best practices required examining the best suspects first. Relying on gut feelings risked cognitive distortion – being so attached to specific information that all other data is adjusted toward it (Stelfox & Pease, 2005).

The American Investigative Society of Cold Cases (AISOCC) offers a free, nonbiased evaluation of cold cases by an interdisciplinary team of experienced professionals (Mains, 2016). Kenneth L. Mains founded the organization in 2013 after he became stuck on an unsolved double homicide in Pennsylvania of a mother and daughter. The AISOCC staff runs annual workshops for case presentations and brainstorming. The investigative team looks at police reports, reading and re-reading, consulting with one another, and pondering what the victim was doing prior to the death. They make a list of leads, determine case solvability factors, and offer a report to the inquiring agency.

Cold case protocols involve more analysis of resources than a normal investigation does. Vergano (2014) reported on 189 cold cases that were examined from the Washington, D.C. area. The purpose was to identify solvability factors and decide what works best for prioritizing resources. The researchers found that cold cases had the best chance of getting solved when there were new witnesses or new information from prior witnesses (such as an ex-boyfriend who had been covering for his then-girlfriend). Cases also had a better chance if there was new physical evidence. Factors that gave the investigation a poor chance were victims from a lower economic status, especially if they used drugs or engaged in prostitution. Better factors included gang membership, a murder that had a clear motive, and investigations that included actions that had not been tried before. Among the worst factors was running an investigation only because the family had pressured for it to be done.

A significant problem with starting an investigation with suspects, as with the Walker homicides described above, is the mental tendency toward cherry picking through the facts to make them fit. Also, confirmation bias, described in Chapter 2, influences how investigators interpret evidence.

At AISOCC's annual conference, a retired NCIS Agent, Joe Kennedy, described lessons he had learned from cold case investigation and offered a list of steps to take. Among them, and coupled with those that Mains advocates, are the following activities:

1. Ensure that evidence has been properly preserved and is available
2. Ensure that all reports are available
3. Contact original investigators and visit scenes, if possible
4. Keep current investigators in the loop
5. Keep files organized

6. Perform a new victimology to brainstorm new approaches
7. List holes and inconsistencies
8. Use public awareness avenues
9. Determine if there exists new technology that might assist
10. Re-interview still-living witnesses – especially if there are changes in their circumstances
11. Put evidence through current databases, if possible and appropriate
12. Weigh solvability factors against costs
13. Consider offering a reward for new information
14. Be aware of assumptions and bias.
15. Use all possible resources, including those not routinely available.

Cold case units are able to spend time and look at various angles, trying out different hypotheses and reconstructions. Investigator tenacity is one of the key factors in solving cold cases, as are changes in former relationships. People break up and get angry, loyalties erode, and people think of something they hadn't before. "I want to know that case like the back of my hand," says Mains. "I want to know what that victim would most likely do given certain circumstances" (2016, p. 9).

Summary

Sometimes investigations have unique factors that require special teams, expertise, or technology. New and unique approaches are developed on a regular basis, and more experts who are not generally within a forensic context seek ways to collaborate. They will often initiate an approach, which means that investigators need to keep an open mind and welcome assistance. Investigators should use all means at their disposal, if costs allow and the chances of success look likely.

Exercise #12.1

Sergeant Jason Moran hoped to identify the John Does from a case dating back to the 1970s. John Wayne Gacy was a notorious serial killer who stored the bodies of at least 28 of his victims in a crawl space beneath his house. Many were identified, with the help of forensic anthropologists and forensic artists, but eight are still waiting for their names.
    What would you suggest for Sgt. Moran?

Exercise #12.2

In 2016, the news media reported that an aging abandoned white horse had been shot more than 100 times with paintballs, as evidenced from the multi-color spots of paint along its neck and sides. People were outraged, calling for the perpetrators to be found and punished for extreme animal cruelty. The horse appeared to be sore in areas where paint patches appeared. Several weeks went by, and a celebrity stepped forward to rescue the horse. At the same time, the horse's former owner said that the media had it all wrong. Doreen Weston said the horse, whose name was Lily, had not been abused. Weston had sold Lily to the auction house, expecting that, due to her numerous medical problems, she would be euthanized. The paint was not from paintballs. It was from finger-painting parties in which children were allowed to paint on Lily, who seemed to enjoy the attention. Weston submitted medical records, communications with a vet, and photos of a finger-painting party. The celebrity who took the horse (which died within months) said that abuse was evident.

What kinds of special resources could help to support one vs. the other side to this story?

References

Death row Scot Kenny Richey admits threatening judge. (2012, April 12). *BBC News*, http://www.bbc.co.uk/news/uk-scotland-17712756

Eveleth, R. (2016, July 21). Police ask this 3D printing lab to recreate a dead man's fingers to unlock his phone. *Fusion*. http://fusion.net/story/327145/3d-print-dead-mans-fingers-to-unlock-his-phone/

Geberth, V. J. (2015). *Practical homicide investigation: Tactics, procedures and forensic techniques*, 5th ed. Boca Raton, FL: CRC Press.

Grann, D. (2009, September 7). Trial by fire: Did Texas execute an innocent man? *The New Yorker*.

Keglovits, S., McCrary, G., & Ramsland, K. (2013, Summer). Solvability and risk factors: A cold case investigation. *The Forensic Examiner*, pp. 17–21.

Mains, K. L. (2016). *Solving the unsolved*. American Investigative Society of Cold Cases.

Stelfox, P., & Pease, K. (2005). Cognition and detection: Reluctant bedfellows? In M.Smith & N. Tilley (Eds.), *Crime science: New approaches to preventing and detecting crime* (pp.194–210). Cullompton, UK: Willan Publishing.

Ventura, F., Fortunato, F., Pizzorno, E., Mazzone, S., Verde, A., & Rocca, G. (2013). The need for an interdisciplinary approach in forensic sciences: Perspectives from a peculiar case of mummification. *Journal of Forensic Sciences*, 58(3), 831–36.

State of Arizona v. Mark Bogan. (1995) April 11). 183 Ariz 507.

Vergano, D. (2014, March 7). Solving cold cases depends on new witnesses, not DNA. *National Geographic.* http://news.nationalgeographic.com/news/2014/03/140306-cold-cases-murder-csi-forensic-science/

Answers to Chapter Exercises

CHAPTER 1

Exercise 1.1

Incident 1. The chief suspect is released, so the investigation begins anew. The man's strange behavior (even the happy face signature), coincidental resemblance, and confession, while compelling, do not outweigh DNA. It would be important to remind yourself that just because the logic and some evidence seemed to support the arrest, this does not make a case.

Nine years later, a rape case in a neighboring state with similar features turned up a new suspect, who also resembled the composite drawing. Kaye did not identify him as her attacker and the fingerprints did not match, but the DNA did. Kaye was stunned. When the first man was let go, she had worked up the courage to go kill him herself. And she had been wrong. Crime scene logic could have convicted the first man, but the second man was the perpetrator. He had lived in the same complex as Kaye and he had a son.

Incident 2. The investigative team first researched the symbolism of the white buffalo, so they could understand the response of the Native American community. They speculated whether the killer was trying to receive spiritual power by killing the calf.

However, conflicting details between Arby's version and his wife's alerted investigators to potential fraud. They brought a veterinarian to the scene and discovered that the hooves were not missing and a lot of the pelt was also intact. The vet was unable to determine a clear cause of death. The place where the calf's body was found had matted hair in several places, as if it had gotten up and lain down several times. Despite Arby's claim, there were no wounds on the mother's body. It turned out that Arby had failed to vaccinate the herd against a bacterial disease called black leg. Other buffalo in the area had died from it.

Arby said he could name seven suspects, but he provided only four. None panned out. When he failed to pay his bills, it turned out that the reward fund was actually his wife's personal bank account.

Ultimately, it seemed that the calf had died from natural causes and Arby had created a narrative that would enrich him and give him status, as well as save face. In the process, he had misused law enforcement resources and committed financial fraud. He had also lied about his ancestry.

It is clear from this incident how important it is to question other people to learn about possible inconsistencies in someone's story. Also, consider what someone gains from claiming that something is a crime, financially and in other ways. In addition, watch for deflections from a thorough investigation or any attempts to hide or distort information.

CHAPTER 2

Exercise 2.2

The plot of a popular Sherlock Holmes story, "Silver Blaze," relies on a hole: the absence of something that should be present. A valuable racehorse has been stolen and its trainer murdered. Holmes mentions "the curious incident of the dog in the night." The dog had done nothing. Its silence suggests that the person who entered was familiar. This narrowed the pool of suspects. So, what was missing in the case of the hanged wife?

When the crime unit processed the bathroom in the alleged suicide, the tub was dry. Although Valerie's hair was damp, there was no evidence that the shower had been running. This inconsistency launched further investigation, which turned up evidence of a troubled marriage. When police identified and interviewed the person to whom Valerie was talking on the phone, this woman said Valerie had been in good spirits. When investigators confronted Joseph with the inconsistencies, he confessed to accidentally killing Valerie during an argument. Her hair was damp because she had just showered.

CHAPTER 3

Exercise 3.1

The detectives in the case of Peter and Greg did not investigate for suicide. They decided that this incident could only have been a homicide. The analysts fired the gun using human blood and calves' livers to replicate the bloodstains on Greg's T-shirt and found consistency from two feet away. They also tossed the gun several times to see if the safety could be jostled into place. They failed. They tried to replicate how Peter would have held the weapon in order to shoot himself in an upward trajectory from behind the head. There had been no blood on his hand, as they thought there should have been. The case against Greg for murder looked solid.

Greg admitted that his brother had come over in an intoxicated state, looking for a fight, but denied touching the gun, because guns scared him. This did not convince detectives of his innocence.

Greg's defense attorney pointed out that the investigators had formed a threshold diagnosis. The detectives had never questioned the family or done an analysis of Peter's potential for suicide. A psychologist performed a psychological autopsy and found that suicide indicators were high. In fact, not only did Peter have a drinking problem and was feeling distraught over the deaths of his parents and former girlfriend over the past nine months (the girlfriend's having been just weeks before), but an older brother had also once killed himself by shooting himself in the back of the head. Peter's blood alcohol level was .30. A sister confirmed that Peter was unstable and depressed. She also said that he had believed his older brother had committed suicide the "right" way.

A blood spatter analyst found evidence from a "shadow" pattern on a chair that, when the gun went off, Greg had been sitting several feet away, not standing. In addition, Peter could have made the shot to the back of his head merely by turning it and holding the gun at a different angle than the detectives had figured (they had considered just one possibility). As for the weapon's safety, an expert said that the attempts to throw and knock the gun around to see if the safety engaged had not replicated the actual conditions at the scene. The gun could have recoiled six feet after the shot and landed on an item on the desk that could have knocked the safety into place. With a gun of this caliber, blood spatter could have reached Greg sitting six feet away. It had actually flown further.

The defense attorney not only answered each of the prosecutor's points with a viable alternative in favor of Greg, he also added information that was pertinent to Peter's state of mind. In addition, Greg had no motive for killing his brother.

The jury accepted this scenario and acquitted Greg.

CHAPTER 4

Exercise 4.1

1. The FSC would examine the methodology and determine whether it had followed accepted scientific procedure, with controlled experiments and hypothesis testing.

2. Legal precedent fails to account for improvements and discovery of methodological error. To say that a practice should continue because it has been allowed before is a logical error, called the fallacy of an appeal to tradition.

3. Odontologists would have to demonstrate that their methods are based on controlled experiments. They would also have to show that the reported discovery of error rates was based on flawed assumptions. Short of this, they would have to admit that they are not using scientific methods.

4. Legal precedents present hurdles in a conservative system that is slow to acknowledge past errors. It has taken an abundance of unjust cases to make legal personnel recognize the need for change and improvement.

5. The judge needs to be educated in scientific methodology, as well as keep up with how science impacts the legal community. The first judge cannot be faulted, since the generic Frye standard would not have caught the error. However, the judge who re-examines the case post-*Daubert* would need to examine the odontological method for scientific rigor and knowledge about statistical claims.

In Chaney's case, the judge threw out his conviction, because the expert had no basis for which to claim that there was a "one to a million" probability. It was scientifically unsound. The Texas FSC determined that odontology groups had not properly vetted their methodology. Remember: 39 forensic dentists, using the standard "scientific" flow chart for the profession to identify human bite marks from 100 genuine photos, had 100% agreement in only four of the cases.

Exercise 4.2

1. No. Requesting volunteers means that the study group is inherently unrepresentative. It risks attracting only those who are interested in supporting standards or are curious about the study. The groups are also too small.

2. The researchers could perform a better quality control study by recruiting qualified judges from among experienced professionals and scientific consultants to devise methods that could be tested for reliability and validity before being used in a comparison study. They could also use the rosters from professional groups of facial forensic examiners to create a method for composing a more representative sample.

CHAPTER 5

Exercise 5.1

1. The determination of a suicidal mindset was likely made via confirmation bias, once the prosecutor accepted that some of John's wounds were hesitation marks. However, the medical examiner was only interpreting such marks. It remained for the prosecutor to do a more thorough analysis to see if John had any psychological flags for suicide. A "stressful job" is not sufficient. In addition, the prosecutor should have used a devil's advocate approach, considering alternative ideas for the DNA on the gas can and for the broken ribs. He seems to have formed a threshold diagnosis and then looked for items to support it.

2. Whenever experts are paid for independent consulting, bias is introduced, even if they insist that they guarantee no specific result. It is an unconscious preference, and they know that they are looking for items to contradict what their employer dislikes in an original report.

Exercise 5.2

1. The detective formed a hypothesis early, based on a boy not reporting a crime, and did not adequately investigate other viable suspects. In addition, there is little research on the reliability of testing on an adolescent. The detective did not recognize the

potential issues with this procedure but accepted results at face value, because they fit his notions.

2. Despite Tim's drawings, they should have also evaluated whether he had skill with a knife to match what the medical examiner had found, and the strength that would have been required to carry Hettrick into the field. They should have wondered why no physical evidence linked Tim, a boy, to a violent crime scene in a snowy field.

3. The prosecutor and judge should have determined whether there was any scientific basis for the psychiatrist to evaluate the drawings as rehearsal for violence. In fact, there was none. In addition, the detective selected the specific drawings he thought were significant from hundreds that Tim had done, thereby cherry-picking those that he then showed to the psychiatrist. The resulting analysis was based on fallacious thinking at all levels.

CHAPTER 6

Exercise 6.1

1. First, it is important to see what the feet had in common. It turned out that most had polymer-based sneakers with air pockets that defied fish nibbling and made them buoyant. As the feet disarticulated, they came loose and floated. So, then, how did they get in the water?

    With only a shoe or a sock, and sometimes just bones, identification proved challenging. The answer was BC's missing persons DNA database. An anthropologist helped determine how long each foot had been immersed, which helped to establish a time frame for a missing person. Vancouver City Coroner Stephen Fonseca and his team cross-referenced the sites of the found feet with missing-persons reports. They also investigated the origins of the shoes, including product data, which told them where the shoes were manufactured and distributed.

    A likely hypothesis is that these were the feet of people who had jumped into the water to commit suicide or fallen in by accident. Feet in such sneakers are commonly found in waterways where high bridges are present. Nearby are bridges that span the Fraser River. British Columbia's average annual rate of recorded suicides is around 500.

    The feet, it turned out, came from eight different people. Seven were identified. An eighth remains unknown, but both feet were found.

Exercise 6.2

1. Some MEs would accept the results and decide that it's an odd coincidence, but Koponen sent the samples to an independent toxicology lab for another opinion.

They found high levels of ethylene glycol in Randy Thompson's blood. It was a component of antifreeze. Death occurs from kidney failure or heart attack.

The medical examiner from Turner's case ordered his remains to be exhumed and re-examined. By the fall of 2001, the cause of death in both cases was antifreeze poisoning. Lynn Turner was charged. An abundance of circumstantial and behavioral evidence linked her to the deaths. The Georgia toxicology lab admitted that it had made an error in its calculations in the original set of tests. Retesting Randy Thompson's blood, the chemist affirmed the poisoning. Lynn Turner was found guilty of both murders. In 2010, she committed suicide in prison by poisoning herself with prescription medication.

CHAPTER 7

Exercise 7.1

1. Investigators over-trusted the polygraph results and relied on a narrative that made logical sense but had no supporting evidence. They failed to do a full background search on Chambers, which would have turned up other odd attention-getting incidents in her past. Nothing in the interactions between Paula and Chambers suggested animosity.

2. Sometimes people do things that are difficult to understand, and investigators generally stick with something that makes sense. Yet Chambers is not the only person to have created such a disturbance. There are many cases of people seeking attention in bizarre ways. Better education in criminal psychology, especially stalking cases, is in order before legal proceedings are instigated. Eighteen months is a long time for someone to have been in dire danger. That, alone, makes this case suspicious.

Exercise 7.2

1. First, detectives put pressure on both men until they got confessions from the online communications that both had had sex with a minor, for which they could be charged and sent to prison.

2. They can use any of the deception detection methods described in Chapter 5, and make it known that they are doing the same with the other suspect. In this case, they used polygraphs. Dos Reis was lying. He finally broke and showed detectives where he had placed Chrissie's body after a sex game that went bad. He said that he had choked her, with her consent, but that her heart gave out. Dos Reis received a twenty-five-year sentence for manslaughter.

CHAPTER 8

Exercise 8.1

1. The immediate problem is that the lead investigator made a decision early, before all the facts were gathered, as to the nature of the incident. He was then prone to confirmation bias, looking for those items that supported his notion and discarding those that did not. There was no attempt to perform a full victimology, which would have shown no red flags for suicide.

2. Before deciding that this is a suicide, perform a full victimology. In fact, this investigation ran aground and was contradicted by three independent investigators, all of whom conducted a victimology and decided this incident was a homicide. Although it remains an unsolved case, homicide is more consistent with the facts than is suicide. As support, the case detectives used an interview with a former girlfriend who had not seen the decedent in several years. Although she tried to help them make sense of a suicide, the next day, she recanted and said that her words had been taken out of context. No knife with the decedent's blood was ever found. The ME believed that the decedent had gone outside to hide it. However, this would have left a double blood trail on the stairs. In addition, he could not have gone far, so they should have found it. Also, the cast-off blood drops meant that he stood on his porch to stab himself three times, but no drugs were found in his system that would explain this bizarre behavior. Some items were missing from his apartment, including a flash drive, which had been removed before he died.

Exercise 8.2

1. A victimology done on each victim might turn up what they had in common. The antiques dealer would be asked for a description of the person who had strangled her, and this could be compared with individuals who might be associated with the other decedents.

   The killer was a female, former nurse Dana Sue Gray. She was caught using one of the victims' credit cards. She had also known two of the victims and was related to the third one. She claimed that she was depressed and addicted to shopping. She had attacked these women to steal from them. Gray tried a plea of not guilty by reason of insanity, but eventually pled guilty and was sentenced to life in prison.

2. Key behaviors would be the specific manner of assault, the weapons used, the time of day, items missing, the shoe print size, the method of entry into each home, the general neighborhood demographics, and the possible need for a vehicle to get to each site.

CHAPTER 9

Exercise 9.1

Another spatter expert had a different interpretation. Dr. Herbert MacDonell stated that there was no blood on Susie Mowbray's nightgown. From the physical and behavioral evidence, including the lack of evidence where there should have been some, he had concluded that the death was a suicide. Mowbray's business was broke and he faced prosecution from the IRS. His closest employee had left and he had threatened suicide in front of a banker who just days before he died had refused him a loan.

Exercise 9.2

The cold case team thought the thumbprint could identify a suspect and the blood trail, with other items, could support the incident reconstruction. Blood on the handkerchief tied it to a suspect, so the traces of paint might be important circumstantial evidence, if they came from a workplace. Samples of the bloodstains from the trail and the car were also tested.

The team believed that the offender had chased Penney from her car on level 8 to 10, and had gotten hurt while stabbing her. He had dripped blood back to her car, and wiped some blood off. He drove Penney's car to level 8, where he left it parked at a slant, returning to his own car on level 7. He dropped the keys and handkerchief there and drove out of the garage, leaving blood on the parking ticket. A time stamp showed that he had entered the lot immediately after Penney.

Enhancing the fingerprints allowed investigators to utilize a new tool not available during the initial investigation. The latent print images were digitized, entered into a computer, and passed through filters and gray-scale programs to produce the clearest images.

Twenty-six years after Penney's death, fifty-six-year-old Edward R. Grant was arrested and charged, due to a fingerprint match in AFIS from an assault charge. The witness descriptions matched Grant's 1973 appearance. A DNA analysis confirmed that the blood from the dropped handkerchief and a tissue in Ms. Serra's car was Grant's. Spray paint on the handkerchief was similar to paint used at the auto body shop that Grant owned. On May 28, 2002, Grant was convicted.

CHAPTER 10

Exercise 10.1

In this scenario, detectives were able to use enhancement equipment from a government agency to see the details of the car dashboard more clearly. It was not the car that the photographer had rented when the model was in his company, as described by her and proven with rental car records. A forensic handwriting expert said the signature was not the model's handwriting, and a background check of the photographer showed not only complaints of aggression against models but also suspicion in a missing persons case.

Exercise 10.2

They can use the route to look for other surveillance videos. They can also tell the girls that they have video footage to see how they react. Investigators determined the likely route the car would have taken to the party and found businesses with surveillance tape. They calculated when the car would have been in the vicinity and identified a car similar to the one in the blurred image. However, they still could not narrow it down to a specific car. Because the two girls' stories failed to match, detectives figured that one or both were lying. They used their discovery of the surveillance footage to pressure the girls about that night, including knowing that they had not dropped Skylar off where they said they had, because no surveillance had captured it. One of them finally cracked and admitted that they had picked Skylar up – the car did belong to one of them – and they had taken her into a wooded area to kill her. They did it because, "We didn't like her." (Deutsch & Valiente, 2014).

CHAPTER 11

Exercise 11.1

The couple had a specific *modus operandi*. First, they accessed a real estate website via a laptop computer and cell phone to identify homes for sale. They entered the addresses into their GPS and drove to the locations. If the home looked vacant, they would return and break in. The GPS locations and timing would be key evidence.

Exercise 11.2

1. Inconsistencies in Bill's story; the fact that he filled his prescription at two pharmacies on the same day and lied about having lost one; he had something to hide (a mistress); he had something to gain by his wife's death; he lied to his daughters about his girlfriend; he did not readily turn over his second computer.

2. They could check with the daughters to see if Sharon was a sleepwalker, or if there was reason to believe there was tension in the marriage. They could see if there were fingerprints on the note, the liturgy book, or Bill's pill bottle. They could talk with the mistress to see if she knew about a plan. They could ask the daughters if the contents of the alleged suicide note made sense. They could look at research on murders staged as suicides to see if there were similar characteristics. They could do a linguistic analysis to see if the note was consistent with Sharon's way of talking (or Bill's), and they could find out if she even used a computer.

CHAPTER 12

Exercise 12.1

Sergeant Moran used Social Security reports, autopsy reports, exhumations, DNA databases, DNA from people who had reported missing persons during this time, and anthropologists to assist. He managed to identify one of the eight unidentified victims, William Bundy (victim #19) and he also solved eleven other cold cases that were unrelated to Gacy. Moran collected eighty missing persons reports and narrowed his parameters to those with a likely profile: male drug abusers, runaways, kids from troubled families, ages 14-24. Andre Drath was identified by a tattoo, fillings in his teeth, and his half-sister's DNA. He was not a Gacy victim. As seen in Chapter 6, the body of 16-year-old Steven Soden, last seen at a New Jersey campground in 1972, was identified with new advances in DNA and the help of a persistent family member.

Exercise 12.2

In fact, the horse had been abused. The horse dealer whom Weston engaged to take Lily, Phillip Price, was convicted of animal cruelty and other charges related to transporting a horse in poor condition. A chemical analysis could be done on the paint on the horse to learn if it was more consistent with children's fingerprints or with paintballs. In addition, the horse could be tested for sensitivity in the areas where paint was on its hide. Weston could show documentation for veterinary treatment of the medical conditions she alleged, and if others were evident that could result from abuse, this would support the other side of the story. Weston could also be questioned about why the horse went to an auction house rather than being euthanized before it left her ownership. Kids who supposedly went to the paint parties could be interviewed, as could Weston's neighbors and acquaintances. It should be determined how long the horse had been out of her hands and who else might have subjected it to poor treatment.

Basic Forensic Terms for the Professional Investigator

Actus reus Latin term that refers to the physical act or omission required for conviction of a crime; the person must have conscious physical control.

AFIS Automated Fingerprint Identification System, a database for storing and making rapid comparisons of fingerprints.

ALS Alternative light source, used for bringing out latent fingerprints, blood, fibers, and other trace materials that are difficult to see under regular light conditions.

Antisocial personality disorder A personality disorder characterized by behaviors that betray or infringe on the rights of others, such as lying, recklessness, aggressiveness, and lack of remorse. See also Psychopathy.

Ballistics The science of the motion and characteristics of projectiles; relevant to wound analysis and reconstruction.

Behavioral evidence Forensically relevant evidence of behavior that assists with incident reconstruction, profiling, and victimology.

Behavioral profiling See Criminal Profiling.

Behavioral Analysis Unit (BAU) The investigative part of the National Center for the Analysis of Violent Crime, specific to threat and terrorism, crimes against adults, and crimes against children; formerly the Behavioral Science Unit.

Burden of proof In a courtroom, the necessity of proving a fact in dispute, according to the standard of proof required in a specific proceeding (beyond reasonable doubt, preponderance of evidence, clear and convincing).

Blood spatter pattern analysis Examining how blood hits a surface to determine how the event took place to spill the blood, and to assess the size and type of wound made.

Cause of death An injury or disease that produces a condition in the body that brings about death.

Chain of custody The method used to keep track of who is handling a piece of evidence, and for what purpose.

CODIS Combined DNA Index System, the FBI's database of genetic material.

Competency   Sufficient ability to participate in proceedings, such as to stand trial, to waive rights, to testify, and to be executed. One must understand the legal proceedings involved and have the ability to consult with an attorney.

Compliant accomplice   A partner in crime, usually female, who is worn down or heavily manipulated into committing murders that the person would not otherwise do.

Confirmation bias   Orientation toward a hypothesis that frames how an investigator observes and analyzes evidence.

Coroner/medical examiner   Official in charge of death investigation, with title dependent on the jurisdiction.

Corpus delicti   Essential body of facts that indicate that a crime has occurred.

Crime reconstruction   Using evidence to determine the sequence and types of actions involved in a crime or series of crimes.

Criminalistics   The science of analyzing physical evidence from a crime.

Criminal investigative analysis   The FBI's structured approach to identifying whether a crime occurred, what type of crime it is, and how it should be profiled and managed.

Criminal profiling   The use of observation of the crime scene and pattern of crimes to determine relevant characteristics of the perpetrator; it guides police in narrowing the field of suspects and devising a strategy for questioning.

Criminology   The study of crime from a sociological perspective.

Dactyloscopy   The technique of developing and identifying fingerprints.

***Daubert* standard**   The 1993 court decision about the admissibility of scientific evidence, which established guidelines for determining if the methodology is scientific and can be applied to the facts at issue.

Deception detection   Methods and measurements that determine if someone being interviewed or interrogated is lying.

Delusion   A false belief based on an incoherent inference about reality.

Diagnostic and Statistical Manual of Mental Disorders (DSM)   The official classification manual of the American Psychiatric Association for mental disorders, revised several times and now in its fourth edition, with text revisions.

Digital forensics   Investigations involving digital data and devices.

Diminished capacity   A psychological defense indicative of an inability to appreciate the nature of the crime or to control one's actions. Not used in all states.

Disorganized offender   Person who commits a crime haphazardly or opportunistically, using weapons at the scene and often leaving clues; usually has a history of mental instability.

DNA profile   The blueprint of a person"s physical identity, as determined by his or her genes.

Evidence   Documents, statements, and all items that are included in the legal proceedings for the jury's sole consideration in the question of guilt or innocence.

Expert witness   A person with specialized knowledge about an area, or with a special skill that is germane to the proceedings, such as linkage analysis or a mental illness. This person's role is to assist the fact finders (judge or jury) in understanding complicated information.

Felony   A serious crime for which the punishment in federal law is generally severe, including capital punishment.

Frye **standard**   A test that governs the admissibility of scientific evidence, such that evidence entered into a case must be generally accepted by the relevant scientific community.

Geographic profiling   Using aspects of a geographical relationship among crime scenes to infer offender characteristics.

Impression evidence   Anything that leaves an impression at a crime scene that links someone to the crime; tire tracks, footprints, fingerprints, tooth marks and bite marks.

Insanity   A legal term for a mental disease or defect that if present at the time of a crime absolves the person of responsibility.

Interrogation   The act of using questions to pressure someone suspected of a crime to confess.

Latent fingerprints   Prints left on something that aren't visible, but can be made visible with certain techniques.

Linkage analysis   Using evidence, particularly behavioral, from a series of crime scenes to indicate that they are associated with a specific offender or set of offenders.

Livescan   Fingerprint technology that allows the fingertips to be scanned rather than rolled in ink.

Locard's exchange principle   The theory that anyone entering a crime scene leaves or takes something, or both.

Luminol   A chemical reagent that makes invisible blood luminescent in darkness.

Malingering   Deliberate simulation of a mental illness to obtain personal gain.

Manner of death   Determination of the mode in which an individual was killed (natural, accident, suicide, homicide, or undetermined).

Mens rea   The mental state that accompanies a forbidden act; required for conviction.

Miranda **warning**   The required statement that a police officer gives to a suspect upon arrest, informing that person of the right to remain silent (not to self-incriminate) and to have legal representation before questioning.

Modus operandi **(MO)**   An offender's method of carrying out the offense.

Narcissistic personality disorder   A personality disorder that manifests as arrogance, entitlement, and the need to be admired by others for one's superiority; often shows up among serial killers.

Organized offender   Person committing a crime in a planned, premeditated manner, leaving few or no clues.

Pattern evidence Evidence that can be read from a specific type of pattern, such as the impression of a shoe or the forcible contact between two surfaces; includes such things as shattered glass fractures and blood spatter patterns.

Personality disorders Enduring patterns of thought and behavior that are maladaptive, causing impairment and distress. For criminal proceedings, the most common are Antisocial, Borderline, Narcissistic, Paranoid, and Schizoid.

Polygraph A machine used to determine through changes in physiological functions whether a person is lying.

Probative Serving to prove.

Profiler (criminal) A mental health professional or law enforcement officer with behavioral science training who helps to determine the traits of an unknown offender from aspects of the victim and crime scene.

Psychological autopsy Methods used to determine the state of mind of a person where the scene of a suicide is ambiguous and therefore questionable; also to make a determination about manner of death.

Psychopathy Personality disorder defined by long-term unsocialized criminal behavior by a person who feels no guilt or remorse and is not inclined to stop; usually diagnosed with the PCL-R.

Psychosis A major mental disorder in which a person's ability to think, respond, communicate, recall, and interpret reality is impaired. The person shows inappropriate mood, poor impulse control, and delusions. Often confused with insanity, which is a legal term, and psychopathy, which is a character disorder.

Schizophrenia A group of disorders manifested in delusions, disturbances in language and thought, mood shifts, and maladaptive behaviors.

Serial killer According to the FBI's new definition (since 2005), an offender who kills at least two different people in two separate events.

Serology The analysis of body fluids like blood, semen, and saliva.

Signature crime A crime scene that bears a personality stamp of an offender, characteristic of a need for ritual or theme. These acts are not necessary to complete the offense. Also called personation.

Staging Arranging a scene to look like something other than what it actually is.

Suicidology The discipline of studying suicide to learn about cause, treatment, and prevention.

Superglue fuming A technique used to bring out latent fingerprints in a lab from surfaces that don't respond well to powders; its fumes adhere to the print when heated and make it visible.

Threat assessment The procedure for determining how likely it is that a certain person or group might become violent in the future.

Trace evidence   The smallest pieces of evidence at a scene, including fiber, hair, grass fragments, seeds, dust, and soil.

Toxicology   The section of the lab that tests tissues or products for contamination by drugs, poisons, and alcohol.

Unsub   The term used in criminal profiling to refer to an unknown suspect.

ViCAP   Violent Criminal Apprehension Program, the FBI's nationwide data information center, designed for collecting, sorting, and analyzing information about crimes.

Victimology   A study of victim information to find clues about the offender's opportunity and selection process.

Index

CPSIA information can be obtained
at www.ICGtesting.com
Printed in the USA
FFHW01n0629040818
47654027-51252FF

9 781524 911621